John Joseph Ogle

The free library

Its history and present condition

John Joseph Ogle

The free library
Its history and present condition

ISBN/EAN: 9783337283650

Printed in Europe, USA, Canada, Australia, Japan

Cover: Foto ©Andreas Hilbeck / pixelio.de

More available books at **www.hansebooks.com**

THE FREE LIBRARY

ITS HISTORY AND PRESENT
CONDITION

BY

JOHN J. OGLE

LONDON
GEORGE ALLEN, 156, CHARING CROSS ROAD
1897

GENERAL INTRODUCTION

THE present age has received divers epithets, mostly uncomplimentary. If ever defined as the Age of Gold, this has by no means been intended in the ancient sense of an age of primitive innocence and simplicity. It has been styled the Age of Steam, the Age of Veneer, and the Age of Talk. As these disparaging epithets have all been affixed by itself, it may occur to some that the Age of Modesty, or at least of Penitence, might not be an inappropriate designation; and after all, we do not apprehend that future ages will consider it so very inferior to most of its predecessors, and are sure that it will be universally preferred to the Ages of Darkness. With these, at least, it has nothing in common. To call it *the* Age of Light were presumptuous, but *an* Age of Light it assuredly is, and, did we seek for a name, we should be inclined to entitle it the Age of Books. Not merely that there never before were so many books in the world, or that there never was a time when books and newspapers were so widely read or so influential; but that there never before was so much interest and curiosity respecting the makers of books, authors—the emitters of books, publishers—or the custodians of books, librarians. This curiosity, frequently frivolous and annoying, bears testimony, at all events, to the place which literature has taken, not merely in fact, but in general apprehension, among the agencies which mould the world. She always has had this place in effect ever since hieroglyphical writing passed into alphabetical, but the man of the world has been singularly unconscious of the agency by which its course was in large measure determined. Alexander has been conspicuous, Aristotle has been overlooked. Now the attention paid to authorship in all its forms shows that mankind has become aware that its destinies may be much affected by what some unknown young man is at the present moment scribbling in a garret.

Those who have especially interested themselves in education, among whom librarians are to be reckoned, may justly regard this general perception as a proof that their efforts have not been in vain. Before men can be interested in trifling details about authors, they must have conceived an interest in books which certainly did not exist in the eighteenth century. The more trivial the gossip—and it is often most provokingly so—the greater the evidence of a demand. And this testimony is corroborated when curiosity is found to pass beyond the persons of authors, and to comprise inquisitiveness respecting books themselves; whether evinced by curiosity respecting particular copies or editions, or by such particulars as the circulation of successful books, the rarity of such as have been for a time neglected, the peculiarities of particular copies, or extraordinary prices realised at sales. That this curiosity exists, the columns of the press afford daily evidence. It is clear that the schoolmaster has been abroad to some purpose, and that one of the results of his mission has been the awakening of an intelligent interest, not merely in the producers and distributors of books, but in the history, the commercial value, the external semblance, and the fitting treatment of the volumes themselves.

The individual book has been ably dealt with of late in monographs referring to the subject of Bibliography. The object of the little series now introduced to the public is to deal with the Book, not so much individually, but collectively, in the aggregated form which is called the Library. Bibliography is neither excluded from the volumes already arranged, nor proscribed as the theme of volumes which may succeed. But it is believed that the most profitable and generally acceptable information which can be given to the public in the first instance is that which relates to the books of the public, the collections which are the property of the entire community, and in whose general administration every citizen should feel interested. Provision has accordingly been made for free libraries in particular. The scheme includes a complete account of the history of the establishment of free libraries in the United Kingdom, including the National Library, with particular details of the progress of the more important, and a brief exposition of the legislation by which they are governed; for a practical discussion on library architecture, illustrated with numerous illustrations of libraries and library appurtenances; and a manual of the leading points in library administration. These little treatises, it is hoped, will be found practically useful by all interested in libraries, and more especially in free libraries, whether practically concerned in their management as librarians or committee men, or merely frequenters and well-wishers. Another volume, dealing mainly with the prices of books, besides its practical utility to purchasers, illustrates a very interesting nook of literary history. Other volumes may not improbably follow. Undertaken, as has been explained, in deference to what appeared the growing popular interest in books and everything pertaining to them, the series, it is hoped, may contribute something to raising the general estimate of the importance of the librarian's office, and the status to which the faithful discharge of its duties entitles him. We have got long past the days when the librarian was defined as "a harmless drudge," and the few posts in his profession worth having were employed to satisfy embarrassing claims on the dispensers of patronage. Much yet remains to be accomplished before the position which the librarian might, and ought to, occupy is sufficiently recognised either by the community in general or the profession itself. Any approximation towards it is doubly welcome, as an index both to an improved appreciation of the supreme importance of knowledge on the part of the public, and to an elevation of the ideals of librarians themselves. The more generous recognition of their services which it is their ambition to obtain can only be insured by a steady increase in the value of these services, and the librarian will be honoured not as the mere distributor of an inferior class of literature, but in proportion as he approves himself a dispenser of information and enlightenment, and a guide qualified to direct the popular taste for reading.

R. GARNETT.

PREFACE

THE aim of this work is sufficiently indicated by the title-page and table of contents. The Library *per se* is its subject, hence only incidental notice has been taken of library buildings and library administration; moreover, these subjects are dealt with in other books of the same series. The information as far as possible has been gathered at first hand; but for the early history Hansard's Parliamentary Debates, the various Returns concerning Public Libraries presented to Parliament, old newspapers and reports have been diligently searched. The publications of the Library Association, and in particular *The Library*, edited by Mr. J. Y. W. MacAlister, have been of the greatest use for the facts they have furnished. Other sources of information are indicated in the work itself. The most conflicting statements are in print, especially regarding the dates of local adoptions of the Public Libraries Acts. Great care has been taken to ascertain the true dates, and these have been given as precisely as could be ascertained in the limits of time set for the preparation of this work.

My thanks for special assistance in my researches are due, and are hereby tendered, to Mr. Peter

Cowell, librarian of the Liverpool Free Public Libraries, and to Mr. Thomas Formby, the sub-librarian; also to Mr. C. W. Sutton, the city librarian of Manchester, and to Mr. W. R. Credland, deputy chief librarian of the same city. To Mr. Charles Madeley of the Warrington Museum I am indebted for access to various monumental documents of the early days of the movement, and for the loan of certain blue-books. Mr. F. T. Barrett, librarian of the Mitchell Library, Glasgow, and Mr. W. E. Doubleday, librarian of the Hampstead Public Libraries, have assisted me with information for Chapter XIII.; and I have also to thank Mr. T. W. Lyster, librarian of the National Library of Ireland, for valuable assistance and suggestions during the reading of the proofs. Finally, my hearty thanks are tendered to the librarians and secretaries of libraries who answered my long list of questions, and whose names are recorded in the statistical tables of the Appendix. Without their valued aid this work could not have been written.

In such a work as this, errors of fact are very apt to creep in; with a view to their amendment in a second edition, the author will be glad to receive any duly authenticated corrections.

JOHN J. OGLE.

BOOTLE, *June* 1897.

CONTENTS

	PAGE
GENERAL INTRODUCTION . .	v-ix
PREFACE . . .	xi-xii

BOOK I

GENERAL HISTORY

CHAPTER I

THE RISE OF LIBRARIES, AND THE ORIGIN OF FREE LIBRARIES IN THE UNITED KINGDOM, WITH THEIR HISTORY UP TO THE YEAR 1855 . . . 3-32

Mediæval libraries—Causes of the formation of libraries—The seventeenth-century city and parish libraries—Norwich, Bristol, Langley Marish, Leicester, the Chetham Library, Boston, Wotton Wawen, Wisbeach, Tong—The eighteenth-century parish libraries—Kirkwood's proposals—Dr. Bray's libraries—Foundation of the British Museum—British Museum influence on free public libraries—Commencement of subscription libraries—Bamburgh Castle Library—Mr. Samuel Brown's itinerating libraries—Itinerating libraries in Scotland, in Yorkshire, in Lancashire, and Cheshire—The rise of Mechanics' Institutions—Their libraries in 1849—Origin of the free library—The Museums Act of 1845—Libraries established under the Museums Act at Warrington and Salford—Edward Edwards and William Ewart—The Select Committee on Public Libraries, and the genesis of the Act of 1850—The debate on Ewart's Bill—Subsequent legislation to 1855—Provisions of the 1855 Acts—Adoptions and rejections of the Acts—Local Acts of Liverpool and Brighton—Inauguration of the Manchester Free Library — Speeches by Lord Lytton, Charles Dickens, W. M. Thackeray, Sir James Stephen, Lord Houghton.

CHAPTER II

THE HISTORY OF THE FREE PUBLIC LIBRARY MOVEMENT FROM 1856 TO 1877 33-46

The parliamentary return of 1856—Adoptions and rejections of the Acts up to 1867—Local powers of Sunderland—The Amending Acts of 1866—Lord Beaconsfield and the Earl of Shaftesbury on library legislation—The Scotch Amending Act of 1867—Adoptions and rejections, 1867-70—The parliamentary return of 1870—Effect of Forster's Elementary Education Act upon the progress of the movement—The new legislation of 1871—Power to make bye-laws in Scotland—Extension to local boards of power to adopt the Acts in England—Review of progress made up to the end of 1870—Adoptions and rejections, 1871-77—The Irish Amending Act of 1877—English Act of 1877—Limitation of rate below one penny—The Philadelphia and London International Library Conferences—Formation of the Library Association of the United Kingdom—The parliamentary return of 1876-77.

CHAPTER III

THE HISTORY OF THE FREE PUBLIC LIBRARY MOVEMENT FROM 1878 TO 1887 47-61

Rejections of the Acts, 1878-82—Opposition tactics—Adoptions of the Acts, 1878-82—The Library Association—The Metropolitan Free Libraries Association and legislation—Proposal of Education Department inspection of libraries—The reopening of the Birmingham Central Free Libraries in 1882—Speeches by John Bright and Joseph Chamberlain—Adoptions and rejections, 1883-86—The Science and Art Department's Bill of 1884—Effect of the Act of 1884 at Worcester—Mr. Hopwood's Bill—The Manx Acts of 1885 and 1886—The year 1887—The publication of Greenwood's "Public Libraries"—"Queen's jubilee celebration" libraries—Adoptions and rejections—The arousing of London—The 1887 Amendment Bill carried—Sir John Lubbock on the Bill—The Scotch Consolidating Bill carried — Professor W. Stanley Jevons on the free library—Notable generosity to free libraries—The Winnard and Taylor bequests at Wigan, Sir Peter Coats's gifts at Paisley, Mr. Keiller's at Dundee, Mr. Carnegie's at Dunfermline, Sir William Gilstrap's at Newark—The parliamentary return of 1885.

CHAPTER IV

THE HISTORY OF THE FREE PUBLIC LIBRARY MOVEMENT FROM 1888 TO 1896 62-95

The rejections during this period—Adoptions—The attack of the " Liberty and Property Defence League "—The support of the Trades Union Congress, 1884—Review of districts in which adoptions had taken place at end of 1896—Large urban districts that have not adopted the Acts—Large donations and bequests to free libraries—£750,000 given in nine years—Comparison of donations, &c., in the United States and in the United Kingdom—Legislation during the period—The Acts of 1888 and 1890—Sir William Harcourt on the free library and the rate limit—The genesis and passing of the Consolidating Act of 1892—The publication of "Public Library Legislation" in 1893—The Amending Bill of 1893—The Museums and Gymnasiums Act, 1891—Effect of the Technical Instruction Acts, 1889 and 1891, and of the Local Taxation (Customs and Excise) Act, 1890, on free libraries—The Local Government Act, 1894, and parish free libraries—Chief provisions of the English Library Acts—The Irish Bill of 1893, and the Act of 1894—Public library law in Ireland—The Scotch Amending Act of 1894—Chief provisions of Scotch library law—Powers of towns under local Acts—Persistent opposition to carrying out of the Acts at Bermondsey, Mile End, and Clerkenwell—The Bristol case, 1892—The Manchester appeal against income-tax, 1893–96, and its success — The distribution of parliamentary papers to free libraries — Mr. Gladstone on the question—The Library Association's new Bill—The attitude of the leaders of opinion towards free libraries—Royalty and free public libraries—Passages from memorable speeches by Mr. Alexander Ireland, Mr. R. K. Causton, M.P., Sir John Lubbock, Lord Rosebery, Mr. Hall Caine, Professor Jebb, Mr. Gladstone—The parliamentary return of 1890—Estimate of the number and extent of free libraries at end of 1896 —Outstanding loans on free libraries—Direction of future growth.

CHAPTER V

THE DEVELOPMENT OF THE FREE LIBRARY . 96–103

Library administration—Early text-books—Edwards's "Memoirs of Libraries"—The United States report of 1876—The American *Library Journal*—The Library Association of the United Kingdom—Its publications and official journals—Branch libraries—Lending and reference libraries—Local history collections—Music scores—Books for the blind—Libraries for the young—Indicators—The card ledger—Free lectures—Half-hour talks to readers—Electric lighting—Photography in libraries—Maps, prints, and drawings—The summer school of library science—Examination of assistants —Open access —American influence on English methods—The card catalogue—The Dewey "Decimal Classification" — Cutter's "Rules for Cataloguing"— Branch delivery stations — Library Association cataloguing rules — Patent libraries and special collections.

CHAPTER VI

SOME PAST WORKERS AND PRESENT BENEFACTORS 104–114

Edward Edwards—William Ewart—Sir John Lubbock—J. Passmore Edwards—Andrew Carnegie.

BOOK II

BRIEF HISTORIES OF TYPICAL LIBRARIES

CHAPTER VII

THE LIBRARY OF THE BRITISH MUSEUM, AND THE GUILDHALL LIBRARY, LONDON . . . 117–133

CHAPTER VIII

LONDON LIBRARIES UNDER THE PUBLIC LIBRARIES ACTS 134–156

Battersea — Chelsea — Clerkenwell — Hampstead — Lambeth — Newington — Poplar — St. George (Hanover Square) — St. Leonard (Shoreditch) — St. Martin-in-the-Fields and St. Paul (Covent Garden) — Wandsworth.

CHAPTER IX

FREE LIBRARIES UNDER THE ACTS IN SEVEN FIRST-CLASS TOWNS 157–194

Manchester — Liverpool — Birmingham — Leeds — Hull — Edinburgh — Dublin — Belfast.

b

CONTENTS

CHAPTER X

PAGE

FREE LIBRARIES UNDER THE ACTS IN SEVENTEEN
   SECOND-CLASS TOWNS 195–241

Bristol—West Ham—Salford—Bradford—Nottingham—Newcastle-on-Tyne—Norwich—Birkenhead—Plymouth—Derby—Wolverhampton—Brighton—Preston—Cardiff—Swansea—Dundee—Aberdeen.

CHAPTER XI

FREE LIBRARIES UNDER THE ACTS IN SIXTEEN THIRD-
   CLASS TOWNS 242–271

South Shields—Southampton—Aston Manor—Wigan—Warrington—Bootle—Cheltenham—Newark-on-Trent—Runcorn—Truro—Wrexham—Paisley—Hawick—Cork—Dundalk—Douglas.

CHAPTER XII

FREE LIBRARIES UNDER THE ACTS IN SMALL TOWNS
   (UNDER 10,000 POPULATION) AND VILLAGES . 272–284

Buxton — Falmouth — Middle Claydon — Brechin — Thurso — Tarves—Drumoak—Suggestions for circuit libraries in villages, and county library authorities—Existing village library schemes.

CHAPTER XIII

PAGE

ENDOWED AND VOLUNTARY FREE LIBRARIES . 285–299

Humphrey Chetham's Library at Manchester—Archbishop Tenison's Library—Dr. Williams's Library—The High Wycombe endowed free library—Libraries at Otley and at Horwich—City Charities' endowed libraries—The Mitchell Library, Glasgow—The Mayer Library, Bebington—Voluntary free libraries at Hull, Bath, Paddington, St. Pancras, Bethnal Green, &c.—The Marylebone Free Public Libraries Association and its voluntary free library.

EPILOGUE 300

APPENDIX (STATISTICAL TABLES) 301–325

INDEX 329–344

BOOK I

GENERAL HISTORY

THE FREE LIBRARY

CHAPTER I

THE RISE OF LIBRARIES, AND THE ORIGIN OF FREE LIBRARIES IN THE UNITED KINGDOM, WITH THEIR HISTORY UP TO THE YEAR 1855.

WHILE books were of necessity written by slow and painful labour large libraries were few, and belonged almost exclusively to rich fraternities and wealthy corporations. The universities, the monastic orders, a rich guild here and there (*e.g.* the Kalendars of Bristol), and the Corporation of London, seem to have been almost the only owners of libraries in Britain in the fifteenth century. But the invention and rapid spread of the art of printing with movable metal types, the diffusion of classical learning, and the free spirit of inquiry awakened by the Reformation, contributed to the multiplication and cheapening of books, and the enlargement and establishment of libraries. Princes and great nobles began to form collections, in which the romances, the chronicles, the poems printed by Caxton, De Worde, Pynson, Machlinia, and the early British printers, were well represented. Reformers gathered about them the works of Luther, of Zuinglius, of Melanchthon, of Erasmus, besides lesser controversial and expository books in which they were interested. Professional men likewise formed libraries of law and jurisprudence and of medicine. Sometimes the owner of a large library was found at his death to have bequeathed his books to his church or college on the one hand, or, on the other, to his professional brethren, to form the nucleus of one of the medical or legal libraries which have now existed since the sixteenth century, some few of them from an earlier date.

In the beginning of the seventeenth century a new fashion began; books were bequeathed to city corporations, and formed the earliest free town libraries in this country. One such was founded at Norwich in the year 1608. The greater part of the original books of this, the oldest city free library with a continuous history to the present day, are now housed in the Norwich Free Public Library. Five years later provision was made by Dr. Toby Matthew, Archbishop of York, and by citizen Robert Redwood, to establish a city library at Bristol. The library was opened in 1615, and is accessible to the reader of to-day in the Central Free Library of that city. Each of these libraries was for a time alienated to the use of a private library society, though it is doubtful whether in either case any authorised seeker after knowledge was ever denied access to the books. A parochial free library was established in 1623 at Langley

Marish, in Buckinghamshire, by Sir John Kederminster, and the books, which consisted of 300 folio volumes of the Greek and Latin Fathers and the chief works of the Reformation controversy, were reported in 1849 to be well preserved. The ancient town of Leicester also has had its free library since 1632, which, after falling into neglect, has been carefully looked after of late years by the corporation, though as yet not included in the "Free Public Library" system of the town. This ancient library contains the famous *Codex Leicestrensis* of the Greek New Testament. Of the free libraries of the seventeenth century which have any record continuous with the present time, next in point of date comes the noble bequest of Sir Humphrey Chetham at Manchester, which was long regarded as the oldest free library in England. The Chetham Library, founded in 1653, appears to have an unbroken record of public use, and its store of antiquarian books and valuable original MSS., chiefly English, as well as its literary associations, justly make it the pride of Manchester citizens. Humphrey Chetham also left books to be chained to desks in various Lancashire churches. In 1635 at Boston, and in 1645 at Wotton Wawen (Warwickshire), the churches were furnished with libraries. Archbishop Tenison's library at St. Martin-in-the-Fields, London, was established in 1684. Other libraries were formed in the seventeenth century at Wisbeach by ten "capital burgesses," and at Tong, in Shropshire, by Gervaise, Lord Pierpoint, the latter, and possibly the former, being for the exclusive use of the clergy. Numerous grammar-school libraries, now for the most part shamefully dilapidated, were also founded late in the sixteenth and early in the seventeenth centuries.

The eighteenth century saw the rise and development of a considerable movement for supplying ministers of the gospel with libraries in connection with their churches. In Scotland the Rev. James Kirkwood issued anonymously, in 1699, "An Overture for Founding and Maintaining of Bibliothecks in every Paroch throughout the Kingdom," and three years later, "A Copy of a Letter anent a Project for Erecting a Library in every Presbytery or at least County in the Highlands." These tracts were not without result. The General Assembly of 1704 approved the project, and adopted rules "about the ordering and preserving the libraries in the Highlands and Islands."

In England, Dr. Bray, founder of the Society for the Propagation of the Gospel, while collecting funds for sending missionaries to America, was met with the objection that the poor clergy at home had more need of libraries than the Americans of missionaries. This led him to collect funds for and establish libraries in various parts of the country while prosecuting his mission work. From 1704 to his death, Dr. Bray established sixty-one so-called parochial libraries, and this work was continued after his death by the "associates of Dr. Bray," who added, up to 1807, seventy-eight parochial and thirty-five lending libraries. Other persons established similar libraries, probably stimulated by Dr. Bray's activity. Dr. Bray induced Chancellor North to obtain the passing of an Act (7 Anne, c. 14) in 1709, entitled "An Act for the Better Preservation of Parochial Libraries in that part of Great Britain called England." In spite of the provisions of this Act, the greater part of these libraries are now neglected or entirely dispersed.

The leading event in the library history of the last century was the foundation of the British Museum in 1753. Into the great national students' free library the collections of the British monarchs from Henry VII. to George III. were ultimately absorbed, so that this great treasury of literature now contains the books from some of the earliest non-ecclesiastical libraries established in this country. Popular free libraries in the days of their beginnings were also largely influenced by British Museum methods and helped by officials from the national library. Indeed, the Parliamentary reports of 1835-36 and 1849 on the management of the British Museum had more than an indirect bearing on the work of the Commission on Free Libraries which sat from 1849 to 1851. Statistics of foreign libraries, prepared by Mr. Panizzi, were given for the first time in the report of 1835-36.

Subscription libraries began to be formed in the more populous places, as early as 1725 in Edinburgh, and 1740 in London. Under the names of Lyceum and Athenæum many of these still exist in various towns, one of the oldest extant being the Liverpool (Lyceum) Library, founded in 1758.

Eight years later it is stated in "Proposals for a Publick Library at Aberdeen," "Public libraries have been established by subscription in most considerable towns where there is a desire of knowledge and improvement." These libraries were for the use of the local gentry, professional men, and the more prosperous tradesmen, but subsequently they formed models for the Mechanics' Institutions, which brought the advantages of public libraries to the smaller tradesmen and the skilled artisans.

A free library for general use was founded in 1778 at Bamburgh Castle, Northumberland, by Nathaniel, Lord Crewe, Bishop of Durham, for the use of all respectable housekeepers within twenty miles of the Castle. Many and valuable accessions were afterwards made to this library, including a large part of the library of John Sharpe, Archbishop of York, which accrued in 1792.

A successful experiment in providing libraries for the people was made in 1817 by Mr. Samuel Brown of East Lothian. His project was described by the Rev. William Brown in a pamphlet which, translated into French and German, circulated even as far as St. Petersburg.

The Rev. J. Crombie Brown has since described the system in his evidence before the Select Committee on Public Libraries, 1849. The plan provided that boxes, each containing fifty volumes, should circulate from village to village; each box was to remain for two years, and at the end of this time it was to be exchanged for another. The success of the scheme was great, but depended much on the ability and enthusiasm of the local unpaid librarians who undertook the charge of the boxes. In 1849 the system was still in proper working order in East Lothian. The plan had been copied in Peeblesshire by the Free Church of Scotland, and in the Highlands and Islands by the General Assembly. Into Russia and into the United States also the same method was introduced. At first these libraries were quite free, but financial necessities soon compelled subscriptions. A similar plan is in excellent working order to-day in connection with the Yorkshire Union of Mechanics' Institutes, and with the Lancashire and Cheshire Union of Institutes. The first Mechanics' Institute at Haddington and at Dunbar, it is said, grew out of the interest in these circulating libraries.

One of the earliest Mechanics' Institutes was formed by George Birkbeck in London in the year 1824. At first these institutes were establishments for instructing mechanics in the principles underlying their trades, for technical instruction, in fact; but the original purpose was soon forgotten or overlaid in their expansion into social institutions, including in nearly every case a collection of books. In the twenties, thirties, and forties, Mechanics' Institutes rapidly increased in number, and a return of 1849 shows that there were four hundred in the United Kingdom, possessing from 300,000 to 400,000 volumes, with an annual circulation of more than a million.

But with all this movement for popularising books

the popular free library had not yet arrived, though the highroad had been constructed, and the heralds of the new institution were already on the way. Mr. William Ewart, M.P., in 1835, had served on the Select Committee on the Condition, Management, and Affairs of the British Museum; and on the School Committee appointed at his instigation; out of the recommendations of which the Government School of Art, now the Science and Art Department, originated in 1836. "Schools of Design" were extended by this department to the provinces in 1841. In 1844, by the efforts of the secretary (Mr. George Jackson) and the treasurer (Mr. George Wallis) of the Manchester School of Design, a public meeting was held in Manchester to discuss the means of improving popular taste. Richard Cobden presided, and Joseph Brotherton, M.P. for Salford, was present. The proposals then considered were subsequently laid by Mr. Brotherton before Mr. William Ewart, M.P., and led to the introduction of the Act of 1845 "for encouraging the establishment of museums in large towns." This Act allowed any town council of a town with 10,000 inhabitants to erect museums of science and art, but not to buy specimens or books. A rate of a halfpenny in the pound might be levied to defray the cost of land and buildings, and entrance-fees of one penny charged and used for paying salaries and establishment expenses. The bill was introduced on 6th March, and passing through both Houses without a division, received the royal assent on 21st July. The Corporations of Canterbury,

Dover, Leicester, Liverpool, Salford, Sunderland, and Warrington established museums under the powers conferred by this Act; and at Canterbury, Warrington, and Salford, books were added to the attractions of the museum—in other words, libraries were formed. At Canterbury a penny per volume was charged for each book issued; but Warrington in 1848 established a library of reference free to the public on certain days and within certain hours, and a lending library, which could be used only by subscribing members. Salford in 1849 followed in the wake of Warrington. The Warrington Museum, therefore, is the earliest example of a municipally-controlled and rate-supported free popular library in the United Kingdom.

Ever to be associated with the name of Mr. William Ewart as a founder of the free library system of this country is that of Edward Edwards (1812–86). He it was who first collected the facts relating to foreign free libraries which so much assisted the Parliamentary Commission on Public Libraries in coming to a conclusion. His statistics were first published in the *Transactions of the Statistical Society of London* in 1848, and followed upon an article of his which had appeared a year earlier in the *British Quarterly Review*, entitled "Public Libraries in London and Paris." Edwards's statistics were brought to the notice of Mr. Ewart, and he obtained in 1849 the appointment of a Select Committee of the House of Commons on the subject of Public Libraries. The work of this committee led to the enactment of the first Public Libraries Act, generally known as Ewart's Act of 1850. The Select Committee examined the librarians of a large number of libraries, British and foreign, large and small, ancient and modern; but by far the most important witness was Edward Edwards. He established conclusively the almost total absence in England of libraries of general interest, accessible of right, and gratuitously, to the people, and the comparative scarcity of easily accessible students' libraries. Possibly he exaggerated the readiness of access in Continental libraries; and certain it is that a vigorous attack was made upon the accuracy of his statistics; yet he vindicated in the report of 1850 their general correctness, and, in fact, proved that perfect accuracy was at that time impossible to be obtained. Further, the information he contributed relative to the history of the formation and management of endowed and subsidised libraries was of the greatest use to the committee by way both of suggestion and of warning. Mr. George Dawson and Mr. Samuel Smiles, with other witnesses, proved the growing intelligence of the working population, and related many instances of the successful efforts of artisans to form libraries for their common use.

The report, which is dated 23rd July 1849, extends to fourteen folio pages, and comments on the success of previous efforts of Parliament to increase the usefulness of galleries of art, museums, and schools of design, and the complaints of authors as to the scarcity of public libraries; gives the number (some 250 in all) of public libraries easily accessible "to the poor as well as to the rich, to the foreigner as well as to the native," in each of the larger countries of the Continent, and proceeds, "yet it is stated that we have only one free library in Great Britain equally accessible with these numerous libraries abroad, the library founded by Humphrey Chetham in the borough of Manchester." Next the fact is stated that the United States "have already anticipated us in the formation of public libraries," and have already more than one hundred, the greater part entirely open to the public. London is compared to its disadvantage with the other capitals and principal cities of Europe. Further, "it would seem," say the committee, "that our ancestors paid much more attention to the formation of such institutions than ourselves. Almost every library in London and in the country, approaching to the character of a free library, is an old library." One by one the libraries that are entitled to copyright privileges, or that have commuted the privilege for an annual payment, are reviewed, also the cathedral and the parochial libraries, and some others. The efforts of the working-classes to form libraries for themselves, and the rise of farmers' and of rural libraries in Scotland, are set forth; while the paucity of libraries and of booksellers' shops in Ireland is dwelt upon. The growing demand for public "lectures" and the improving taste of readers is given as a reason for not abandoning the people to "low, enfeebling, and often pestilential literature, instead of enabling them to breathe a more pure, elevated, and congenial atmosphere." The general want, they say, is, above all, buildings to receive books and objects "secured in some fixed and lasting society or corporation." The materials to fill the buildings they believe will be provided by voluntary effort; the buildings should be provided by a local rate. "It is evident that there should be in all countries libraries of two sorts: libraries of deposit and of research, and libraries devoted to the general reading and circulation of books." Fruitful suggestions for improving the older libraries are made. "Every witness examined on the subject has given an opinion favourable to the grant of assistance for the formation of public libraries, on certain strict and clear conditions, by the Government." Then follow recommendations which were embodied in Ewart's Act of 1850, and suggestions as to village libraries and workpeople's libraries. On the question of lending libraries they say, "Many men, in order to derive the fullest advantage from books, must have them not only in their hands, but in their homes. A great public library ought above all things to teach the teachers; to supply with the best implements of education those who educate the people, whether in the pulpit, the school, or the press. The lending out of books, therefore, which is a general characteristic of foreign libraries, should be an essential element in the formation of our own. Nor to such classes as those we have just described and to the labouring classes is the opening of libraries during the evening a point of less importance." The necessity of precautions against fire is insisted on, and fire-proof buildings and iron shelves and furniture recommended. Printed catalogues are held to be a necessity for effective use. The committee regret that more has not been done to facilitate the international exchange of books, and discuss the effect of our fiscal regulations on the circulation of books in Europe and America. The report concludes with the following passage :—

"Your committee feel convinced that the people of a country like our own—abounding in capital, in energy, and in an honest desire not only to initiate, but to imitate, whatsoever is good and useful—will not long linger behind the people of other countries in the acquisition of such valuable institutions as freely accessible public libraries. Our present inferior position is unworthy of the power, the liberality, and the literature of our country. Your committee believe that on such a subject as this, inquiry alone will stimulate improvement. Even while they are concluding their report, they observe with pleasure that, in addition to the library formed at Warrington, the creation of a large public library has been planned and accomplished in the public-spirited borough of Salford. It will be a source of sincere satisfaction to your committee if the result of their labours shall be still further to call out, to foster, and to encourage among their countrymen, that love of literature, and reverence for knowledge, of which during the course of their inquiries they have had the gratification to trace the spontaneous development."

On 14th February 1850, Mr. Ewart asked leave to bring in a " Bill for enabling Town Councils to establish Public Libraries and Museums." In view of the importance of this measure an epitome of the debate on the bill is given. Many of the arguments advanced against the bill in the light of present-day experience appear very absurd. Mr. Ewart compared Continental towns with English as to provision of public libraries. "Here there was only a sort of small public library in Manchester; but there was none in Glasgow, Leeds, Sheffield, and other great manufacturing towns; whilst in Amiens, Rouen, Lyons, Marseilles, and other towns in France, the working-classes resorted in numbers to the fine public libraries that were open to them." He dwelt on the advantages to the labouring population of libraries as an instrument of self-teaching. Americans had in every State a State library, accessible to the public. "A few years ago his honourable friend the member for Salford (Mr. J. Brotherton) and himself had introduced a bill enabling town councils to establish public museums of art and sciences. That bill was carried under the auspices and with the assistance of the Right Hon. Baronet the member for Tamworth" (Sir Robert Peel). "They relied upon books being supplied by the donations of individuals. . . . Was it called for by the people?" Warrington and Salford had established libraries, Birmingham and Sheffield had held meetings about the subject. They were not about to ask the Government for any assistance ; they asked merely that those popular institutions might be legally "founded by the people, supported by the people, and enjoyed by the people."

The bill was ordered to be brought in by Mr. W. Ewart, Mr. J. Brotherton, and Mr. George Alexander Hamilton. The first reading was taken on the 20th of the same month, and the second reading on 13th March.

Mr. Ewart explained the object of the bill. He wished to extend the principle of the Museums Act, and said he had received communications from several large towns in Ireland and Scotland desirous of having the bill extended to those countries.

Colonel Sibthorp said this was an attempt to impose a general increase of taxation. "He would be happy at any time to contribute his mite towards providing libraries and proper recreations for the humbler classes in large towns, but he thought that however excellent food for the mind might be, food for the body was now most wanted for the people. He did not like reading at all, and he hated it when at Oxford; but he could not see how one halfpenny in the pound would be enough * to enable town councils to carry into effect the *immense* powers they were to have by this bill." He objected to the borrowing powers proposed, and suggested that Mr. Ewart was unconstitutional in introducing a bill to levy taxes. He proposed that the bill be read that day six months.

Mr. Buck "approved of the objects of this bill, but objected to the unjust mode it proposed for carrying them out." He opposed it in the interests of the landed and manufacturing classes.

Mr. Brotherton was much surprised at the opposition.

* Colonel Sibthorp was not so far wrong here, but the promoters of the bill were no doubt afraid of asking too much.

"The manner in which the money could be applied was restricted to the erection of, or the paying rent for, a building for holding a public library and museum. No power was given to lay out the funds in the purchase of books and specimens or pictures; all these were left to depend on the voluntary contributions of the inhabitants. In the popular boroughs of the country this was a popular measure." "This bill would provide the cheapest police that could possibly be established; and what was the use of education for the people unless they were enabled to consult valuable works which they could not purchase for themselves."

Mr. Goulburn "did not think this bill would exactly impose a tax upon the landed classes; but he feared it would tend to make the poorer inhabitants of boroughs pay extensively for the enjoyments of those who were better off than themselves." "The library would become a mere news-room, which only those well-to-do people who had plenty of leisure . . . would be able to avail themselves of." Again, who was to select the books? "Was there to be a supervision of the different works to be introduced, thereby establishing a kind of censorship for these public libraries?"

Mr. Bernal[-Osborne] "found fault with the bill because it would enable any town council desirous of carrying out the views of any small section of the inhabitants to tax the general body of the ratepayers for an institution that might soon degenerate into a mere political club." "A halfpenny in the pound was really a serious addition to the burden of taxation." "Had the bill been really permissive he would not have opposed it, but it proposed to clothe town councils with imperative powers."

Mr. Hume said: "In the United States there were 10,000 libraries, and this country would do well in that respect to imitate America. He should vote for the second reading, and his further concurrence would be dependent on a provision requiring the concurrence of two-thirds of the ratepayers."

Mr. G. Hamilton said: "Any one who had read the evidence would see how great the desire was on the part of the middle and lower classes, especially in boroughs, for access to libraries, and the means of acquiring useful information." "He thought that libraries were at least as useful as museums."

Lord J. Manners (now Duke of Rutland) said: "Why were not schools, hospitals, and churches to receive the same benefit as the proposed bill gave to libraries and museums? He wished for public libraries and museums in all towns, but objected to the increase of local taxation. The bill "would impose an additional tax upon the agricultural labourers." He had himself been desirous to introduce a bill for providing greens and places of amusement for the public, "and suggested that the Government should bring in a bill combining all the valuable suggestions heard in the debate."

Mr. Labouchere: "Every one who had experience in country towns must know that there was a great want of access to good books. . . . Nothing he believed could be more visionary than the fear that these libraries would be filled with novels and the worst description of publications —bad and useless as literature—or that they would be mere receptacles for newspapers." "Why should they distrust the discretion of town councils? Libraries would have a good effect in promoting education." "His opinion was that the libraries should be lending libraries, or their usefulness might be much impeded."

Mr. W. Miles objected that the bill allowed town councils to tax without consent. He understood the bill to provide that loans for buildings should be paid out of the general rate. He would like a clause inserting that consent of three-fourths of the ratepayers should be obtained before a town council could levy the rate.

Mr. Bright noted the great accordance of opinion on both sides of the House with regard to the object of the bill.

Mr. Spooner objected to taxing the whole community for objects which would benefit only a few, and feared that by the institution of lectures hereafter these libraries would become normal schools of agitation. He anticipated the probability of a call for increased rates, and that it would be urged that another halfpenny would not be too much.

Mr. Slaney contended that "these libraries were to be established upon the lending system, and if that system were fairly carried out, the honourable gentleman's (Mr. Spooner's) objection would be at once met. Where libraries had been established on that principle they had been found highly beneficial to the working-classes." " By encouraging habits which kept the working-man from the public-house they lessened the incentives to a dissolute life, and consequently to idleness and crime, which cost the country much more than all the libraries they could build under the bill."

Mr. Roundell Palmer (afterwards Lord Selborne): The principle of this bill was taxation without the consent of the persons to be taxed. "He strongly dissented from this principle." "What town council would be justified in erecting buildings in anticipation that charitable persons would afterwards present them with books and curiosities?" "It was evident that the bill was intended for ulterior objects, by which powers would be given for the purchase of books, and perhaps also for the fitting up of lecture-rooms. He hoped the House would consider well before they applied to institutions of this nature the principles of public management and compulsory rating."

Sir R. H. Inglis spoke in a similar strain.

Mr. Heywood believed that in all towns the bill would prove of the greatest utility, by the improvement of the morality of the public to which it would lead.

Mr. Wyld regarded it in the light of an economic question, believing that the improvement in the condition of the people would lessen the rates for crime. He referred to an experiment which proved that improved education increased the quantity of work which a given number of people would do.

Mr. Howard (afterwards Baron Howard) thought that such a bill should have come out of a spontaneous movement of the people. He objected to it because it would check private enterprise in Mechanics' Institutions and the like.

Mr. Oswald said the object of the bill ought to be accomplished by private enterprise, as at Ayr and Kilmarnock, and in almost every other burgh of Scotland.

Mr. Ewart replied.

Sir J. Graham, Mr. Muntz, Sir G. Grey, and Mr. Law also spoke.

The second reading was carried by a majority of 17 votes. (Ayes, 118; noes, 101.)

On 10th April the bill went into committee.

Mr. Brotherton said: "Here were £2,000,000 a year paid for the punishment of crime, yet honourable gentlemen objected to permitting communities to tax themselves a halfpenny in the pound for the prevention of crime. In his opinion it was of little use to teach people to read unless you afterwards provided them with books to which they might apply the faculty they had so acquired. It was well known that the large bulk of the labouring classes had not the means of buying books of their own; and, therefore, the next best thing was to collect in every town libraries for their free use. He was satisfied that expenditure upon this object would be productive not only of immense moral good, but of very material public economy in the long run.

It was a melancholy thing to find the members of the Universities taking a foremost position in this opposition to the spread of knowledge. Did these gentlemen and their constituents imagine that no one but themselves was to know anything?"

Mr. Walter said: "If the books were to be lent out in considerable numbers great inconvenience, he thought, must arise; and, on the other hand, if the public were not allowed to take the books they wanted home with them to their own fire-sides, but were compelled to read them in the library, he conceived the bill would be of very little practical use, since it would be quite impossible to afford accommodation in the library for so large a population as that contemplated for each district."

Mr. Hume said that the libraries in the United States were supported by taxation and by voluntary contributions in equal proportions.

Mr. Bernal[-Osborne], Mr. Plowden, and Mr. Muntz came round to the support of the bill.

Mr. W. J. Fox said that books were not contributed to libraries often because there was no secure place of deposit, and considerable collections were sometimes scattered because of the difficulty of providing building accommodation.

Mr. Ewart and Mr. Bright answered objectors.

On a division the ayes were 99; noes, 35.

On 16th May the committee stage was resumed, and continued on 13th June, when Colonel Sibthorp was again in vigorous opposition.

"Instead of endeavouring to afford [the people] industrious and profitable employment, he supposed they would be thinking of supplying the working-classes with quoits, peg-tops, and footballs. . . . He supposed that the honourable member and his friends would soon be thinking of introducing the performances of Punch for the amusement of the people. The bill was wholly uncalled for. There were no petitions presented in favour of it." He moved that the committee stage be taken that day six months.

Mr. Heald had objected to the former bill, but should now vote for going into committee.

Mr. Stanford believed the bill would be as inoperative as the Museums Act, and made the astounding assertion that *not one museum had been erected under that Act.*

Colonel Sibthorp's motion was defeated by 87 votes to 21.

Mr. Law moved an amendment that the committee sit again that day six months, and was defeated by 85 to 47.

On 30th July the third reading was taken, and the undaunted Colonel Sibthorp was again on his feet to move that it be read that day three months. The ayes for the bill were 64; noes, 15.

The bill went through the Lords without comment, and received the royal assent on 14th August 1850.

The Act thus passed allowed the establishment of libraries and museums of art and science together or separately, but applied only to municipal boroughs in England. The mayor, on the request of a town council, was to ascertain whether the Act should be adopted by a poll of burgesses, but a two-thirds majority was required for adoption. The same population and rate limits which appeared in the Museums Act, which this Act abrogated, reappeared, but entrance-fees were abolished. Still no provision was made for buying specimens or books.

On 21st June 1853 a bill to extend the operation of Ewart's Act to Ireland and Scotland was introduced, passed without comment through both

Houses of Parliament, and became law on 20th August of that year.

In the very next year this second Act was altered as regards Scotland by an Act dated 31st July, which is notable as the first admission into library law of the "penny rate in the pound," and the principle of adoption by a public meeting of £10 householders. Strange to say, the bill passed without discussion.

Mr. Ewart sought to extend the benefits of the Act of 1850 to non-municipal towns and vestries by a bill read the first time on 20th March 1854, to raise the halfpenny rate to a penny in England, and to give power to expend rates on books. This bill did not get beyond a second reading owing to the opposition of the Government, though the majority against the bill was only 3 votes out of 173 that were cast. In the debate on the second reading Mr. Monckton Milnes (afterwards Lord Houghton) spoke warmly for the bill. Mr. Ewart stated that thirteen towns had adopted the Act of 1850.

The library law for Ireland was amended on 26th June 1855. This Act still (1897) remains the principal Act for Ireland. There was no opposition to its passage through Parliament. The principal provisions of the Act were that any town council or board of municipal commissioners in a town of 5000 inhabitants might call a public meeting of householders, and a two-thirds majority decide adoption, and that the limit of the library or museum rate be fixed at one penny in the pound.

Undaunted by his defeat in the spring of 1854,

Mr. Ewart on 20th December obtained the first reading of another bill for increasing the usefulness of the 1850 enactment. The second reading took place on 7th February 1855, and the committee stage was reached on 7th March. There was great improvement in the tone of the debate as compared with that on the bill of 1850. Criticism was directed chiefly against the incidence of taxation on the rural parts of large borough areas, and a lively debate took place on the proposal to allow newspapers to be purchased out of the product of the rate.

Mr. Spooner said it was monstrous that poor people residing out of towns should be taxed to enable the townspeople to enjoy the luxury of reading newspapers. More than that, he doubted whether their introduction would be beneficial to the libraries themselves, as it might have a tendency to convert them into mere newspaper reading-rooms and "sedition shops."

Mr. Seymour Fitzgerald objected "it would be most unfair that newspaper rooms should be established at the expense of the agricultural districts."

The Attorney-General (afterwards Lord Chief-Justice Cockburn) said he did not consider the insertion of the word "newspaper" at all objectionable. "The bill sought to accomplish two great objects—first, to lead the labouring population from animal to intellectual pursuits, and, in the second place, to give them as much information as possible. However attractive general knowledge might be, nothing was so attractive as political knowledge, and if they shut out newspapers from libraries, they would deprive them of one of the principal attractions to be found in public-houses. Why should they deprive the labouring classes of the opportunity of acquiring political knowledge? . . . they might trust the selection [of newspapers] to the good sense of those who had the management of the libraries."

There were two divisions in the committee stage, one of them on a proposal to make all the libraries to be established under the Act lending libraries, for which proposal 32 votes were cast, and 49 against it.

Mr. Ewart wanted to exempt libraries and museums from taxation, but in deference to opponents withdrew his amendment. The later stages of the bill were passed without remark, and the royal assent was received on 30th July 1855.

This Act remained the principal Act for England and Wales until 1892, and was without amendment for more than eleven years. The Act repealed the 1850 Act, and provided—

1. In places of more than 5000 inhabitants for the adoption by a two-thirds vote of burgesses and ratepayers at a public meeting convened by a town council or district board.
2. In parishes of 5000 population by a similar vote at a meeting convened by the overseers, on the requisition of ten ratepayers. If the population reached 8000, a poll might be demanded. Commissioners were to be appointed in parishes, agricultural and horticultural land was to be subject to rates on one-third of the assessment, and the library rate was not to exceed one penny in the pound. Vestries of adjoining parishes might co-operate. Books and specimens might be purchased, and money borrowed for buildings.
3. The case of the City of London was specially provided for by the Act.

ADOPTIONS OF THE ACTS

What was the effect of these various enactments? How far were they efficacious?

Well! Ewart's first Act had been passed only about two months when the city of Norwich adopted its provisions by 150 to 7 votes. Winchester, Exeter, and Sheffield considered the question in the following year. Winchester adopted, Exeter and Sheffield rejected the Act, though in a later year both these places reversed the decision. In 1852 a majority declared for adoption at Birmingham, though it was not sufficiently large legally to carry its will into force, but this defect was set right for ever in 1860. In the same year Bolton, Manchester, and Oxford were registered the third, fourth, and fifth adoptions respectively; while Liverpool, for reasons connected with the conditions of a large bequest to its museum, obtained a local Act, which virtually secured the same benefit to that city. In 1853, Blackburn and Sheffield in the north, and Cambridge and Ipswich in the east, accepted the new Act, and the amending Act for Scotland was adopted at Airdrie, the first Scotch town to benefit by a library rate. The next year appears to have been a blank in these annals; but in 1855 adoptions were recorded for Maidstone and Kidderminster before the passing of the Act of that year, and by Hereford two months after the passing of that Act. The Irish Act of the same year was adopted by the city of Cork, though not until recently have the rates actually been applied in that city to the support of a library. The City of London rejected the Act at a public meeting held on 5th November, and on the 16th of the same month Islington began the long series of rejections of the Libraries Acts which have rendered that part of the metropolis unenviable. Paddington about this time took a similar course, and has since obtained a like character.

It should be noted also that a local Act was passed for Brighton in 1850, under which, at a much later period, a public free library was established in the town.

Thus it will be seen that, including the two towns which had established free libraries under the Museums Act, and the two which had obtained local Acts, there were no fewer than eighteen places in England, Ireland, and Scotland which had obtained powers to support free libraries out of a municipal rate, whilst not more than five had declared for the rejection of the Acts conferring such powers.

This chapter of library history may fittingly conclude with a few extracts from speeches delivered at the inauguration of the Manchester Free Libraries on 2nd September 1852. To do justice to this, the inauguration of the public library of the fourth town to adopt Ewart's Act of 1850, but the first to open its doors to the public, would require more space than the plan of this book admits of. The occasion was fittingly honoured by the Manchester people and the Manchester press. Indeed, one may quote the significant words of the *Manchester Courier* of the time in speaking of the occasion: "In our remembrance Manchester has never yet had so rich an intellectual banquet, producing so fair a promise of social amelioration."

Sir Edward Bulwer Lytton (afterwards Lord Lytton) said—

"You have voluntarily contributed to diffuse amongst the poor the means of intellectual wealth. I confess, however, that there are two things which I value still more than this library itself: and the one is, the generous spirit of emulation with which the poor have co-operated with you for their own improvement; and next, the proof you have given that you sympathise with all that can elevate and instruct the classes whose industries you employ. So that this library is a new, an enduring, and a truly conservative link between your wealth and their labour, between the manufacturer and the operative, for every time that the operative shall come into this library he will feel that you have invited knowledge to be the impartial arbiter between all the duties of property and all the rights of labour. . . . Education rightly considered is the work of a life, and libraries are the schools of grown-up men. I was exceeding touched and affected when . . . I was taken . . . to see the library and museum at Peel Park . . . when I saw so many intelligent young faces bending over books with such earnest attention, and when I felt what healthful stimulus had replaced the old English excitements of the alehouse and gin-palace. . . . What minds may be destined to grow up and flourish under the shade of this tree of knowledge which you have now planted none of us can conjecture, but you of the present generation have nobly done your duty, and may calmly leave the result to time, sure that you have placed beside the sorrows and cares and passions of this common sensual life the still monitors that instruct our youth, that direct our manhood, and comfort our old age."

Mr. Charles Dickens said—

"I have seen so many references made in newspapers, Parliamentary debates, and elsewhere, to 'the Manchester School,' that I have long had a considerable anxiety to know what that phrase might mean, and what the Manchester School might be. . . . Now, gentlemen, I have solved this difficulty by finding here to-day that the Manchester School is a great free school, bent on carrying instruction to the poorest hearths. It is this great free school, inviting the humblest workman to come in and to be a student,—this great free school, munificently endowed by voluntary subscription in an incredibly short space of time—starting upon its glorious career with twenty thousand volumes of books—knowing no sect, no party, and no distinction; nothing but the public want and the public good. Henceforth, ladies and gentlemen, this building shall represent for me the Manchester School."

Mr. W. M. Thackeray said—

"Those who know the educated mechanics of this vast city, or of this empire, are aware that they are in the habit of debating the greatest literary and political questions among themselves; that they have leisure to think and talent to speak, much greater than that of other men, who may be obliged like myself to appear for a moment before you; they have their poets and philosophers; their education is very much changed from that of a hundred years ago, when, if you remember, Hogarth represented the idle mechanic as occupied with 'Moll Flanders,' and the good mechanic as having arrived at reading the history of that good apprentice who was made Lord Mayor of London. The mechanics of our day have got their Carlyles to read, their Dickens on the shelf, and their Bulwers by the side of them. . . . I know that our novels are but what we may call the tarts for the people, whereas history is bread, and science is bread, and historical and spiritual truth are that upon which they must be fed. And as every one knows that with every fresh book that is written a new desire springs up for better and better reading, I feel sure that your attempt to open hitherto inaccessible means of acquiring knowledge will be attended with complete success."

Sir James Stephen, Professor of Modern History at Cambridge, after referring to the advantages possessed by students in his University, said—

"If in the midst of such associations and of such associates I had disobeyed your summons to come hither, and to show by my presence, as far as I could, the profound interest which the teachers of youth at Cambridge feel in the moral and in the intellectual welfare of this great city, I should not have known how to justify to myself this strange superiority of my accidental fortunes, and I should have failed in one of the most grateful of the duties which I owe to my own University."

How marked a change from the opposition of the members for the University to the early public library bills!

Mr. Monckton Milnes, M.P. (afterwards Lord Houghton), in the course of a long speech, said—

"In the committee of the House of Commons on which I sat ... in the committee, among the great amount of evidence brought before us, I am not aware that any one sentence touched me more than the evidence given, if I remember right, by some person intimately connected with the manufacturing districts, that books were a good deal more sought for and read by artisans when they had short time and less work than when they were in full employment. I own I thought that I saw in this something more than met the eye. I saw that it was possible for the artisan not enjoying the full produce of his strength and his labour to find at least some consolation for the increased difficulties and self-denial to which he was subject in communing with the minds of others through the various channels of literature, and deriving, perhaps, comfort and advantage for himself in seeing how other men toiled and suffered before him, and beginning to hope for the future time by seeing how full of glorious prospects this world is for the good and the industrious man."

The Earl of Wilton, the Bishop of Manchester, Mr. John Bright, Mr. (afterwards Sir) William Brown, M.P., Mr. Charles Knight, and Mr. Peter Cunningham also spoke at the morning meeting; and in the evening a special meeting for workingmen was held and addressed by the Earl of Shaftesbury, the Rev. Dr. Vaughan, and many of the speakers of the morning.

CHAPTER II

THE HISTORY OF THE FREE PUBLIC LIBRARY MOVEMENT FROM 1856 TO 1877

BY a Parliamentary return made in 1856 on the motion of Mr. Ewart, it is possible to measure the progress made in establishing free popular libraries under municipal control. In eleven towns there had been founded nineteen libraries, with a stock of about 120,000, and an annual use of nearly 650,000 volumes. Subscriptions amounting to more than £26,000 had been received for providing books for libraries and specimens for museums, chiefly the former, and thirteen out of eighteen towns which had adopted the Acts, or obtained local powers for the same ends, had levied rates, producing more than £10,000 per annum, for the support of free libraries and museums. Museums were established in few of the places concerned, though at Winchester, Ipswich, and Maidstone they were more important than the associated libraries, and of quite equal importance in Warrington and in Salford.

In 1856, Birkenhead, Leamington, and the parishes of St. Margaret and St. John at Westminster adopted the Public Libraries Act ; Walsall and Lichfield took a like course in 1857; and Canterbury, which had adopted the Museums Act in 1846, adopted the new Act in 1858.

In the metropolis the parish of Marylebone in May and that of St. Pancras in June of 1856 rejected the Act; Camberwell followed suit in 1858. In January 1857 the borough of Kingston-upon-Hull rejected the Act, this being the first of several rejections that earned the seaport an unenviable name, from which it was not redeemed until five years ago. Cheltenham likewise in 1856 began the record of a series of rejections extending over a long period, but happily terminated in 1883. In February 1857 Haslingden, in Lancashire, considered and rejected the Act. In 1860, Cardiff, by a majority of one in a small public meeting, determined against adoption, but two years afterwards triumphantly reversed the decision. In 1860, also, Bridgwater, Birmingham, Northampton, and Stockport adopted the Act—each of the two last-named places to establish a museum, which after many years was supplemented by a free library. The City of London recorded a second rejection in July 1861. At this time, with the exception of Exeter, Haslingden, Hull, and the London parishes, all the places which had once recorded a rejection had now registered their adoption of the Act. In 1860 the town of Ennis recorded the second adoption of the Irish Public Libraries Act of 1855. For some reason, however, that adoption has been ineffectual even to the present day, for Ennis is yet without a free public library.

In a Parliamentary return it is stated that Leicester adopted Ewart's Act in 1862; it has also been stated that in that year Leicester rejected the Act, but the truth is, that Leicester never did formally adopt the Public Libraries Act, though the town established a museum in 1848, and in 1849 the council resolved to apply an additional halfpenny rate to the establishment of a free library. The year 1863 added to the list of adoptions the name of Burslem, and 1865 that of Warwick. In 1865, too, Oldham by a local Act obtained powers even greater than those in Ewart's Act for the establishment of libraries, museums, and art galleries. In 1866, Dundee adopted the Scotch Act of 1854, thus recording the second instance of the acceptance of the powers of a Public Libraries Act in Scotland. Paisley took a similar course in 1867, aided to a decision by the princely generosity of Sir Peter Coats. In that year, too, it is said that Berwick adopted the Public Libraries Act, but a committee having been appointed, the members refused to act, hence the adoption became abortive.

Another English town, Sunderland, obtained local powers in reference to libraries and museums by a private bill in the year 1866.

The first bill, amending the 1855 Act, was brought in by Mr. Ewart and Mr. Dunlop on 27th February 1866. In introducing the measure, Mr. Ewart said that twenty-five public libraries had been established under the Public Libraries Act, besides schools of art and museums. The Chancellor of the Exchequer, the Right Hon. B. Disraeli (Lord Beaconsfield), said : " I cannot refrain from seizing this opportunity of cordially congratulating my honourable friend on having been permitted during a long and honourable Parliamentary life to see the gradual development of the fruit of his labour, and to watch these institutions spread throughout the great centres of population, where it is so desirable they should exist. My honourable friend's name is associated with many achievements of public utility, but with this act of legislation, I think, he may feel assured that his name will be associated not only during his life, but after he is gone."

In the committee stage of the bill Mr. Cheetham moved a new clause to the bill, exempting libraries and museums from payment of rates. Considerable discussion ensued, and the motion was rejected by 54 to 10 votes.

The measure passed through both Houses without opposition, and on its second reading in the Lords (3rd August) the Earl of Shaftesbury said : "The Act (of 1855) had proved very useful ; twenty-seven free public libraries had been established under it throughout the country, which were quite unrestricted as to their admission, and were resorted to by rich and poor. To every one of these libraries a lending library was attached, which added very much to the public value of these institutions. The operation of the present bill was to extend the operation of the original Act by one or two trifling provisions, and to assimilate the law in Scotland to that in England and Ireland."

The bill received the royal assent on 10th August. It extended the initiative as to adoption so as to include a requisition from ten ratepayers, did away with the population limit, enlarged the power of co-operation among authorities, reduced the two-thirds majority of the 1855 Act to a simple majority, and withdrew the right to demand a poll.

In the following year a further Amending Act was found necessary for Scotland, and on 26th March a bill introduced by Mr. Ewart and Sir John Ogilvy was read a first time. There was no discussion at any stage, and the bill received the royal assent on 15th July 1867.

The principal differences between this Act and the preceding related to the constitution of the library committee (which in the Scotch Act was to consist of ten members of a board or council and ten non-members), and the period which must expire between rejection and another attempt at adoption, viz.: in the English Act one year, in the Scotch, two years.

Adoptions of the English Acts took place at Nottingham and at Coventry in 1867. At the former place there was but a single dissentient in the public meeting, and he became one of the earliest and most frequent borrowers from the free library after its establishment! Leeds and Doncaster followed in 1868; Tynemouth, Wolverhampton, and Ashton-under-Lyne in 1869; and in 1870, Newport (Monmouthshire), Swansea, Exeter, Bilston, West Bromwich, Derby, Rochdale, and

Middlesborough. The Scotch Act of 1867 was also adopted in this year by the town of Forfar. The borough of St. Helens in 1869 obtained a local Act, under which, at a later date, the town established its free public library. In the list of rejections during the period 1867-70 are the names of two of the towns which occur in the list of adoptions, thus the repentance of Swansea and Wolverhampton was not long delayed. The last-named town is said to have twice rejected the Acts before adopting them in 1869. At Gloucester a hostile meeting prevented the taking of a vote on the question at issue in 1867, though now the city is in course of organising a free library, having adopted the Act in 1894. Margate rejected the Acts in 1867, Edinburgh by a vote of 1025 to 68, and Reading in 1868, Bath in 1869, Thurso in 1870. Besides these towns, Macclesfield rejected the Acts sometime before 1869, and Portsmouth twice before the same year; though the evidence of a Parliamentary return points rather to the fact that the legal adviser of the corporation at the time did not understand the provisions of Ewart's Act which refer to the mode of adoption. Every one of the places except Bath which rejected the Acts during 1867-70 has since reversed the decision, and in most of them very flourishing free libraries now exist.

On the 6th May 1869 Mr. Baines, M.P., moved for a return, which was furnished to Parliament on 11th April 1870. The figures in this return do not all refer to the same year, but one may take them as very nearly representing the state of the free public libraries of the country at the end of 1868. Forty-six adoptions, or local Acts equivalent thereto, had been obtained; twenty-nine places had established fifty-two libraries, with nearly half a million volumes and a yearly use of 3,400,000 volumes. The amount raised by rate for public libraries and museums was at least £25,400 per annum.

To compare these figures with those of the return of fourteen years before is interesting and instructive, but the progress thus indicated is slow in comparison with that of later years. A no inconsiderable cause of the later successes was the passing of the Elementary Education Act of 1870 —a law for ever honourably associated with the name of the Right Hon. W. E. Forster, M.P. The amount of illiteracy among the working-classes before and for a few years after the passing of that Act, it is now very difficult to realise; and the present improvement can probably be appreciated only by one who has had long experience as polling clerk or as presiding officer at municipal and parliamentary elections. That improvement, due to Forster's Act and its successors, has had a great effect on the use of existing public libraries and reading-rooms, and the establishment of such instruments of civilisation in fresh localities. This progress was assisted by the improvements in library law which were obtained in 1871.

The Scotch Public Libraries Act was amended by an Act dated 31st July 1871. Mr. Armistead, Sir John Ogilvy, and Mr. Kinnaird brought in the bill on 20th June, and it passed through all its stages in both Houses without remark, except for a short debate in the Lords on the second reading (11th July). The Act had reference chiefly to the borrowing powers of authorities, which it limited, so as to prevent the pledging of resources by extravagant initial expenditure on buildings. Power is also given to enact bye-laws, a power not yet possessed under any English Act, though still greatly needed in English libraries.

An Amending Act, extending the operation of free libraries to local boards under the Public Health Act 1848, received the royal assent on 14th August. The bill was introduced by Mr. J. G. Talbot, Mr. George Gregory, and Mr. Lyttleton, and passed through both Houses without debate.

Before proceeding to chronicle the further adoptions of the Acts, it may be well to pause and review the progress of the movement throughout the kingdom. In Scotland it had made slight headway; Airdrie, Paisley, Dundee, Forfar, and Berwick alone had adopted the Act. As for Ireland, only Cork and Ennis in all that large country had taken a similar course. In Wales, the two largest towns, Cardiff and Swansea, had availed themselves of library legislation; and in England, towns in twenty-four out of the forty counties had begun the organisation, or were actually enjoying the benefit, of free libraries. There are now (1897) only two counties in England where there is not a free library, but at the end of 1870 there were sixteen counties without that advantage: Cumberland, Westmorland, Lincoln, Rutland, Essex, Surrey, Wilts, Dorset,

ADOPTIONS, 1871-77

Cornwall, Gloucester, Herefordshire, Shropshire, Berkshire, Buckinghamshire, Bedford, Huntingdon.

Watford and Darwen dispute the honour of being the first Local Board District to adopt the Amending Act of 1871 in the year in which it was passed. Bangor, in Wales, adopted the Acts the same year, and Plymouth, Hereford, Bradford, and South Shields in England, and Coleraine in Ireland. The year 1872 produced four rejections and three adoptions, the latter at Aberystwith, at Galashiels, and at Thurso. In the following year no places declared either for or against the Acts, but in 1874 the following seven places declared their acceptance of their provisions, viz. : Bristol, where the second oldest free library in England was to form the nucleus of the free popular libraries of the city, Chester, Macclesfield, nobly aided by the gift of the Chadwick Library (building and books), Willenhall, Heywood, Newcastle-on-Tyne, and Stockton-on-Tees. In 1875 Brierley Hill, Stoke-on-Trent, Darlaston, Chesterfield, and Southport, the last-named place aided by the handsome gift of Mr. Atkinson, adopted the Acts ; and in 1876, Portsmouth, Handsworth, Smethwick, Rotherham, Wednesbury, and Wigan increased the number. In 1877, Bideford, Reading, and Aston Manor declared in the same sense, and Inverness adopted the Scotch Public Libraries Acts.

During the period 1871-77 rejections were declared at Newcastle-on-Tyne, through informality, Bath (the second time), Worcester, and Aberdeen— these in 1872 ; at Arbroath in 1873, at St. Pancras for the second time in 1874, at Islington also for the second time in 1874 or 1875 (by 1435 votes to 338), at Accrington in 1875, at Chatham and at Bath (for the third time) in 1877, and at Kensington in 1878. Newcastle, Worcester, Aberdeen, and Kensington have long ago brought forth fruits meet for repentance, and Arbroath much more recently, but the five other parishes or towns are still unmoved.

Thus in these seven years, although good and steady progress was made, but one English county (Gloucester) was newly conquered, thus leaving fifteen counties at the end of 1877 without a single free public library.

For the last year of the period additional legislation has to be recorded. A bill was introduced to Parliament in 1877 (19th April) by Mr. Murphy, Mr. Maurice Brooks, Mr. James Corry, and Mr. O'Shaughnessy, and received the royal assent on 28th June. It extended the range of objects for which the penny library rate might be applied in Ireland so as to include schools of music, added to the powers under the Irish Act of 1855 that of borrowing on a mortgage of the borough or town fund; and provided that non-members of the local council or board might be members of the library committee. This bill became law without comment during its progress in either House.

A Public Libraries Act Amendment Bill was also introduced this year by Mr. Mundella, Sir John Lubbock, Mr. Chamberlain, and Mr. Anderson, but was subsequently dropped. Mr. Anderson's and Mr. Mundella's names, however, together with Mr. O'Shaughnessy's, appear on a second bill, which was read a first time on 16th April, and became law on 14th August. The object of this Act was to provide an alternative method of adopting by "voting papers," and to allow of a limitation of the rate below "one penny," where ratepayers vote to that effect. No doubt the Act was a concession to the ratepayers of London, but it is doubtful whether it has diminished the forces of opposition, while it has had a very injurious effect on the development of particular free libraries.

The free public library had now existed as a municipal institution of a popular character for nigh upon thirty years, with no national organisation to advocate its claims in untried fields of possible extension. The Parliamentary opposition to library legislation of early days had now ceased, and public library bills were allowed to pass through Parliament without debate or with a word of unchallenged praise. In the United States of America also the establishment of free town libraries had been contemporaneously active and progressive. The time, therefore, seemed ripe for an international congress of those immediately concerned in the administration of libraries, to compare plans and methods, with a view to increasing the prosperity and usefulness of public libraries of every kind. During the Centennial Exhibition of 1876 a general conference of librarians had been held at Philadelphia, the second of such conferences in America, the first having been held in 1853 at New York. The Philadelphia conference was so successful that Mr. E. W. B. Nicholson, at that time librarian of the London Institution, but now of the Bodleian Library, Oxford, in an article in the *Academy* of 27th January 1877, urged the desirability of a similar meeting in London. This was followed up by correspondence with the responsible heads of many libraries, a meeting at the London Library, and the formation of an organising committee, consisting of Mr. George Bullen, at that time Keeper of the Printed Books, the editor of the present series of public library manuals, then Superintendent of the Reading-room, and the present Principal Librarian of the Museum, Mr. (now Sir) Edward Maunde Thompson, at that time Assistant Keeper in the department of manuscripts, besides the librarians of all the important libraries in the metropolis, Mr. Henry Stevens (of Vermont), and Mr. J. Leighton. The result of the committee's labours may be summed up in these words, quoted from the introduction to the published *Transactions of the London Conference*, edited by the secretaries, Messrs. E. W. B. Nicholson and H. R. Tedder :—

"The first conference of librarians in Europe was held in the lecture theatre of the London Institution on October 2nd, 3rd, 4th, 5th, 1877. The transactions and proceedings form a [handsome folio] volume of nearly three hundred pages, which includes descriptions of the visits to some of the most representative metropolitan libraries, as well as of the exhibition of library designs, catalogues, and appliances. The list of names enumerates

218 members, nearly all of whom came to the meetings, among the most assiduous attendants being the sixteen visitors from the United States. The French Government, with that enlightened zeal for progress and new ideas which is so marked a quality of the national character, deputed a special commission to report on the conference. The German and Greek Governments were likewise represented. . . . To the 139 libraries represented, Belgium contributed 1, Denmark 2, France 4, Italy 1, the United States 17, Victoria 1, and Great Britain and Ireland 113. [There were about thirty delegates from free public libraries in municipalities.] Nearly every point of library economy received more or less attention, and one action of the conference was the thorough ventilation of the great question of printing the catalogue of the British Museum."

References are also made to the formation of the new Library Association of the United Kingdom which resulted from this international gathering. About this Association more will be said in a succeeding chapter. Its formation marks the commencement of a new period in the history of the free library in Great Britain.

Another Parliamentary return appeared in 1876, and was continued in 1877. The return is very defective, there being no particulars given as to sixteen places which had adopted the Acts, or acquired library clauses in local Acts, before the end of 1876. Nevertheless, the positive information given is of great value as showing the progress since the date of the previous return. In the fifty-seven places named there were eighty-nine free libraries established, with considerably more than a million volumes, and an annual issue of more than five millions. The annual rates levied in the aggregate amounted to no less than £70,750.

At the end of 1877 there had been eighty adoptions of the Public Libraries Acts, three free libraries had been established under the Museums Acts, and five towns had acquired powers to establish free libraries under local Acts. Thus in all, eighty-eight places had acquired the legal right to a free public library. In the period covered by this chapter, the gifts of the Brown Library at Liverpool, the Atkinson Library at Southport, the Chadwick Library at Macclesfield, and the Free Library at Derby, show that the springs of private munificence were not dried up by the legal enactments which allowed the application of local rates to every purpose connected with a public free library.

CHAPTER III

THE HISTORY OF THE FREE PUBLIC LIBRARY MOVEMENT FROM 1878 TO 1887

THE rejections of the Public Libraries Acts during the following five years (1878-82) may be thus set forth :—

1878. Cheltenham (second rejection); Hackney (4369 against, 631 for); Whitechapel (496 against, 261 for).
1879. Camberwell (second rejection), where the adverse vote was to the favourable as two to one, but only one voter in eleven voted; Arbroath (second rejection).
1880. Northwich; Bath (for the fourth time).
1881. Huddersfield, where, out of 15,000 voters, 2425 went against, and 1264 for adoption; Edinburgh (second rejection), with 15,708 votes against, and only 7619 for; York (where a statutory meeting had voted favourably, but a poll went adversely, there being 4939 against, and 3044 in favour of the proposal).
1882. Ayr; Hastings; Hull (second rejection, 5889 to 4212); Lynn (504 to 201); Merthyr-Tydvil (where after a six days' poll 2010 votes were recorded adverse, and 1758 favourable to adoption); Putney (where the poll reversed the decision of a previous public meeting).

In this list there are four places in the metropolitan district, but the decisions have since been reversed in three of them, and six other places in the list have since established free public libraries. Indeed, the only places still unconverted are Hackney, Bath, Huddersfield, Hastings, Lynn, and Merthyr Tydvil. In some of these places it is probable that a wisely directed agitation would now lead to a reversal of former decisions. As a type of the kind of resistance which the friends of free libraries have had to contend with, the following may be taken. In February 1881 two huge bills carried by sandwich-men through the streets of Edinburgh bore these words—

RATEPAYERS!

RESIST THIS FREE LIBRARY DODGE,

AND SAVE YOURSELVES FROM THE BURDEN OF £6000

OF ADDITIONAL TAXATION.

RETURN YOUR CARDS MARKED "NO."

BE SURE AND SIGN YOUR NAMES.

The opponents of the movement had a committee sitting daily and vigorously canvassing the city, while the friends of libraries had no organisation at all. Out of more than 41,000 voters, more than 15,500 did not trouble to return the voting paper. A few years served to change all this, and the beneficence of a millionaire in 1886 neutralised the unfortunate decision of 1881.

It is more agreeable to observe the good side of

the picture. The following statement exhibits the new adoptions in yearly sequence :—

1878. Wrexham, Folkestone, St. Albans, Dudley, Clitheroe, Preston, Hawick.
1879. Richmond, Worcester, Stafford, Blackpool.
1880. Devonport, Gateshead, Sligo, Dunfermline.
1881. Kingston-on-Thames, Tamworth, Newark-on-Trent, Runcorn, Halifax, Barrow-in-Furness, Dumbarton.
1882. Tunbridge, Twickenham, Penrith, Belfast.

During these five years the improvement of public library legislation was much under the consideration of the administrators of public libraries and their friends. The Library Association at their annual meeting listened to papers from Mr. E. W. B. Nicholson and Mr. G. L. Campbell in 1879, and appointed a committee to cause to be introduced in Parliament a bill to remedy the defects pointed out. This committee learned that the Metropolitan Free Libraries Association—a body which did useful pioneer work in the metropolis—had already drafted a bill to secure similar ends. A bill, the result of mutual deliberations, was introduced by Sir John Lubbock on 7th January 1881. Several features of the bill, however, met with strong disapproval in the country. The Birmingham local committee of the Library Association, and a conference convened at Manchester by the Mayor, condemned several of its proposals; and although Sir John Lubbock desired to press the second reading, and to introduce later amendments to bring the bill into harmony with the views of library managers, the bill was not proceeded with.

It is interesting to find that the proposal of the Act of 1877 regarding the limitation of the rate to a fraction of a penny was considered reactionary, and the promoters of the bill proposed, in consolidating the library laws, to omit the power of limitation below one penny. A clause which would have allowed the Education Department to appoint an inspector seems to have aroused special opposition. At that time probably the suggestion was premature, but surely no evil and much benefit would accrue if it were to be revived in the near future and associated with grants to the weaker libraries from the imperial exchequer. The fear of a dead uniformity of method resulting therefrom may now be characterised as a groundless fear. The whole trend of opinion of present-day educationalists is in the contrary direction, and State Education Departments are reflecting that opinion more and more. Another reasonable proposal of the bill was that annual reports should be furnished to the Education Department and summarised in Parliamentary returns.

In 1879 a destructive fire reduced the free library of Birmingham to ashes; but out of this disaster, and through the energy and generosity of the people of that city, a newer and ampler library arose, though alas! deficient in some never to be replaced treasures of the older library. This new Central Free Library was opened in great state on the 1st June 1882, under the presidency of the Mayor (Mr. Alderman Avery). The speeches delivered on the occasion were of more than local importance. As the utterances of leaders of thought and action of that time they indicate a favourable advance in public sentiment respecting the free library as an institution, and the arguments uttered for a local case are of very wide, nearly universal, application. Space precludes the reproduction of more than selected passages from the speeches at the opening ceremony and at the banquet following. The story of the Birmingham Free Libraries was briefly but ably told by the Mayor, and the episode of the fire, with the noble response to the needs created by it. The treasurer of the Restoration Fund reported that subscriptions exceeding £15,000 had been received. Mr. John Bright then delivered the inaugural address, which abounded in autobiographical interest through its display of his love of books and libraries. He said—

"Books, it is true, are silent as you see them on their shelves, but silent as they are, I think—to me it is so—that when I enter a library I feel as if almost the dead were present, and I know if I could put questions to these books they would answer me with all the faithfulness and fulness which have been left in them by the great men who have left the books to us. Have none of us, or, may I not say, are there any of us who have not felt some of this feeling when in a great library—I don't mean in a library quite as big as that of the British Museum or the Bodleian Library at Oxford, where books are so many that they seem to overwhelm one—but libraries that are not absolutely unapproachable in their magnitude? . . . There are hundreds of libraries throughout this country which are of the kind which I describe—such, that when you are within their walls, and see their shelves, and these thousands of volumes, and consider for a moment who they are that wrote them, who has gathered them together, for whom they are intended, how much wisdom they contain, what they will tell to future ages, it is impossible not to feel something of solemnity, and of tranquillity, when you are spending time in rooms like these. You may have in a house costly pictures and costly ornaments, and a great variety of decorations, yet, so far as my judgment goes, I would prefer to have one comfortable room well-stocked with books, to all which you can give me which even the highest art can supply."

Amongst other things Mr. Joseph Chamberlain said—

"I am a great believer in the advantages of miscellaneous reading. I believe that by it we open our minds to new ideas, we widen our sympathies, and expand our intellectual and moral horizon; and I know also, that for the student who desires to pursue thoroughly any subject, it is absolutely necessary that he should have access to books, many of which are costly, many of which are difficult to obtain, even to the richest of single individuals, but which it is in the power of a community to provide for all its members alike. And in this provision there is no favour conferred; it is a right which is enjoyed by all. Sir, I have often thought that that is a kind of communism which the least revolutionary amongst us may be proud to advocate. It imparts, it gives to every man a sense of possession and knowledge of the rights and privileges of property which cannot, I think, constitute any danger to the property of others. It behoves us all to make it a point of honour, that for the benefit of this generation, and as an example to those who shall succeed it, we will endeavour to show that trade and commerce have not the narrowing effect which some people have attributed to them, and that even in the eager pursuits of material interests, which is at once a sign of the times and an evidence of our enterprise and activity, we have yet found time to leave behind us a striking proof of the estimate which we have set upon the teaching of literature and of art, and of the value which we ascribe to their potent influence in forming the character, the manners, and in contributing to the happiness of the population."

Returning now to the consideration of the progress of the free library movement in the country, the following adoptions of the Acts occurred in the four years 1883 to 1886 :—

1883. Ealing, Wimbledon, Cheltenham, Shrewsbury, Tipton, Northwich, Darlington, Wandsworth (the second adoption in London).
1884. Newcastle-under-Lyme, Hanley, Hucknall Torkard, Bootle, Kingston, Tarves (the first adoption in a purely rural district), Aberdeen.
1885. Truro (the first adoption in Cornwall), Poole, Yarmouth, Loughborough, Tunstall, Widnes, Hindley, Alloa.
1886. Gosport and Alverstoke, Weston-super-Mare, Buxton, Harrogate, Fulham, Lambeth, Edinburgh, Douglas (under the Manx Act).

Against these thirty-one adoptions are to be set the following thirteen rejections :—

1883. Battersea (where a poll reversed the vestry's acceptance), Brentford (295 to 242 votes), Cambuslang, Colchester, Taunton (2039 to 484 votes), Wheatley, near Doncaster (66 to 14).

1884. Elgin, Peterborough (1632 to 1115 votes).
1885. Glasgow (29,946 to 22,755 votes).
1886. Deptford (3080 to 1090), Ramsgate (hostile meeting, no resolution submitted), Newton Heath (poll demanded, adoption declared the following year), Croydon (1024 to 576).

Eight of these places reversed their decision in a very short time.

Legislation during these four years was extended by the Act of 1884, and the Manx Acts of 1885 and 1886. The bill of 1884 was introduced in the House of Lords by the Lord President of the Committee of Council on Education (Lord Carlingford) on 13th May, and passed through both Houses with no more comment than an explanation of the scope of the bill by its promoter. The royal assent was declared on 28th July.

This Act, probably originating out of the circumstances of the free library committee at Cardiff, which, as a local committee, had conducted for years a school in connection with the Science and Art Department, provided that library authorities might accept Parliamentary grants in aid from the Committee of the Privy Council on Education for purposes connected with the teaching of science and art, and made clear that buildings might be erected for public libraries, public museums, schools for science, art galleries, schools for art, or for any of these objects. Where the Acts had been adopted for one of these purposes, others could be added without further proceedings. It will be perceived that this Act greatly extended the educational scope of the free library, whilst providing for imperial aid for the added work of committees. It was a weakness in the Act that the penny limit was left unaltered, although the grants contemplated by the Act were not sufficient to meet the expenses incurred for their receipt by any library authority. The Act itself demonstrated the acceptance of the belief in official quarters that the free library had become a valuable educational instrument and ally. At Worcester one result of the Act was that notice was given at the October meeting of the free library committee that a series of resolutions would be moved in favour of bringing the science and art schools under one management with the free library and museum. Mr. Downes's proposal for "the creation of one institution combining libraries, museums, art schools, science school, and art gallery" was the seed out of which has grown up the magnificent "Victoria Institute" in this beautiful city.

Out of the wreck of the Metropolitan Free Libraries Association Bill, and from the dissatisfaction it produced in the provinces, grew up the bill then known as Mr. Hopwood's, which came to a second reading in 1883, and was talked out by Mr. Warton. This bill was under discussion among library managers in the Northern Counties for several years, and at the annual meeting of the Library Association in 1886 a resolution affirming the desirability of the re-introduction of Mr. Hopwood's bill was carried. Nothing seems to have come of it in the end, probably because the bill of 1887, backed by Sir John Lubbock and others, met many of the needs which it was designed to supply. Mr. Hopwood's bill proposed a twopenny library rate, and better machinery for combining local authorities for common purposes than any Act yet has provided.

In 1885 the House of Keys of the Isle of Man passed a Public Libraries Act, clearly modelled on the English law, while simpler in its provisions. This was promulgated on 6th July, but the following year the Isle of Man Local Government Act, 1886, passed 16th July, promulgated 14th December, superseded the earlier Act, by embodying its powers and provisions in sections 220 to 226. As yet, however, only one town, Douglas, has put into operation this beneficial enactment.

The year 1887, the jubilee year of our beloved Queen's happy and glorious reign, is noticeable in free library annals for the great activity of both friends and foes. In 1886, Mr. Thomas Greenwood published his useful epitome of information, "Public Libraries," and circulated it widely. His enthusiastic advocacy of free libraries found a response in many hearts, and the erection or establishment of free libraries became for the time a popular form of celebration of the Queen's jubilee. No year has witnessed so many adoptions of the Acts as the year 1887, and though the rejections numbered fifteen, they are well outweighed by thirty adoptions. Seven of the rejections have since been reversed.

The rejections were Croydon (1090 to 1017 votes), Droylesden, Gloucester (2509 to 916), Huddersfield

(2385 to 1303), Paddington (second rejection, 5845 to 1652), Islington (third rejection, 15,776 to 10,152), Acton (1145 to 788), Woolwich (2310 to 895), West Ham (1220 to 800), Alnwick (664 to 456), Skelmersdale (300 to 15), York (2832 to 2015), Falkirk (a gift of £1000 declined), Mountain Ash (111 to 52, out of 2724 voters), Scarborough (2105 to 1408).

The adoptions were Welshpool, Pontypridd, Carnarvon, Queenborough, Sittingbourne, Southampton, Carlton (Notts), Leek, Nantwich, Winsford, Denton and Haughton, Middleton, Moss Side, Newton Heath (since absorbed into Manchester), Fleetwood, Dewsbury, Millom, Whitehaven, Battersea, Bermondsey, Chelsea, Clapham, Clerkenwell, Hammersmith, Kensington, Putney, Rotherhithe, St. Martin-in-the-Fields, Rathmines and Rathgar, Grangemouth, Wick.

An interesting feature of these lists is the place occupied by the county of London; four rejections and ten adoptions show that at length the interest of London was really aroused. That interest was still further accentuated by the passing of the Act of 1887, which gave power to any district, as defined by the Metropolis Management Act, 1885, to adopt on the lines of a parish. The same Act placed an English library authority on the same footing as an urban sanitary authority as to borrowing of money, with many other improvements of a minor nature.

On 28th January a bill had been introduced into the House of Commons by Sir John Lubbock,

Mr. Arthur Cohen, Mr. Collins, Sir John Kennaway, and Sir Lyon Playfair, and had been withdrawn on 30th March, but on 6th April the same names, with the addition of Mr. Baggallay's and Mr. Justin MacCarthy's, appeared on the back of a new Public Libraries Acts Amendment Bill. On the occasion of the second reading (4th July) Sir John Lubbock said—

"That the extension of free libraries in the metropolis had been much checked, because the area prescribed under the law as it stood was the parish. Some of the metropolitan parishes were, of course, large, and they constituted a very suitable area. Many, however, were very small, and in them the parishioners naturally felt that if they established a free library the whole expense would fall on them, while their neighbours would share the benefit. For various administrative purposes those parishes were already grouped in district boards, and it was believed by the supporters of free libraries that their adoption would be much encouraged by permitting the area adopted to be either the parish or the district as preferred. The only other provision to which he need refer applied to small places, and villages where the rateable value was so small that the maximum rate—namely, a penny in the pound—was insufficient to erect, or even rent, a building, and when it would permit the application of the Act to lending libraries. The provision was, however, applicable to larger places, which might prefer, before going to greater expense, to establish a lending library. He hoped that the adoption of the bill would promote the establishment of free libraries, and he trusted it would meet with the approval of the House."

The principle of the bill was accepted without division, but in committee, on 19th July, Sir John

THE CONSOLIDATING ACT FOR SCOTLAND 59

Lubbock proposed various amendments, which were agreed to.

The Secretary to the Treasury (Mr. Jackson, Leeds, N.) proposed a new clause (transfer to Local Government Board of certain functions of the Treasury), and a new clause (provisions as to a parish partly within and partly without a borough or district) was proposed by Mr. O. V. Morgan (Battersea).

In the same session of Parliament a consolidating bill for Scotland was carried. Mr. Caldwell, Dr. Cameron, and Mr. Cameron Corbett introduced a measure on 28th January, which was withdrawn on 23rd February. A new bill, bearing the names of Mr. Cameron Corbett and Mr. Graham, took the place of the one withdrawn, and was read on 24th February. No discussion took place at any stage, and the royal assent was obtained on 16th September.

This Act had been prepared by Mr. Richard Brown under the auspices of the Glasgow Public Libraries Association, and it is now the principal Act for Scotland.

In the periodical press the free library did not occupy a very large space, neither did it lack able defenders who could wield the pen when the occasion demanded their services.

One of the most important articles which appeared in the decade 1878–87 on the question of the free library was contributed to the *Contemporary Review* of March 1881 by Professor W. Stanley Jevons, and was afterwards reprinted in his "Methods of Social Reform," 1883. The author writes:—

"The main *raison d'être* of free public libraries, as indeed of public museums, art galleries, parks, halls, public clocks, and many other kinds of public works, is the enormous increase of utility which is thereby acquired for the community at a trifling cost. If a beautiful picture be hung in the dining-room of a private house, it may perhaps be gazed at by a few guests a score or two of times in the year. Its real utility is that of ministering to the selfish pride of its owner. If it be hung in the National Gallery, it will be enjoyed by hundreds of thousands of persons, whose glances it need hardly be said do not tend to wear out the canvas. The same principle applies to books in common ownership. If a man possesses a library of a few thousand volumes, by far the greater part of them must lie for years untouched upon the shelves; he cannot possibly use more than a fraction of the whole in any one year. But a library of five or ten thousand volumes opened free to the population of a town may be used a thousand times as much. It is a striking case of what I propose to call *the principle of the multiplication of utility*, a principle which lies at the base of some of the most important processes of political economy, including the division of labour. . . . We must remember that, in addition to the borrowing and consulting of books, the readers have in most cases a cheerful, well-warmed, and well-lighted sitting-room, supplied with newspapers and magazine tables. To many a moneyless weary man the free library is a literary club, an unexceptionable refuge from the strife and dangers of life. . . . Even if they were very costly, free libraries would be less expensive establishments than prisons, courts of justice, poor-houses, and other institutions maintained by public money; or the gin-palaces, music-halls, and theatres maintained by private expenditure."

THE PARLIAMENTARY RETURN OF 1885

This paper also contains many most interesting and permanently valuable remarks on the provision of free libraries for village populations, remarks which might do much good if reprinted and circulated widely at the present time.

Notable instances of private generosity during the period 1878-87 were the splendid Winnard and Taylor bequests at Wigan, the gifts of Sir P. Coats to Paisley, and Mr. J. M. Keiller's gift of 10,000 guineas to Dundee, Mr. Andrew Carnegie's to Dunfermline, and Sir William Gilstrap's to Newark-on-Trent. These the reader will find recorded in the second part of this book, with many other instances of public subscriptions of great value contributed in the jubilee year towards the founding of free libraries. And better things were yet to come.

At the end of 1884 there had been 130 adoptions of the Public Libraries Acts in the United Kingdom. A Parliamentary return printed in 1885 gives particulars which may be taken as fairly representing the state of free libraries at that time. The return mentions only 112 places, and gives particulars of 100. In these there were 251 libraries, 1,910,630 volumes, and the rates levied for their support came to £120,337 for the year. The annual issues were certainly more than ten millions, three times as many as in 1868, two years before Forster's Elementary Education Act was passed.

By the end of 1877, 176 places had adopted the Public Libraries Acts, or had provided the same advantages for their residents under local Acts.

CHAPTER IV

THE HISTORY OF THE FREE PUBLIC LIBRARY MOVEMENT FROM 1888 TO 1896

THE history of the free library movement in the years subsequent to 1887 is in many respects more remarkable than in any equal period of earlier time. Opposition, and that of no feeble order, was encountered here and there, yet no less than 150 adoptions of the Acts against about 40 rejections are to be chronicled.

The rejections of this period are here set out; the numbers following names indicate the noes and ayes recorded at the voting :—

1888. Newington (4319, 3606); Monk Bretton (74, 20); Taunton (956, 309); West Cowes (204, 120); Tunbridge Wells (1570, 567); Glasgow, second refusal (22,987, 13,550); Marylebone, second refusal (4964, 1946); Hull, third refusal (13,664, 5370); Plumstead (2988, 1353); Woolwich (2098, 766); Luton (majority of 3 to 1); Stroud.

1889. Llandudno (771, 626); Colne (1317, 660); Tottenham (156, 70—out of 8000 voters).

1890. Plumstead, second refusal (2857, 2291)—diminished majority; Hastings (1927, 595); Bowden (public meeting against); Deptford, second refusal (1758, 666)—here 11,000 voting papers were issued.

1891. Greenwich (2592, 1633); Marylebone, third refusal (4701, 1080)—smaller poll, increased adverse majority; Paddington, third refusal (majority of 3 to 1); Hackney, second refusal (7076, 5703); Bethnal Green (3098, 2966); Islington, fourth refusal (10,912, 7542); Gainsborough (1057, 211).

1892. Ilkeston (1284, 532).

1893. Cockermouth (382, 260); Deptford, third refusal (2873, 2673)—much diminished majority on a much larger poll; Grantham (1729, 460); Marylebone, fourth refusal (4726, 3454)—opposition nearly stationary, poll of the ayes three times that of 1891.

By the English Acts of 1893, and the Scotch of 1894, a large class of constituencies were delivered from the turmoil of a poll; indeed, London and the rural parishes (the latter not necessarily) are the only places left to decide adoption by this means, consequently there are few popular rejections to record for the later years.

Such as they are, here they are noted :—

1894. Deptford, fourth refusal (3552, 2316)—nearly 700 more opponents than in 1893, and 350 fewer friends; St. Pancras, third refusal (6248, 4574 —out of 26,000 voters); Southend-on-Sea (787, 201). The local board of Sevenoaks, the town council of Maidenhead, and the town commissioners of Downpatrick, rejected proposals to the same end; also an attempt to carry a favourable vote in the vestry at Mile

End was defeated by 25 votes to 11. The town council of Londonderry rescinded a former resolution to adopt the Acts. The legality of their action is doubtful, but a recent valuable gift to the town will probably lead to fresh consideration of the later resolution.

1895. Campbeltown voted against the adoption of the Acts.

Eight of the places named above adopted the Acts at later dates. A successful attempt was made to get the halfpenny rate limit increased to a penny by public vote at Lambeth in 1891, and at St. Giles', Bloomsbury, in 1893; while unsuccessful attempts of a like nature were made at Hammersmith in 1893, and at Lewisham in 1895.

The list of adoptions of the Acts in the same period is as follows : in the list Welsh names occur first, then English (except metropolitan, proceeding from the south northwards), next London parishes and districts, and finally Irish and Scottish towns and parishes :—

1888. Croydon, Barking, Christ Church (Southwark), Hinckley, Oldbury, Glossop, Staleybridge.

1889. Brentford, Bedford, Leominster (afterwards declared void), Middlewich, Nelson, Altrincham, Crompton, Camberwell, Streatham, Whitechapel, Limerick, Selkirk.

1890. Salisbury, Chiswick, West Ham, Rugby, Mansfield, Oswestry, Woolton (near Liverpool), Sale, Bingley, Barnsley, Carlisle, Workington, Thornaby-on-Tees, Lewisham, Newington, Poplar, St. George (Hanover Square), Stoke Newington, Banbridge, Ayr, Brechin, Kirkwall, Peterhead.

1891. Barry and Cadoxton, Hove, Edmonton, Tottenham, Wood Green (Middlesex), Willesden, Leyton, Colchester, Leighton, Lowestoft, Peterborough, York, Longton, East Hartlepool, West Hartlepool, Arlecdon and Frizington, Kendal, Bromley-by-Bow, Penge, Holborn, St. Giles' District (Bloomsbury), St. Saviour's (Southwark), St. Leonard (Shoreditch), Lurgan, Elgin.

1892. Worthing, Bromley (Kent), Gravesend, Enfield, Walthamstow, Lincoln, Hull, Morley, Rawmarsh, Lancaster, Leigh, Waterloo-with-Seaforth, Cleator Moor, St. Paul (Covent Garden), Jedburgh.

1893. Falmouth, Penzance, Bournemouth, Grays, Middle Claydon, New Mills, Sowerby Bridge, Stretford, Hyde, Hampstead, Kilmarnock, Drumoak.

1894. Blaenau Festiniog, Penarth, Ramsgate, Rochester, Camborne, Redruth, Gloucester, Luton, Grimsby, Burton-on-Trent, Bury St. Edmunds, Rothwell, Dukinfield, Lower Bebington, Colne, Waterford, Nenagh, Newburgh (Fife).

1895. Broughton, Llanuwchllyn, Bodmin, Liskeard, St. Austell, Tunbridge Wells, Woolwich, Teddington, Ilford, Kettering, Burwell, Ibstock, Atherstone, Worksop, Pleasley, Halton, Trimdon, Ratcliff, Newry, Dalkey, Newtonards.

1896. Corwen, Holyhead, Halkin, Towyn, Bexley Heath, Eastbourne, Andover, Hornsey, St. George (Bristol), Stroud, Grandborough, Shouldham, Nuneaton, Sheepshed, Todmorden, Ashton-on-Mersey, Leadgate, Mile End, St. George-the-Martyr (Southwark), St. George-in-the-East, Bow, Kirkmichael (Banff), Campbeltown, Perth, Falkirk, Arbroath.

The "Liberty and Property Defence League" was an adverse force to be reckoned with in some of the metropolitan parishes. A publication of this ultra-individualist body, entitled a "Plea for Liberty," contains an attack on free libraries; but, perhaps, it will be enough to say that it also contains one on the Post Office! On the other hand, the Trades Union Congress passed a resolution in favour of the establishment of free libraries in 1884.

At the end of 1896 the Public Libraries Acts had been adopted, or an equivalent course taken, in 334 places in the United Kingdom. The English adoptions were distributed over every county of England except two, and these but small ones, viz. Rutland and Huntingdon. The Acts had also been adopted in thirty-seven London districts and parishes, and not a single town of 100,000 inhabitants in England or Wales was outside their operation. Indeed, the only town of larger size in the United Kingdom which has not yet adopted the Acts is the city of Glasgow; though, in justice, the disgrace should be shared by several large and populous districts in London; and it should be added that Edinburgh waited until a private benefactor, Mr. Carnegie, made a munificent contribution.

Forty-six urban districts, with populations of 20,000 or more, have yet to adopt the Acts; thirty-two of these have each a population of more than 25,000, twenty-two exceed 30,000, and ten 50,000. The names of the ten are as follows: Bath, Burnley, Bury, Hastings, Huddersfield,

Merthyr Tydvil, Ystradyfodwy, Glasgow, Greenock, Leith.

Not less remarkable than the increase in the number of adoptions of the Public Libraries Acts in this period is the generosity called forth in the establishment or aid of free libraries. Many valuable gifts had been received for similar objects in the earlier days of the movement, but readily will it be conceded that the chronicled benefactions of the past nine years far surpass any earlier record. The munificence of Mr. Passmore Edwards and of Mr. Andrew Carnegie are chronicled in a later chapter. In this place only the more striking gifts and bequests are recorded.

GIFTS TO LIBRARIES

A library building (£2000) at Hucknall Torkard, from Mr. J. E. Ellis, M.P.

The Brassey Institute (£15,000) at Hastings, from Lord Brassey. (The library may be used as a free library when the Acts are adopted by the town.)

A new reading-room (£1000) at Chester, from the Mayor of Chester.

A building and two years' expenses at Selkirk, from Mr. Craig-Brown.

A library, complete, at Falkirk, from Mr. R. Dollar (of the United States).

A park, hall, and library (£30,000) at Alloa, from Mr. Thomson Paton.

£500 for books at Hinckley, from Mr. Stephen Malin.

£500 to the library funds at Chelsea, from Sir Charles Dilke.

£350 to the library funds at Chelsea, from Lord Cadogan.

£500 to the library funds at Winsford, from Mr. J. T. Brunner, M.P.

A library building at Camberwell, from Mr. Minet.

£800 in books at Clerkenwell, from Mr. R. M. Holborn.
£1,200 for extensions at Galashiels, from a public subscription.
A library, complete, with endowment (£11,000) at Hull, from Mr. J. Reckitt.
The Nicholson Institute, with money gifts, annually, at Leek, from the Nicholson family.
£5000 towards a library at Brechin, from Mr. G. M. Inglis.
A library, complete, with partial endowment, at Newark, from Sir William Gilstrap.
£3000 towards a library and institute at Denton, from a public subscription.
A library, complete (£2700), at Poole, from Mr. J. J. Norton.
£2000 towards a library at Bingley, from Mr. Alfred Sharp.
Property valued at £12,000 at Barnsley, from Mr. C. Harvey.
£555 to the library funds at Barnsley, from a few gentlemen.
£900 to the library funds at Kidderminster, from three donors.
£10,570 towards a technical school and library at Ashton-under-Lyne, from Mr. G. Heginbottom.
A park, library, and hall (£50,000) at Kirkcaldy, from Mr. M. Beveridge.
£1000 towards a library at Poplar, from Mr. Bullivant.
£2000 additional towards a library at Poplar, from a public subscription.
£1000 towards a library at Colchester, from Mr. R. Catchpool.
£25,600 for buildings, &c., at Lambeth, from Mr. H. Tate.
£4000 at Lambeth, from Mr. W. Noble.
£10,500 for buildings, &c., at Lambeth, from Miss Durning Smith.
£3700 for buildings, &c., at Lambeth, from various donors.
£5000 towards converting Tullie House at Carlisle, from the Bishop of Carlisle, the Earl of Carlisle, and the Duke of Devonshire.
The Openshaw branch library, café, baths, &c., at Manchester, from the Whitworth Legatees.
£6000 for books at Exeter, from Mr. Kent Kingdon.
Freehold and buildings (£8000) at Bromley, from the School of Science and Art.
A boys' reading-room (£500) and £50 per annum at Wigan, from Sir F. S. Powell, M.P.

GIFTS AND BEQUESTS, 1888–96

Free library and endowment at Otley, from Mr. Robinson Gill (of New York).

£4000 at Aberdeen, from the "Common Good," Mr. and Mrs. Carnegie, and others.

£500 towards a technical school and library at Leigh, from Lord Lilford.

£550 towards a technical school and library at Leigh, by subscription.

A reading-room and library at Wensley, from Mr. Joseph Taylor.

A building (£5000) and endowment of working expenses at Hythe, from Mr. Bull.

£10,000 to library funds in Truro and other Cornish towns, from Mr. A. O. Ferris.

850 square yards of land at West Bromwich, from Mr. Alderman Farley.

£2600 for library funds at Colchester, from five donors.

A branch library complete, also baths, at Lochee, Dundee, from Mr. J. H. Cox.

A technical institute and library (£25,000) at St. Helens, from Colonel Gamble, C.B.

A technical institute and library (£20,000) at Lancaster, from the managers of the Storey Institute.

Building and funds (£105,000) at Preston, from the trustees of the Harris Bequest.

A reading-room (£5000) at Wolverhampton, from Mr. Butler.

£4000 to the Mitchell Library, Glasgow, from Mr. E. L. Campbell.

£1200 towards a library at Lincoln, from Colonel Seeley.

£5000 towards a building at Hampstead, from Mr. H. Harben, J.P.

A legacy of £500 to the library at Cheltenham, from Miss Isabella Buchanan.

£500 to the Mitchell Library, Glasgow, from Mr. Donald MacPherson.

The Hanson Library of 10,000 volumes at Bradford, from Mr. J. Moser.

£200 a year to the free library, and a deferred bequest of £4000, at Kendal, from Mr. H. Hewetson.

A library, complete (£4000), at Elswick, Newcastle, from Mr. Stephenson.
A library and working men's institute (£10,000) at Canterbury, from Mr. Beaney (of Australia).
A library and museum at Campbeltown, from Mr. J. M. Hall.
A library building (£6000) at Staleybridge, from Mr. J. F. Cheetham.
£3500 for purchase of Welsh MSS., &c., at Cardiff, from Lord Bute and others.
£30,000 for a library at Perth, from Professor Sandeman.
A library of 8000 volumes and a new building (£3000) at Todmorden, from the local Co-operative Society.
A building (£1000) at Arbroath, from Mr. David Corsar.

The gifts above named certainly represent a value exceeding half a million. When the gifts of Mr. Passmore Edwards and Mr. Andrew Carnegie are added, and the numerous smaller sums gathered in all parts of the country, it will be seen that the aggregate of gifts for free libraries in the past nine years, and in the United Kingdom alone, cannot be less than three-quarters of a million pounds. What an answer to those who contend that rate-aid kills voluntary effort! Great, however, as have been the gifts to British free libraries, the United States can show a much more splendid gift-roll. Mr. T. Formby, sub-librarian to the Liverpool Free Libraries, estimated, in 1889, that no less than £6,000,000 had been contributed to American libraries during the preceding thirty-five years, while the United Kingdom could only claim to have received £1,000,000 for free libraries in the same period.

Public library legislation during the period under review has been much simplified and improved. Lord Monkswell introduced into the House of Lords, on 1st May 1888, a short Amending Bill, designed to lessen the expenses of collecting the public library rate. The bill was prepared by request of the Chelsea Commissioners of Public Libraries and Museums, who had been put to an expense of £150 for the separate collection of the rate. As a money bill, which the Lords had not authority to originate, it was ruled out of order, but was taken up by Mr. H. Gardner in the House of Commons, where it was read a first time on 22nd February 1889. On its third reading in the Commons Mr. J. T. Brunner drew the attention of the Government to the anomalies under the Acts in the rating of agricultural land. When this Act was passed on 31st May it provided not only that the expenses of collection be paid out of a rate raised with and as part of the poor-rate, but also that an abatement of two-thirds of the sum assessed in respect of agricultural land should be made. A further improvement (which has been of practical effect in the parishes of Camberwell and Lambeth) allowed bodies of commissioners separately appointed to co-operate by agreement in the carrying out of the Acts in adjoining parishes.

The Amending Bill of 1890 was introduced on 25th February, and bore the names of Sir John Lubbock, Mr. Baumann, Mr. Sydney Buxton, Sir William Houldsworth, and Mr. Justin MacCarthy. In the House of Lords, Lord Houghton had charge of the measure, and it received the royal assent on 18th August. Several of the speeches in debate on this bill have a more than passing interest. Procedure by public meeting to determine adoption was abolished on the motion of Baron Dinsdale. The Act provided that adoption was to be by voting papers only. Mr. Rankin carried an amendment, of which the effect was to allow the rate to be levied in different proportions on defined parts of a library district. He said his object was to encourage rural and urban districts, or scattered parishes, to combine in establishing free libraries. "It was obviously unfair that those who were a considerable distance from the place should pay in the same proportion as those who were near. The difference in rateable value also worked injustice in some cases."

Differences which had arisen amongst his constituents at Leominster as to the adoption of the Acts seem to have been in Mr. Rankin's mind during his speech. It is almost certain that his amendment has not assisted the spread of free libraries in any degree. During the debate on the limitation of rating power, Sir William Harcourt said—

"To listen to honourable gentlemen, one would think there is some terrible danger about to be incurred. What is it? That a given community may wish to spend more than one penny in the pound on a free library. I do not regard that as a very terrible danger. I can quite understand very poor communities wishing to be limited in their expenditure, but I do not see why rich communities should not be allowed to spend twopence in the pound, if they so desire. I think it is a great evil that the rate under the Public Libraries Act should have been confined to one penny. It is not in the least necessary that Parliament should legislate against the terrible danger that a community should spend what it thinks fit on so excellent an object as a free library."

In the Upper House there was much fear expressed by the law lords as to the effect of a clause conferring power to grant charity lands for library purposes. The clause had been introduced at the desire of Mr. Kelly when the bill was under consideration in the Lower House. He had pointed out that the Governors of Dulwich College had expressed a desire to grant some of their land for library purposes, but there was no power in the Dulwich Estate Act that would authorise them to do so. In the end the clause was passed. Power was also given to allow co-operation with the governing body of any endowed library under a scheme of the Charity Commissioners. Metropolitan parish vestries and district boards of works were allowed to appropriate lands for library purposes. Both these excellent provisions were embodied in the Consolidating Act of 1892.

The greatest legislative achievement of the period undoubtedly was the passing of the Public Libraries Act, 1892. Long had it been perceived that the Acts relating to public libraries in England and Wales needed to be consolidated and harmonised. The Library Association had frequently discussed the inconsistencies of the law, and the growing sentiment in favour of consolidation was brought to a focus by the offer of a prize by Mr. J. Y. W. MacAlister for the best draft bill to consolidate and amend the Public Libraries Acts, 1855–90. A number of drafts were sent in and submitted to the consideration of Chancellor Christie, at that time president of the Library Association, and of Sir John Lubbock. The award of the prize was made known at the annual meeting of the Association in London in 1889. The prize draft Bill, besides consolidating existing enactments, would have limited the borrowing powers of library authorities to "a sum or sums of money not exceeding the capital sum represented by one-fourth part of the library rate capitalised at the rate of twenty years' purchase of such sums." This was to be repaid by not more than fifty annual instalments. A special inauguration rate, not exceeding a penny in the pound, for the purchase of books and objects, was to be levied during the first year, in addition to the annual rate; one penny in the pound for a library or museum alone; three-halfpence for a library and museum, or in addition to the other objects, not being all the objects authorised; twopence where a library, museum, art gallery, and school of science and art were provided. Exemption of institutions from local rates, and power to demand free copies of government and local official publications, were included, besides proposals to legalise public free lectures, which many thought to be of doubtful legality. The draft bill formed the basis of a long discussion at the next annual conference of the

Library Association (at Reading in 1890). Later the authors were desired by the Association to undertake the preparation of a manual of the existing law, and this work, emphasising many inconsistencies in the existing Acts, appeared in 1893.

Discussion on the state of the law continued until Mr. Fanshawe, a Parliamentary draughtsman of high repute, was commissioned by the Library Association to prepare a Consolidating Bill; and the manuscript of "Public Library Legislation," the work referred to above, was placed in Mr. Fanshawe's hands in order to facilitate the preparation of a bill. The new draft Bill was discussed by library authorities all over the country, and amendments suggested by library authorities were discussed at monthly and special meetings of the Library Association. Sir John Lubbock undertook to bring in the bill, but on his advice none but the very simplest amendments were inserted, as owing to the state of public business in the House there was a doubt whether it could be passed that session. The bill bore the names of Sir John Lubbock, Sir John Kennaway, Mr. Justin MacCarthy, Mr. John Morley, and Mr. Powell, and was introduced into the House of Commons on 11th February 1892. No debate took place in its progress through either House. Under Lord Sandhurst's charge it was read a first time in the House of Lords on 17th June, and finally received the royal assent on 27th June 1892. This Act has consolidated no fewer than seven previous enactments, and harmonised several conflicting provisions and definitions of the earlier laws. Its provisions are restricted to England and Wales.

In the very next session an Amending Bill was brought in by Sir F. S. Powell. Its object was to provide for the adoption of the Acts in any urban district by a resolution of the urban authority, and to give power to two urban districts to combine in carrying out the Acts. The Bill was brought in on 1st February 1893, and received the royal assent, after a peaceful passage through both Houses, on 9th June.

Another Act which has favourably affected free libraries is the Museums and Gymnasiums Act, which was first introduced into the House of Commons by Mr. Powell in 1890, and re-introduced in 1891. Under this Act several library authorities have levied a special museum rate, and transferred the charge for museum maintenance, which was upon the penny library rate, to the new fund, thus setting free a part of their funds for library extension and improvement. Bristol, Cardiff, and Liverpool now levy a halfpenny museum rate; Bradford, a farthing; Buxton, a sufficient rate to supply £25 per annum in support of a small museum; while several corporations now have under consideration the question of applying its provisions.

A number of communities have adopted the Technical Instruction Acts, 1889 and 1891, and have transferred from the library account the charge for science and art classes held at free libraries. Similarly the Local Taxation (Customs and Excise) Act, 1890, by providing for the distribution throughout the

THE LOCAL TAXATION ACT

country of a very large amount of money arising from increased beer and spirit duties (about £750,000), and empowering local authorities to use these funds for purposes connected with technical instruction, gave relief to many free libraries, sums of money being voted for the purchase of books on technical training in science and on local industries.

But the operation of these collateral Acts has not in any way interfered with the machinery of the Public Libraries Acts. The same cannot be said of the Local Government Act, 1894, which, in giving power to parish councils to levy a rate for certain adoptive Acts, including the Public Libraries Acts, confused the law relating to free libraries in rural parishes. Those who desire full information on this difficult part of library law are referred to a sixpenny pamphlet, entitled "Adoption of the Public Libraries Acts in England and Wales," by Mr. H. W. Fovargue, the honorary solicitor to the Library Association. Briefly, the position may be stated thus: In rural parishes, on the requisition of ten or more voters, the chairman of the parish meeting or council convenes a parish meeting, at which a resolution to adopt the Act must be moved. If this be carried and no poll demanded, the adoption is complete. If a poll be demanded, it must be taken by ballot, and according to the regulations prescribed by the Local Government Board, and the poll will determine adoption. Where there is a parish council, it will be the authority to carry out the Acts when they have been adopted. Where there is no council, the parish meeting must appoint a committee or commissioners of public libraries and museums.

The English Library Acts provide that adoption must be—

> (1.) In an urban district by resolution of the local authority.
> (2.) In the City of London by a poll on the requisition of the Common Council.
> (3.) In a metropolitan district by a poll on the requisition of ten or more voters.

A poll may also be taken on any matter for which the consent of the voters is necessary; for example, agreement to combine with neighbouring districts, and fixing, raising, or lowering the rate.

The library rate may not exceed a penny (except in the City of London), but may be fixed by the voters at $\frac{3}{4}$d. or $\frac{1}{2}$d. in the pound. The authority to carry out the Acts is to be—

> (1.) In an urban district the urban authority (town council, urban district council).
> (2.) In the City of London the Common Council.
> (3.) In a metropolitan parish or metropolitan district the Commissioners for Public Libraries and Museums, appointed by the vestry or district board.

This last case may be altered by an order of the Local Government Board, under the powers of another Act making the vestry the library authority.

Two or more neighbouring parishes or districts may combine by agreement to carry out the Acts, and the agreement may specify the proportion in which the expenses are to be borne by each vestry or board. A library authority may provide—

> (1.) Public libraries.
> (2.) Public museums.
> (3.) Schools for science.
> (4.) Art galleries.
> (5.) Schools for art.

No charge can be made for admission to a library or museum, or for the use of a lending library to the inhabitants of the district, but others than inhabitants may be charged for the use of a lending library. Land (limited to one acre) held for purposes following may be granted or conveyed for purposes of the Acts—

> (1.) Ecclesiastical, with the consent of the Ecclesiastical Commissioners.
> (2.) Parochial, with the consent of the Local Government Board and the local board of guardians.
> (3.) Charitable, with the consent of the Charity Commissioners; but land held on trust as an open space is not to be taken in London or any place of more than 20,000 inhabitants.

An urban library authority may delegate all or some of their powers to a committee, members of which need not be members of the urban authority. A library authority may make an agreement for joint-use with the governing body of an endowed library, museum, school, or art gallery, or with the Charity Commissioners, and may accept grants from the Science and Art Department, and execute instruments relating to the same. A two-thirds deduction must be made from the assessment of cultivated lands. Provisions are also included relating to the necessary sanctions for raising the rate, the borrowing of money, the keeping of accounts, and the termination of agreements.

Fuller details on these points will be found in Fovargue and Ogle's "Public Library Legislation," 1893.

Turning back again to the progress of legislation, the introduction by Mr. Field, on 1st March 1893, of a Public Libraries (Ireland) Amendment Bill is to be noted. This passed rapidly through the House of Commons, though on the third reading Mr. Macartney protested that it was unworkable. But the Lords soon found out its defect, and on 29th August its consideration was adjourned *sine die*. In an improved form it was presented in the following session, and had better success. The royal assent was given on 17th August. It is a great pity that this Act did not consolidate as well as amend the Irish law relating to libraries; some of its provisions seem to be little more than re-statements of unrepealed clauses of previous Acts.

The effect of the Public Library law for Ireland is now practically the same as that in England, with the following important exceptions or additions: —Only urban districts can adopt the Acts. If an urban authority do not adopt the Act, a requisition of twenty ratepayers can compel the taking of a poll of the voters by ballot. If an urban authority

LIBRARY LAW IN IRELAND AND SCOTLAND

after the adoption of the Act do not in a reasonable time appoint Commissioners of Public Libraries and Museums, on the application of ten voters the Local Government Board may appoint them. Copies of the accounts of the Library Commissioners after audit have to be sent to the Lord Lieutenant. Money may be borrowed on mortgage of property with the consent of H.M. Treasury. The Local Government Board may make rules for the carrying into effect of the provisions of the Amending Act, having the force of law after submission to Parliament. Schools of music may be established under the Acts.

On 17th April 1894 Mr. Dalziel introduced a bill to amend the Public Libraries (Scotland) Act, and, like the Irish Act of the same session, this had the good fortune to go through Parliament without opposition. This bill, like the Consolidating Bill of 1887, which it was to amend, was prepared by Mr. Richard Brown of Glasgow. In its provisions it is parallel to the English Amending Act of 1893.

It will be convenient to set forth here the chief provisions of the present Scotch law relating to public libraries, emphasising the points of difference from English procedure.

(1.) On the requisition of ten householders in any parish, the opinions of the householders must be ascertained as to the adoption of the Act; in places of more than 3000 inhabitants, by voting papers; in other places, either in that way or by public meeting. (2.) In burghs the magistrates and council determine adoption by resolution. No new effort must be made within two years after a defeat. Where any Act allows differential rating on lands or premises, it is not to apply to the library rate. Accounts are to be open, and published annually. Lands may be appropriated, purchased, or rented, sold, or exchanged. Borrowing powers are regulated and limited to a sum not exceeding a quarter of the library rate capitalised at twenty years' purchase; provisions as to repayment of loans are inserted. A committee of from ten to twenty persons must be appointed annually, of whom half shall be magistrates or councillors or members of the board. The powers of the committee are set out in great detail. The committee may make byelaws, which are to be published, and can be enforced. Penalties and forfeitures are recoverable by an ordinary small debt action. Estimates in advance are to be made annually. Libraries, museums, and art galleries are to be free and open to the public, and no charge is allowed for the loan of books or magazines.

Besides the progress in general legislation, we must record the fact that several corporations, impressed with the insufficiency of a penny rate for all the library and museum and associated educational work which they had commenced or were projecting, secured by local Acts power to levy a higher rate. Wolverhampton by an Act of 1887, Swansea in 1889, Sheffield in 1890, and Manchester in 1891, obtained power to levy up to twopence in the pound, and Warrington, by an Act of 1890, up to three-halfpence. In 1891 Ashton-under-Lyne and Salford by provisional order and local Act raised the limit to three-halfpence. An unsuccessful attempt was made to obtain a similar power at Birkenhead. Increased rating powers have also been obtained by the corporations of Birmingham, Leamington, Newcastle-on-Tyne, Walsall, Oldham, St. Helens, Preston, Sunderland, and Wigan. Since 1888 Kingston-on-Thames has had power to levy, with the consent of ratepayers, a rate not exceeding twopence in the pound. Manchester has power to make and enforce bye-laws under an Improvement Act of 1871. Nottingham, under a local Act, can apply profits arising from the municipal gas undertaking to educational purposes, and actually devotes £2000 per annum, in addition to the product of the penny rate, to its public libraries and museums. The Brighton Pavilion Act, under which the Free Library at Brighton is established, did not allow the opening of branch libraries; accordingly a local bill to acquire the power was promoted in 1893.

Notwithstanding the general improvement in public sentiment towards free libraries, here and there—and particularly in London—the opposition did not always stop on the adoption of the Acts. At Bermondsey the Vestry succeeded in baulking for a period of eighteen months the appointment of Library Commissioners; and within the last few months the Mile End vestry has obtained notoriety by its adoption of the same policy in antagonism to the mandate of the voters. At Clerkenwell, in

1888, two warrants to question the election of commissioners were applied for. The judgment of the court in this case (Reg. *v.* Morris) was favourable to the legality of the adoption of the Acts and appointment of the commissioners, so the application was refused.

At various times and with varying success free library committees and commissioners applied for relief from taxation under the provisions of the Act 6 and 7 Vict. c. 36. In 1892 the case of Andrew *v.* the Mayor of Bristol was tried, and the decision of the court was that the free library committee of Bristol were liable for income-tax. Accordingly applications for payment of income-tax on free library buildings and on free library income became general after 1892. There was, however, great dissatisfaction among library authorities, a dissatisfaction at length publicly expressed by the Manchester Free Libraries Committee, who resolved to resist the payment, and with the assistance of other committees and the Library Association to appeal even to the highest court. The Bristol case rested on an opinion that a free library building was not technically "the property of a literary and scientific institution." The appeal against the assessment of four buildings at Manchester was heard before the Income-Tax Commissioners on 16th October 1893, and naturally enough the appeal was dismissed by the Divisional Court. The corporation then went to the Court of Appeal, which confirmed the decision of the Income-Tax Commissioners, although the Master of the Rolls dissented. Next the case was carried to the House of Lords, and was heard on the 6th and 9th of March 1896 before the Lord Chancellor, Lord Herschell, Lord Macnaghten, and Lord Morris. Judgment was reserved, but on 31st July their lordships delivered judgment, reversing the decision of the Queen's Bench Division. The Lord Chancellor alone dissented. Thus was won a victory for free library committees, whose property by this judgment of the highest Court in the land is declared exempt from income-tax, provided that the buildings are used solely for the purposes of free libraries, that no payment is received or demanded for instruction therein, that no officer of the institution occupies them, and that no person pays rent for their use.

Another matter closely associated with the legal history of the free library question is that of the gratuitous distribution of Parliamentary papers to free public libraries. As far back as 1875 Mr. Wheelhouse, M.P., tried to obtain a concession for the Leeds Public Library, and at various times the subject was revived by questions in the House of Commons. The Library Association also sent a deputation to the Government in 1885, soliciting this boon, and urging the claims of public representative institutions to papers of national importance printed at the public expense. The application was unsuccessful; yet in 1889 Dundee obtained the gift of certain Blue-books, the local member of Parliament, Mr. (now Sir) John Leng acting as agent for their transmission to the public library;

and on the general question being revived in the House on 27th December 1893, in answer to Mr. Fisher, the Right Hon. W. E. Gladstone, then Prime Minister, said : " Arrangements have been in operation since 1886 whereby any public library is supplied gratuitously with any Parliamentary papers for which it might apply to the Stationery Office. The expense of doing this is charged to a special sub-head of the stationery vote. A small sum which is amply sufficient for the purpose has been yearly provided on that account." Recently the Labour Department of the Board of Trade has seen that it is advisable to distribute important reports on labour questions to public libraries without waiting to be asked.

From what has been said, it may be seen that there is still room for much improvement in the law relating to libraries. The Library Association has not abandoned the amendments proposed for incorporation with the Act of 1892, but has embodied them with other improvements in a bill which it is hoped may be brought in during the next session of Parliament. By this bill it is proposed to give voters the power of adoption by ballot where an urban authority refuses to adopt by resolution ; to simplify the methods of adoption ; to give the Local Government Board power to appoint commissioners where the local authority neglects its duty ; to define the qualifications of a commissioner in a rural parish ; to follow the precedent of the Scotch law as to the making and enforcement of bye-laws ; to enable parishes to agree with urban districts as to the joint use of a library; to remove the vestry's power of limiting the rate; to settle a few questions at present in doubt; and to protect library managers from actions in respect of the circulation of alleged libellous matter contained in books in their libraries. Should this bill succeed in becoming law in the next session of Parliament, the period 1888-97 will prove to have been a most remarkable decade for the improvements effected in library law.

In the course of the foregoing review of the bills in Parliament, the reader must have noticed the names of several distinguished public men who have put the seal of their approval on the free library. More remarkable will appear a list of some of the eminent names associated with the stone-laying, opening, or re-opening of free library buildings during the past nine years (the list has no pretension to completeness): The Right Hon. Sir John Lubbock, the Right Hon. W. E. Gladstone, the Right Hon. Lord Rosebery, the Right Hon. A. J. Mundella, the Right Hon. G. J. Goschen, Sir Lyon (now Lord) Playfair, the Earl Cadogan, the Marquis of Ripon, Professor Jebb, Sir Arthur Arnold, Mr. Hall Caine, Mr. Alexander Ireland, and the philanthropists Mr. Andrew Carnegie and Mr. J. Passmore Edwards.

The Prince of Wales has on five occasions at least attended public functions at free libraries in these years, viz.: St. Martin-in-the-Fields (stone-laying), 1890; Lambeth Central (opening), 1893; Camberwell Central (opening), 1893; Croydon (opening),

1896; Cardiff (re-opening), 1896. H.R.H. the Princess Louise, Marchioness of Lorne, opened the Kensington Free Library in 1889, and H.R.H. the Princess Christian the North Lambeth Free Library in 1894.

A few passages from memorable speeches may be reproduced here. Mr. Alexander Ireland, in opening the Longsight Branch Free Library at Manchester on 23rd July 1892, said that—

"He was the last survivor of the original committee which in 1852 originated the Manchester Free Libraries, and that since then, a period of forty years, 250 free libraries had been established throughout the kingdom, containing probably two and a half million volumes [much too low an estimate]. Notwithstanding all this, we were far behind the United States in the matter of free libraries. In the State of Massachusetts there were a few years ago 182 free town libraries. One of the most telling points in favour of these institutions was the fact that one could take home for reading, free of any cost whatever, the latest book of travels, of biography, of essays, or fiction, or philosophy."

Mr. R. K. Causton, M.P., speaking at the stone-laying at St. Saviour's Free Library, Southwark, on 31st July 1893, said that—

"He was not surprised at the demand for free libraries. The great Education Act of 1870 was just beginning to show its effect, and he thought his hearers would agree that the time and the money spent on education since then had not been thrown away. In 1871 the average attendance in the primary schools of Great Britain was 1,500,000, but in 1891 it had grown to 4,250,000. The expenditure on primary education in 1870 was under £2,000,000. In 1892 it had risen to five millions and a quarter. The result was a generation of educated people, with a demand for free libraries, and for improvement in everything social."

At the opening of the Rotherhithe Free Library on 1st October 1890, Sir John Lubbock gave an address which subsequently appeared in an article on Free Libraries in the *New Review*. He said—

"No one now denies the advantage of free libraries. The only objection ever raised to them now is on the score of expense. But we do not grudge the cost of schools, and the free library is the school for the grown-up. Moreover, I doubt whether either the one or the other is really an expense.

"A great part, at any rate, of what we spend on books we save in prisons and police. Only a fraction of the crime of the country arises from deliberate wickedness or irresistible temptation; the great sources of crime are drink and ignorance.

"There is a general impression that our schools are very expensive, and that the cost is increasing. I think, however, it may be shown that ignorance, in reality, costs more than knowledge. What are the facts? The annual cost of elementary schools in England and Wales amounts, in round numbers, to £8,500,000, but out of this sum the parents provided £1,860,000, and subscriptions amounted to £746,000, leaving something under £6,000,000 as contributed from rates and taxes.

"To this must be added the Science and Art Department, £500,000; museums, &c., £250,000; and public libraries, £150,000—say together, £7,000,000.

"Now let us look at pauperism. The nominal poor-rate

includes several other matters, but the part devoted to the maintenance of the poor is no less than £8,500,000.

"The cost of police, prisons, and criminals amounts to over £4,000,000. The police, of course, perform various useful functions besides protecting us against criminals. On the other hand, the cost of the criminal population is not to be measured by the mere cost of police and prisons, and the real expense to the country far exceeds that sum.

"Now let us consider what our expenditure in these directions might have been if it had not been for our expenditure on education. First, let me take the criminal statistics. Up to 1877 the number of prisoners showed a tendency to increase. In that year the average number was 20,800. Since then it has steadily decreased, and now is only 14,700. It has, therefore, diminished in round numbers by one-third. But we must remember that the population has been steadily increasing. Since 1870 it has increased by one-third. If our criminals had increased in the same proportion, they would have been 28,000 instead of 14,000, or just double.

"In that case, then, our expenditure on police and prisons would have been at least £8,000,000.

"In juvenile crime the decrease is even more satisfactory. In 1856 the number of young persons committed for indictable offences was 14,000; in 1866 it had fallen to 10,000; in 1876, to 7000; in 1881, to 6000; and the last figures I have seen, to 5100!

"Turning to poor-rate statistics, we find that in 1870 the number of paupers to every thousand of the population was over forty-seven. It had been as high as fifty-two. Since then it has steadily fallen to twenty-two as an average, and in a parenthesis I may say I am proud to find that in the metropolis we are substantially below the average. The proportion, therefore, is less than one-half of what it used to be. Supposing it had remained as it was, our expenditure would have been £16,000,000 instead of £8,000,000, or £8,000,000 more than the present amount.

"Of course I am aware that various allowances would have to be made, and that these figures cannot claim any scientific accuracy, but I believe that the additions would be larger than the deductions, and am convinced that the £7,000,000 of public funds spent annually on education save us a much larger sum in other ways.

"I have dwelt on this, because the question of expense is the one argument generally used against public libraries. But I need hardly assert that I should be one of the last to look on this as a mere matter of £. s. d.

"I doubt very much, therefore, whether free libraries really cost the ratepayers anything, whether they do not save more than the penny rate."

Speaking at the opening of the Passmore Edwards Free Library at Hammersmith on 25th June 1896, Lord Rosebery said—

"I believe intellectual apathy is the great danger of our nation at the present time. . . . I believe that this great work of public libraries is a great counter-irritant to that intellectual apathy; I believe it furnishes an inducement to those who wish not merely to improve their bodies, but their minds; who wish not merely to play, but to think; who wish to have an opportunity of retirement from the second-hand impressions of the world, and to form impressions for themselves, to come to some temple of reading and of thought where they can form their own conclusions and their own convictions. I believe that the experience is that a fair proportion of thoughtful books are taken and digested, and pre-eminently, I believe, by the artisan class."

Less than a fortnight later (7th July 1896) Mr. Hall Caine opened the Eastbourne Free Library, and criticised Lord Rosebery. Yet both speakers are heartily in favour of the free library. The well-known novelist said that—

"With regard to public libraries and the trade of bookselling, these were not in any degree antagonistic to each other, and he had found that in the great centres the public library and the booksellers kept pace together. The great success of the public library was a proof that the intellectual vigour of a nation was from within and not from without. Intellectual apathy would lead by sure and speedy consequence to the decline of literature, and the decline of literature would mean the decline of the nation. . . . There had never been a period when books played so large a part in the life of England as now."

Professor Jebb, speaking at the opening of the Lincoln Free Library on 19th October 1895, said that—

"Among the varied activities of that great educational movement which had marked the second half of this century in England, history will assign a very important place to the establishment of rate-supported libraries. . . . A public library when organised with judgment and in [a] comprehensive spirit . . . offers two great advantages to the reader. The first is the great variety of subjects among which he can choose, an advantage which scarcely any private library could attempt to offer in a similar degree. The other advantage is the opportunity for a systematic study of a given subject. There is a large class of minds to which it is congenial to make all their reading systematic. . . . The supporters of a library such as this ought not to feel any discouragement if the lighter literature, and especially the fiction, is found to be very largely in demand. Let them remember, first, the gain implied in the mere fact that literature in any worthy form is the chosen recreation of hard-working men and women; and next, let them not undervalue the importance of exercising the imagination. In addition to the more direct and obvious benefits which libraries such as this confer, there is another consequence of a very valuable kind which may be expected to flow from them, viz., a strengthening of local patriotism. The studies in English history and English literature which such a library invites, will from time to time remind the reader of the part which his own town has borne in that history and that literature, and of the distinguished names with which it has been connected."

Nothing would be easier than to continue giving quotations from the speeches of distinguished men strongly laudatory of the free library, but space cannot be spared for more than one more, and that the weighty utterance of Mr. W. E. Gladstone, M.P., at the opening of the St. Martin-in-the-Fields Free Public Library on 12th February 1891—

"To all classes there is great utility in the power of reference and use which these institutions afford; but for the masses of the community these institutions are particularly valuable, and it is by those masses that I believe they will be still more and more largely appreciated. There is one kind of appreciation which I cannot help contemplating with greater interest than any other, and that is the case of the very young, the case of the intelligent, growing lad, the case of the lad who is just beginning, perhaps only in the humble capacity of a messenger, perhaps as an apprentice, but, in one way or another, beginning to show that he has got in him the metal of a man, and the faculty which, if well used, may develop into something comparatively great for the future. It is in a library like this that every such youth may derive the greatest benefit. Here, if a youth has the material within him, he may be inspired with a vital spark, with ideas altogether new, with ideas which may enable him to attain some valuable end. All these things he may learn from the occasions which life affords; but there is hardly any place where he is likely to receive more enormous benefit than within the walls of institutions of this kind."

The latest Parliamentary return concerning public libraries was issued in 1890; from this we gather that 170 places possessed 408 libraries, 3,056,658 volumes, and annually issued 16,350,508. The rate raised for the support of these libraries amounted in a year to £204,972. The return is deficient, for at the end of 1889, 194 places either had adopted the Public Libraries Act, or had local powers to establish free libraries.

At the present time (1897) the writer estimates that there cannot be fewer than six or seven hundred free libraries established in 300 towns, parishes, or districts under the Public Libraries Acts of the United Kingdom. These libraries contain 5,000,000 volumes, and have an annual issue of from twenty-five to thirty millions. The outstanding loans on free public library property in England and Wales only amount to not less than £800,000, despite the fact of the very considerable gifts of buildings in every part of the country. But the end is not yet. The movement is yet young, and it is vigorous with the strength and activity of adolescence. The towns will yet show advances neither few nor small; but the villages, the counties, have yet to reap the advantages the towns enjoy; the metropolis has yet to do much to equal the provision of the larger provincial centres, whose libraries of twenty, thirty, or forty years' formation are one of the glories of this mercantile age.

Shades of Edward Edwards and William Ewart! little did you dream of the fertility of the land where you sowed in hope, where we reap in gladness! Small space at present do your biographies fill in the national chronicles; large space will you occupy in the estimation of generations yet unborn!

CHAPTER V

THE DEVELOPMENT OF THE FREE LIBRARY

THE development of the free public library has naturally brought to a point many scattered questions concerning the proper administration of libraries of a public character. Points of library administration were to some extent discussed in the evidence taken by the Parliamentary Commission on the British Museum in 1835-36, and to a much larger extent in the Commission on the same subject which reported in 1849. Manuals of library management in French and in German were not wanting even before 1850, but nothing of equal importance to Edward Edwards's "Memoirs of Libraries" had been published before 1859. A considerable part of the second volume deals with questions of library management as adapted to the English free library system. This long remained the only systematic general treatise in the English tongue on the subject, but in 1876 another important publication was issued by the United States Bureau of Education, entitled "A Report on Public Libraries in the United States." In the same year the American Library Association was born, shortly after the International Conference of Librarians which met at

Philadelphia; then followed in 1877 the London International Conference of Librarians, out of which originated the Library Association of the United Kingdom. The movement possessed no regular organ until quite a recent date. The *Library Journal*, published first in New York in September 1876, still continues its useful existence. For a•time (1877-79) this was the official organ both of the American and of the home Library Associations. In 1879 the English Association commenced an official journal of its own, entitled *Monthly Notes;* to this succeeded in 1884 the *Library Chronicle*, which for five years was ably edited by the late Mr. E. C. Thomas, and was followed by *The Library*, commenced in 1889, and still flourishing under the zealous editorship of Mr. J. Y. W. MacAlister. All these publications are of importance not merely for the history they contain, but for their papers on and discussions of matters which concern the everyday labour of library governors and officials. The excellent article on "Libraries" in the ninth edition of the *Encyclopædia Britannica*, by Mr. H. R. Tedder and Mr. E. C. Thomas, appeared in 1882.

As another work in this series deals with library management it is not necessary here to give more than a few historical notes on some of the principal developments of the public library system, as reflected in the reports of various libraries, and in the publications aforesaid.

Manifestly a free library could not long exist in a large town without the necessity for subordinate or collateral centres of distribution being forced on the attention of its managers. From the very first the city of Liverpool provided two branch libraries, almost synchronously with the central establishment. Manchester early met a similar need; and now the magnitude of free library operations is such, that in several large towns the branch libraries rival in extent and value many really important independent libraries in towns of from 30,000 to 50,000 inhabitants. Lending libraries for a time kept even pace with reference libraries, but in later years the former have outstripped the latter in number and use, but not in importance or value.

The idea of making a town library a museum of local history and local topography was early considered, as appears from the debates on various public library bills; but the subject seems to have first acquired practical importance from the efforts of Mr. George Pryce, librarian of the Bristol City Library, who, as early as 1856, was vigorously engaged in collecting the materials and records of Bristol history. This subject was brought prominently forward at the Library Association's meeting in 1878, being introduced by a paper of Mr. W. H. K. Wright's. At various subsequent meetings it was discussed, until now there is hardly a free library of any importance where it is not recognised that the local collection is an important section.

Liverpool seems to have led the way in providing music scores in 1859, and books for the blind in 1857; and Mr. J. P. Briscoe of Nottingham brought the usefulness of these features of library work into greater prominence, by papers published, the latter in 1886, the former in 1892. At the annual meeting of the Library Association in 1879, Mr. W. H. K. Wright called attention to the possibilities of the Board School as an auxiliary distributing agency for children's books; and in 1885 Mr. Briscoe read to the Association a paper on libraries for the young. Nottingham established the first separate children's library as part of its public library system in 1882. Special juvenile sections are now included in all the principal public libraries and in most of the smaller ones, and the issue of special children's catalogues has done much to secure good reading for the young.

The labour-saving device known as an "indicator" was brought under the notice of the first annual meeting of the Library Association by Mr. J. Yates. Several gentlemen lay claim to the merit of inventing the indicator. Mr. John Elliott of Wolverhampton had one in use in 1869; but Mr. Charles Dyall, of the Walker Art Gallery, Liverpool, devised an indicator, which was used in a Manchester branch free library as early as 1863, though its use was limited to the members of the staff. The recording indicator is almost certainly the invention of Mr. Alfred Cotgreave, librarian of the West Ham Public Libraries; and although the Robertson, the Bonner, and the Chivers indicators are favoured in some libraries, the Cotgreave Indicator is that most largely used. There are, however, many libraries without an indicator, where a modification of the card ledger of Mr.

George Parr, brought under the notice of the Manchester (1879) annual meeting of the Library Association, is in vogue.

Mr. (now Sir) W. H. Bailey called the attention of the same conference to the advisability of free lectures in connection with free libraries; but the Library Committee at Liverpool had been carrying out a programme of free lectures ever since 1865. The Oxford and Manchester Library Committees had organised lecture courses in the early years of their existence, but they have not been continued with regularity. Free lectures are now an important part of the education obtainable at many free libraries in the United Kingdom. About 1890 Mr. J. Potter Briscoe introduced a modification of the lecture system, consisting of half-hour talks to readers about books and book-writers, which has proved very popular at Nottingham, and been widely adopted elsewhere.

Mr. Peter Cowell of Liverpool introduced the subject of electric lighting in public libraries at the Cambridge (1882) meeting of the Library Association, and now in a large number of free libraries gas has been superseded by the healthier illuminant.

Mr. Henry Stevens, at the International Conference (1877), and the editor of this series of manuals, at the 1884 meeting of the Library Association, introduced the question of the uses of photography in libraries; and at the 1891 meeting Mr. Ballinger of Cardiff read a paper advocating a photographic survey of the counties and the storage of photographs in free libraries; while in 1895, at the

Cardiff meeting, Mr. Sheppeard pleaded for the care of old maps, prints, and drawings illustrative of the locality, and submitted plans for their safety and accessibility.

In 1892 the writer made a proposal for the formation of a summer school of library science, which has since become a reality, and a valuable accessory help in the training of library assistants. The Association in 1885 inaugurated a system of examinations in special knowledge for assistants, and then first issued certificates on the results. Much care has been given to the subject of examinations by several committees, and it is hoped that in time the Library Association's certificate will be much sought after. At nearly every annual meeting questions on the classification of books, cataloguing methods, binding, legislation, and the extension of free libraries have been discussed, but in some of these matters it is not so easy to indicate specific improvements, though the discussions as a whole have undoubtedly been productive of advantage.

One of the most recent experiments in free libraries is that of admitting the public direct to the library shelves, allowing them to choose what they want without the intervention of the librarian. This plan, introduced at Clerkenwell on the advice of Mr. J. D. Brown, has been followed as yet by few libraries, and it remains to be seen under what circumstances, if any, it may be safely or advantageously adopted. In America "open access" appears to be much more general than at home.

Little has been said hitherto about the influence of American methods on English libraries. No doubt that influence has been and is considerable. The *American Library Journal* is widely read by British librarians, and although there is a feeling that American methods are unnecessarily complex, many improvements in English libraries are due to American influence.

The card catalogue, though not an American invention, owes much to American use and advocacy, and it is doubtful whether it would otherwise have been so largely used in English reference libraries. The most important contributions to English libraries, from the American side, have been Dewey's "Decimal Classification," and Cutter's "Rules for making a Dictionary Catalogue." Dewey's system is now followed in many libraries, and has been much, and favourably, discussed in this country.

Another benefit received from over sea is that of branch delivery stations, which have been recently organised, much after the American plan, in several large English towns.

In 1883 the Library Association accepted a code of cataloguing rules, drawn up by a committee of experts. This code refers only to author and title entries.

The growth of free public libraries in large centres of population is already showing signs of developing specialisation. The accounts of particular libraries, which follow, well illustrate this fact. Liverpool, Manchester, and many large towns have splendid accommodation for inventors in their separate rooms for the consultation of the English and American specifications, and the other literature of patents. Even many of the small libraries contain comprehensive collections of the books of particular authors, or relating to a particular, more or less limited, subject. Kept within the limits prescribed by good sense, this development is likely to prove of great value. The librarians, who collect, become in time repositories of much valuable information, which is freely at the service of literary workers and the public; and this advantage is gained without interference with the general efficiency of the library's management, however large a demand it may make upon the time and energies of its chief officer.

CHAPTER VI

SOME PAST WORKERS AND PRESENT BENEFACTORS

THE brief outlines which follow, of the lives of a few of the men who have made the free library a permanent institution in the United Kingdom, or who are helping in a national spirit to spread its blessings, make no pretensions to original research, and are compiled from easily accessible and well-known sources.

EDWARD EDWARDS was born in 1812, probably in London. In 1836 he came into prominence by a pamphlet which he wrote on the affairs of the British Museum. In February 1839 he was taken as a supernumerary assistant at the British Museum Library to help in the compilation of a projected catalogue, and was forthwith included in the committee of five which drew up the ninety-one cataloguing rules of the British Museum. He catalogued the Thomason collection of Civil War Tracts, and this duty seems to have absorbed his attention for several years. In 1847 he published in the *British Quarterly Review* an article on "Public Libraries in London and Paris," and in the following year he contributed to the *Transactions of the Statistical Society of London* an important paper on Public Libraries in Europe. This latter paper was brought under the notice of Mr. William Ewart, M.P., and led to his obtaining the Select Committee of the House of Commons on Public Libraries, which reported in 1849, 1850, and 1851. Thus it will be seen that to Edward Edwards belongs the credit of taking the first steps towards the establishment of the free library as a British institution, while hardly less honour is due to Mr. William Ewart as the foreseeing and energetic statesman who made Edwards's plans a reality.

Indiscretion on his own part had much to do with the termination in April 1850 of Edwards's engagement at the Museum. In 1850 Manchester secured his services for the upbuilding of the Free Library, which was the first opened under Ewart's Act. Here Edwards did most useful work, and determined the main lines of internal administration now followed in the principal free libraries of this country. In the formation of the magnificent libraries of Manchester he proceeded on broad and catholic principles. He was soon attacked for disregard of economy, and for insubordinate conduct towards the committee, and despite his great abilities his position became most irksome. In 1858 he was compelled to resign. In the following year he published in two large octavo volumes his *magnum opus*, " Memoirs of Libraries," a book which must be the foundation of every subsequent history of libraries.

"Libraries and their Founders" appeared in 1865, "Free Town Libraries" in 1869, and "Lives of the Founders of the British Museum" in 1870. In the last-named work there is shown no particle of ill-feeling towards Sir Anthony Panizzi, the principal under whom he had served at the Museum, nor against Mr. Thomas Watts, whose criticisms of Edwards's statistics of libraries in 1848 have been spoken of in some quarters as though they were an attack on Edwards's veracity. On the contrary, there is a beautiful spirit of appreciation of the labours of both those eminent men, and the highest praise given to their respective qualities. The articles "Libraries" in the eighth, and "Newspapers" in the ninth, edition of the *Encyclopædia Britannica* were from the pen of Edwards. Several scholarly works of a non-professional character also were published by Edwards, the best known of them being his "Life and Letters of Sir Walter Raleigh," never completed. He did much work for private libraries, especially for that of Queen's College, Oxford, where he was engaged for many years. In 1883, on Mr. Gladstone's recommendation, Edwards was granted a civil list pension of £80 per annum. He died in retirement at Niton, Isle of Wight, on 10th February 1886.

Mr. E. A. Bond, late principal librarian of the British Museum, refers to Edwards as "distinguished for his great capacity and power of work," and says, "I know no one to whom I can point as having taken wider and more liberal views on the administration of public libraries." The late

Mr. E. C. Thomas, formerly secretary of the Library Association, said of him, "His name will always be associated by librarians not only with the history and management of libraries, but with the great movement for the establishment of popular libraries, the full development of which none of us may live to see."

The present writer thinks that even higher praise should be his, for it was Edward Edwards who made possible the successful issue of the Select Committee of 1849 in the subsequent Public Libraries Acts of Ewart. His work was that of a pioneer, and as such it would be fitting that some public recognition of that work should take permanent form in the approaching jubilee year of the free library movement.

One who introduced a bill into Parliament (in 1834) which abolished hanging in chains, and (in 1837) another which did away with capital punishment for stealing and sacrilege ; who (in 1836) drew the report which led to the establishment of the Schools of Design at Somerset House, since developed into the Government Science and Art Department ; who (in 1841) moved for an annual statement on education from a minister of the Crown, and subsequently saw his motion carried into effect ; who took the first public steps which led to the establishment of the system of civil, army, and diplomatic service examinations ; who obtained the Select Committee on Public Libraries, and the Public Libraries Act of 1850, needs must be a considerable public benefactor. When the din of political party strife shall have died away, and the history of the nineteenth century in Britain shall be written by the impartial historian of the twentieth century, it is not improbable that the name of WILLIAM EWART will have a distinguished place when that of many a more applauded politician shall have shrunk into oblivion.

William Ewart was the second son of a Liverpool merchant of the same name, and was born in Liverpool on 1st May 1798. He was educated at Eton, and passed in due course to Christ Church, Oxford, where, in 1819, he carried off the college prize for Latin verse. In the following year a poem of his obtained the Newdigate prize. He obtained a second-class in classical honours, and graduated B.A. in 1821. Nearly six years later he was called to the bar at the Middle Temple, and in the following year (1828) he entered Parliament for the borough of Bletchingley, in Surrey. In 1830 he was elected by a narrow majority a member for Liverpool, for which town he sat until 1837, when he was defeated by his opponent. In 1839 he was elected for Wigan, and in 1841 for the Dumfries burghs, which he continued to represent until his retirement from public life in 1868. He died at Broadleas, near Devizes, on 23rd January 1869.

The important services of Mr. Ewart as Parliamentary leader of the public library movement have been recounted in the earlier chapters of this book. No celebration of the jubilee year of the Act of 1850 can be satisfactory which does not leave behind some permanent public memorial of the greatness of this truly modest, accomplished, and patriotic educational reformer.

The Right Hon. Sir JOHN LUBBOCK, Bart., M.P., was born in London on the 30th April 1834. He was the son and heir of Sir John William Lubbock, eminent as astronomer and mathematician. The baronetcy to which he succeeded in 1865 was created in 1806 in favour of his great-great-uncle. Sir John was educated at Eton, but at the early age of fourteen was withdrawn from school to assist in his father's banking business, owing to the sudden illness of several of the partners. In 1856 he became a partner, and he has since distinguished himself in the banking world by his introduction of the "country clearing" and other financial improvements. Sir John Lubbock has served on many Royal Commissions dealing with educational, scientific, and financial questions. Among scientists he has become distinguished for his valuable original work and popular studies in anthropology, botany, entomology, and other branches of science.

His writings are numerous, and for the greater part well known. "The Pleasures of Life" and "The Uses of Life" are among the most attractive of his works. He has been President of the British Association for the Advancement of Science (in the "jubilee" year, 1881), of the Linnæan Society, of the Ethnographical Society, of the Entomological

Society, of the Anthropological Institute, and Vice-President of the Royal Society. In 1878 he became a Trustee of the British Museum. In 1870 he entered Parliament as representative of Maidstone, but in 1880 he lost that seat and was returned for the University of London, the constituency which he still represents. His Parliamentary activity has been great; a very considerable number of bills which have passed into law were introduced by him. Amongst them are the Bank Holidays Act, 1871, the Shop Hours Regulation Act, and the Ancient Monuments Act, besides many dealing with banking and finance and medical education. In 1878 he became LL.D. *honoris causa* of Dublin. He is also LL.D. of Cambridge and of Edinburgh, D.C.L. of Oxford, and M.D. of Würzburg. He was Vice-President of the first London County Council, and succeeded Lord Rosebery as President in 1890.

Sir John Lubbock may be justly regarded as the successor to Mr. William Ewart in the Parliamentary leadership of the free library movement. The part which he has played since 1877 in the improvement of library legislation may be gathered from the history contained in the early chapters of this work, where it will be seen that nearly every library bill considered by Parliament has been backed with his name and received his support.

Mr. JOHN PASSMORE EDWARDS was born at Blackwater, near Chacewater, in Cornwall, on the

24th March 1824. In 1842 he was employed in Truro as a solicitor's clerk, and he has stated that he left Truro involuntarily and went to London, where he arrived with three shillings and fourpence in his pocket. In London he took to press work, and successively edited many useful periodicals. In 1860 he succeeded Mr. E. J. Reed as editor, and became the proprietor, of *The Mechanics' Magazine*. This ran until 1868, and was succeeded by *The English Mechanic and World of Science*, which has been his property from its first appearance in 1869. In 1861 Mr. Edwards acquired the *Building News and Engineering Journal*, a technical paper like the preceding one, with a very large weekly circulation. He became the proprietor of the *Echo* in 1876. From 1880 to 1886 he sat as member of Parliament for Salisbury. Before 1889 he had already given 10,000 volumes to free libraries, and in that year he made a gift of £20,000 to the Bethnal Green Free Library. In 1896 his gifts to the Shoreditch Public Libraries amounted to £8250. The benefactions of the parish of Camberwell made by him to the Public Library Commissioners amount to £13,500. A Passmore Edwards Library at Hammersmith has been built at his expense, and he has offered £5000 towards a free library in the poor parish of St. George the Martyr, Southwark. The St. Bride's Foundation Institute has acquired a library of modern works on printing, for which purpose Mr. Edwards gave £500 to the managers. His gifts of 500 and of 1000 volumes to various libraries are too numerous to be recorded here. Mr. Edwards has built or promised to build no fewer than nineteen institutions for his native county. Most of these are free libraries, the remainder are institutes, cottage hospitals, and technical schools. The free libraries erected at Truro, Camborne, Redruth, Bodmin, Liskeard, and St. Ives may be taken as representative institutions connected with his name. His usual donation for the erection of a building in a country town is £2000. Mr. Passmore Edwards frequently makes the local adoption of the Public Libraries Acts a condition of his gift, as by this means he considers that he secures the permanence and efficiency of the institutions inaugurated by his munificence. In February 1894 he was elected an honorary member of the Library Association of the United Kingdom.

Mr. ANDREW CARNEGIE was born at Dunfermline, in Scotland, on 25th November 1835. His family removed ten years later to Pittsburg, Pennsylvania. At the age of twelve he commenced to work by attending a small stationary engine; afterwards he entered the telegraph service, and rapidly rose to an important position. He was made superintendent of the Pittsburg division of the Pennsylvania Railroad Co.'s lines, then he acquired an interest in some oil wells, which turned out very profitable. His means enabled him to found and work up "the largest and most complete system of iron and steel industries in the world ever controlled by one individual," hence his popular appellation, "the Iron King."

Mr. Carnegie has also bought up a number of English Radical newspaper properties. He is the author of "An American Four-in-Hand in Britain," 1883; "Round the World," 1884; and "Triumphant Democracy," 1886. The *Critic* says: "Altogether, Mr. Carnegie has within the last few years given more than four million dollars (say, £800,000) to the cause of public education in its wider sense, for the libraries erected by him almost invariably are devoted to music, art, and science as well. The principal of these institutions are at Alleghany, Homestead, Braddock, and Johnston, Pennsylvania; and Edinburgh, Ayr, and Dunfermline." In an article on "The Gospel of Wealth" published in the *North American Review*, Mr. Carnegie writes: "The result of my own study of the question, What is the best gift which can be given to a community? is that a free library occupies the first place, provided the community will accept and maintain it as a public institution, as much a part of the city property as its public schools, and indeed an adjunct to these. It is no doubt possible that my own personal experience may have led me to value a free library beyond all other forms of beneficence. When I was a boy in Pittsburg, Colonel Anderson of Alleghany—a name I can never speak without feelings of devotional gratitude—opened his little library of four hundred books to boys. Every Saturday afternoon he was in attendance himself to exchange books. No one but he who has felt it can know the intense longing with which the arrival of Saturday was awaited, that a new book might be had. My brother and Mr. Phipps, who have been my principal business partners through life, shared with me Colonel Anderson's precious generosity; and it was when revelling in these treasures that I resolved, if ever wealth came to me, that it should be used to establish free libraries, that other poor boys might receive opportunities similar to those for which we were indebted to that noble man."

Mr. Carnegie's gifts to British libraries have been confined to his native country. The principal places are Edinburgh (1886), £50,000; Ayr (1890), £10,000; Dunfermline (1880), £8000; Peterhead (1892–95), £4000; Inverness (1890), £1750; Aberdeen (1892–96), £2000; Airdrie (1892), £1000; Arbroath (1896), £1000. Smaller sums have been given by Mr. Carnegie, and also by Mrs. Carnegie, to a large number of Free Library Committees in struggling circumstances in Scotland.

BOOK II

BRIEF HISTORIES OF TYPICAL
LIBRARIES

CHAPTER VII

THE LIBRARY OF THE BRITISH MUSEUM, AND THE
GUILDHALL LIBRARY, LONDON

THE present work, although not primarily concerned with the free library in any but its local and popular developments, could not reasonably pass over without mention the great National Library of the British Museum. The British Museum Library has three special claims to notice here : it is supported out of public moneys ; it is almost as free as the municipal free library ; it has been the arena in which theories of library administration have been largely tested in practice, and where a large body of library doctrine has been collected and crystallised. To these claims one may also add that its leading officials have shown the deepest practical sympathy with the popular free library of the towns and country places.

The Museum Library like a great river has been formed by the union of several sources, and like a great river it has been increased by many tributary collections combining with the broadening stream as it flows through the sands of time. Sir Hans Sloane, of Chelsea, long eminent as a physician, died in 1752, and directed by his will that his library of 50,000 volumes of printed books and MSS., and his collections of medals, coins, cameos, precious stones, &c., which had cost him £50,000, should be offered to the nation for £20,000. An Act was obtained to this end, providing also for the acquisition by purchase of the Harleian MSS. at the price of £10,000, and directing that the Cottonian MSS., already the property of the nation, should form part of the new national collection. The Act further provided for the appointment of Trustees, and for the raising of money by means of a lottery. The lottery was held, and realised a net profit of more than £95,000; Montague House, the mansion of the deceased Duke of Montague, was bought from Lord Halifax for £10,250, and adapted and furnished at great expense as a repository for the collections; while £30,000 was set aside as a fund for payment of salaries, taxes, and other expenses.

Montague House had been built by a French architect in 1686, on the site of an earlier house of the same name. At different times it was enlarged. In 1823 the eastern wing, from designs of Smirke, was built to receive the King's Library. The building was not finished before 1847, and then the Reading-room had yet to be added. At that time the building was a hollow square, with a columnar façade 470 feet long, in the Ionic style of architecture. About fifty years ago Montague House still existed as a red-brick mansion, fronted by a high brick wall. Visitors entered through an aperture guarded by a French-looking lodge. Where the present Reading-room is there existed a spacious grass plot, enclosed by the quadrangle of Montague House. "It was pleasant," says one, "to steal away to it from the gloom of the library proper, and in stillness and solitude look up at the blue sky."

The British Museum was opened on 15th January 1759, but before that event an accession of immense importance had been received from the King (George II.), viz., the Royal Library of the Kings of England. The British Museum Library at its origin therefore consisted of four important libraries or collections, viz., the Royal Library, the Cottonian, the Harleian, and the Sloane Collections.

The Royal Library existed in the reign of Henry VII., and contained many beautiful books printed in France, notably a series of vellum copies by the famous printer Verard. In the next reign it was still small, for we find 329 volumes described as its greater part. In Edward VI.'s time Bucer's MSS. were added, and Roger Ascham served as librarian. In James I.'s reign Prince Henry secured the valuable collections of Lord Lumley, who died in 1609. During the Commonwealth the library was endangered, but there were not wanting both soldiers and preachers ready to defend it. Richard Bentley, the classical scholar, when appointed librarian in 1694, turned his attention to enforcing the copyright privilege. This valuable privilege was transferred to the Museum with the books, and at a later date Mr. (afterwards

Sir) Anthony Panizzi made it a valuable means of adding to the library. The books in the Royal Library, when handed over to the nation, were 10,200, and the manuscripts 1800 in number.

The Cottonian Collection, rich in documents relating to English history, was acquired by the nation as far back as 1700. Many original letters of royal and illustrious personages, two originals of *Magna Charta*, and the *Durham Book* written about A.D. 720, are among its greater treasures.

The Harleian Collection began to be formed by Robert Harley (afterwards Earl of Oxford and Mortimer) in 1705, and was increased by Edward, the second Earl. Illuminated manuscripts, ancient records, manuscripts of the Classics, including a very important *Odyssey*, and early English poetry, are the glory of the collection.

The Sloane Library of 50,000 volumes chiefly consisted of medical works and books on natural history.

Other important libraries have accrued, some of which may be briefly mentioned. The foundation of the present remarkable collection of Hebrew books in the Museum was made by a gift of 180 volumes from Mr. Solomon da Costa, in the opening year of the institution. In 1763 the Thomason Collection of books and tracts published in England from 1640 to 1662 was presented by George III. This collection of 30,000 distinct publications has yielded, in the hands of Thomas Carlyle and Samuel Rawson Gardiner, most valuable results to study. The Cracherode bequest of 4500 volumes, made in 1799, embraces early editions of the Classics, and books printed on vellum or bound for Grolier and De Thou, besides other choice copies and bibliographical rarities. The Banksian Library, received in 1827, is rich in works of natural history, voyages, and travels, transactions of learned societies and scientific journals, and was collected and bequeathed by Sir Joseph Banks. George III., finding his palace without a library when he came to the throne, at once set about to form one, employing as his librarian Sir Frederick Augusta Barnard. His success was great, and benefited the Museum through the transfer by his successor on the throne of about 84,000 volumes (including pamphlets). This splendid library is said to have cost the King £200,000. Next in value was the bequest made by the Right Honourable Thomas Grenville, received in 1846. The books numbered 20,240, and cost £54,000. Many are among the rarest in the world, many among the most beautiful. Italian and Spanish literature, and early voyages and travels, are well represented. The libraries of musical works once belonging to Sir J. Hawkins and to Dr. C. Burney, the old English plays formerly owned by Garrick, the Croker collection of pamphlets relating to the French Revolution, the Hargrave, Colt Hoare, Moll, and Ginguené collections, the Waterton collection of editions of the "Imitation of Christ," the Chinese books of Robert Morrison, and the Chinese "Cyclopædia," a single work in upwards of 5000 volumes, can only be mentioned; as likewise the

Lansdowne (historical), Burney (classical), Howard-Arundel (historical and philological), and the Stowe (historical) manuscript collections.

From books and manuscripts to readers is an easy transition. In 1894 the number of readers was more than 200,000, a daily average of 670; in 1886 it was 580 per day; but in far away 1810 the number of visits to the Reading-room was no more than 1950 for the whole year. Even in 1832 the annual visits (46,800) were only about one-fifth of what they now are.

For the benefit of readers who have not seen the Museum Reading-room, the following description is borrowed :—

"The Reading-room is circular. The entire building does not occupy the whole quadrangle, there being a clear interval of from twenty-seven to thirty feet all round, to give light and air to the surrounding buildings, and as a guard against possible destruction by fire from the outer parts of the Museum. The dome of this Reading-room is 140 feet in diameter, its height being 106 feet. . . . The new Reading-room contains 1,250,000 cubic feet of space, its suburbs or surrounding libraries 750,000. The building is constructed principally of iron, with brick arches between the main ribs, supported by twenty iron piers. . . . Upwards of 2000 tons of iron have been employed in the construction. The weight of the materials used in the dome is about 4200 tons."

Throughout the interior of the new building walls are dispensed with; double ranges of books in their cases form the partitions. Of the beautiful appearance of the interior of the Reading-room no description can convey a proper sense; it must be seen, and once seen, it will never be forgotten. Probably no modern building so perfectly answers the purposes of its construction as this magnificent *salon* which the British people owe to that prince of library administrators, Sir Anthony Panizzi; who, amid incessant attacks from enemies and much discouragement, persevered in bringing the Museum Library from the inferior position in which he found it in 1837, to the splendid state of efficiency in which he left it on his retirement in 1866.

The British Museum is governed by a Board of Trustees, consisting of official trustees, representing State departments and national academies; elected trustees, usually men of the highest eminence in literature, science, and art; and family trustees, being representatives of great families who have contributed very important collections (*e.g.* the Sloane, the Cottonian, the Townley). For the first sixty years of the existence of the British Museum the money available for purchases and management, with the exception of the initial funds and gifts, did not average £500 per annum. Later the grants were increased, and in the years 1833-37 the sum of £10,250 was allotted for the purchase of books alone. In 1845 Mr. (afterwards Sir) Anthony Panizzi made strong representations to the Trustees of the inadequacy of the funds allowed, and obtained £10,000 per year for a very few years succeeding, followed by a largely reduced grant until 1857, then increased again to £10,000, and so continued annually for many years. Seven thousand pounds was also allowed in 1857 for the laying down and binding of catalogue slips. About ten years ago the allowance to the Museum was greatly reduced, and notwithstanding the protests of important bodies of literary and scholarly men, that unfortunate policy of retrenchment has not yet been entirely reversed.

At first the British Museum consisted of three departments—printed books, manuscripts, natural history; now there are no fewer than twelve—four relating to natural history, four dealing with antiquities, and four literary, viz., printed books, manuscripts, prints and drawings, and Oriental printed books and MSS.

In 1835-36 there was a Parliamentary Commission of inquiry on the management of the British Museum. A very slight acquaintance with the bulky volumes of evidence taken will convince any one of the immense advances of recent years in every department of its work.

The later inquiry, which resulted in the report and valuable body of evidence published in 1849, is a still more interesting document, especially from the literary workers' point of view. The variety of opinions, crude and expert, on the single subject of cataloguing, for instance, which are there set forth, are a mine of ideas to the librarian who wishes to avoid pitfalls, or to consider the pros and cons of the very latest suggestions.

The absence of any adequate catalogue, then so much deplored, is now a complaint of the past. In

1880 the old manuscript catalogue filled more than 2000 folio volumes. In a year or two the gigantic author-catalogue of the printed books, now only a letter or two short of the completed alphabet, will have been wholly printed. Mr. Bullen's catalogue of the English books before 1641, in three octavo volumes, has been very warmly welcomed ; and is an excellent, finished piece of work. The thousands of books of reference on the ground floor of the Reading-room—books freely available to every reader without formality of application—are now properly entered in a catalogue, which has attained to a third edition. A Bibliography of Bibliographies in the Museum is also in print for literary searchers' use. A catalogue of books, placed in the galleries of the Reading-room, opens up another section of 40,000 volumes, which is virtually a well-selected library to that extent.

Further, the additions to the library of the period 1880–95 are indexed by subject, in three handsome octavo volumes, dealing with about 120,000 works, and there is no doubt that this admirable work, for which the public are indebted to Mr. G. K. Fortescue, late Superintendent of the Reading-room, and now Assistant Keeper of Printed Books, will be regularly kept up. Mr. Fortescue's work has been chiefly performed in non-official time. There are also catalogues of great value of the maps and plans and of the various Oriental books. All these catalogues are of far greater use than the limits of the Museum would suggest. Librarians all the world over are grateful for such carefully compiled bibliographic aids to their labours. The manuscript treasures of the Museum also are carefully catalogued. An index to the catalogue for 1854-75 appeared in 1880. Catalogues, each covering a period of six years, have made available the additional MSS. The acquisitions 1854-75 amounted to 10,000 ; 1876-82, 2000 ; 1882-87, 1500 ; 1889-93, nearly 1300. These catalogues of additions contain notices of many mediæval manuscripts, illuminated *Horæ*, romances of chivalry, monastic chronicles, writings of the ancients, works of classic British authors from Chaucer to George Eliot, music scores, and letters of distinguished men and women. The Department of Manuscripts has also issued a catalogue of the Stowe Collection, with its 1085 manuscripts and 646 charters, including documents of the greatest interest for their bearing on our national history, from the seventh to the eighteenth century, besides a few rarities of a literary character. The Oriental MSS., the Romances, the Greek and Latin Classical MSS., have also their special published catalogues.

When it is remembered that the enormous activity of recent years so imperfectly described or suggested here is a characteristic of the remaining departments of the Museum in perhaps no less a degree, one becomes overpowered by the thought of the vastness of this great academic repository of the fruit of intellect.

The Natural History Departments were removed from Bloomsbury to South Kensington in 1881, a course made necessary through the natural growth of all the departments. This transference left room to expand for what remained in the old home. Since that time exhibitions of great value have from time to time been organised in the King's Library, and in the Grenville Room. Wycliffe and Caxton have each had fitting honour done to their fame; while a valuable array of bibliographical monuments and curiosities is now to be seen in the King's Library. In another room manuscripts of great importance, enshrined in strong glazed cases, are laid open to the curious eyes of the casual visitor, no less than to those of the student. Useful and popular handbooks to these collections are published and sold at the Museum.

Space, however, is still a desideratum, and ere long further extensions will be necessary. On account of this possibility the authorities have recently secured five and a half acres of land adjoining the Museum at Bloomsbury. In the meantime, the invention and adoption of the sliding and revolving presses which are now in use in the library have almost doubled the capacity for book storage in the present building.

Of necessity there are many important things here lightly touched upon or omitted, but enough will have been said to convince the reader that the National Library is worthy of the pride of every Englishman, a great national heritage nobly managed, an institution deserving of no niggardly treatment by the Treasury, and progressive as the times in which we live. The library, now consisting of nearly 2,000,000 volumes, holds a foremost place among the libraries of the world, and its pre-eminence is in no degree so marked as in the accessibility of its treasures. The additions of printed books of all descriptions average 46,000 per annum.

A quotation from a paper written forty years ago by one of the most learned of the Museum's past officers, Mr. Watts, may fitly close this section :—

"The Museum is now supposed to possess the best Russian library in existence out of Russia, the best Hungarian out of Hungary, the best Dutch out of Holland; in short, the best library in every European language out of the territory in which that language is vernacular. The books are in every case the standard books of the language —the laws, the histories, the biographies, the works on topography and local history, the poets and novelists in most esteem; in short, all that moulds or paints the life and manners of a nation, and which now a student of any European language need travel no further than to the Reading-room of the Museum to see and make use of."

THE GUILDHALL LIBRARY

If Lord Protector Somerset about the year 1549 had not borrowed, never to return, the whole of the books in the City Corporation Library, it is very probable that to-day the City of London would possess the oldest municipal free library in the country. The original City Library was founded by the executors of the renowned Richard Whityngton and of William Bury early in the fifteenth

THE GUILDHALL LIBRARY

century. The city records contain a first entry regarding it under date 4 Henry VI. (1425). In 1442 the will of John Carpenter, an executor of the celebrated Whityngton, and the founder of the City of London School, was proved. Part of it ran: "If any good or rare books shall be found among the residue of my goods, which by the discretion of the aforesaid Master William Lichfield [founder of a school which afterwards became Mercer's School] and Reginald Pecock [author of *The Repressor*] may seem necessary to the common library at Guildhall, for the profit of the students there and those discoursing to the common people, then I will and bequeath that those books be placed by my executors, and chained in that library, under such form that the visitors and students thereof may be sooner admonished to pray for my soul." Various entries in the records of the corporation show that the library was well looked after until, as Stow relates, Edward Duke of Somerset descended upon the collection.

Thenceforward until 1824 the history of the Guildhall Library is a blank, but on the 8th April of that year Mr. Richard Lambert Jones proposed a resolution in the Court of Common Council which led to the re-founding of the library. A special committee which reported in favour of allotting rooms for a library in the east wing at the front of the Guildhall, asked for £500 for the outfit, and £200 annually for maintenance. Purchases were confined to works relating to the manners, customs, laws, privileges, and history of the City of London and the neighbouring locality. The newly-founded library was thus entirely different in character from the original one, which evidently had been in the main theological. In June 1828 the library was opened with 1380 works in 1700 volumes. By the 5th November 1829, 2800 volumes (more than 1000 by donation), 2000 prints, and 100 drawings and portraits had been received. In 1840, nearly 10,000 volumes and an extension of premises, so as to include a room for a museum of local antiquities, could be reported. In December 1840 evening opening was tried, soon to be discontinued. The celebrated autograph signature of Shakespeare to the purchase deed of a house in Blackfriars was obtained in 1843 for the price of £145. About 400 Hebrew books were presented by Mr. Philip Salomons in 1847, a special collection which has been very much increased by purchases out of part of a munificent bequest of £1000 left by Alderman Sir David Salomons. The additions were made under the advice of the Rev. Albert Löwy, who prepared a catalogue of the Hebrew and Jewish books, published in 1891.

Among the treasures of the library may be reckoned Aggas's map of the ancient city (one of two copies in existence); a collection of writings by Hackney Nonconformist ministers, formed by the donor, Mr. J. R. D. Tyssen; and a "Golden Legend," printed by Wynkyn de Worde. The library of the Dutch Church in London was deposited for many years in the Guildhall Library, but has now been withdrawn to be placed in a new building adjoining the church. The British Museum in 1889 presented a large number of its duplicates. In 1890 the corporation purchased a fine collection of English plays and poems printed by London printers; and in 1894 a very fine manuscript of an English Missal, which once belonged to the Church of St. Botolph, Aldersgate. From the Gennadius sale in 1895 were acquired valuable illustrated books on the topography of Greece and the East.

The library is supported entirely out of corporate income, without falling upon the rates in any degree. The annual allowance for the purchase and binding of books has been increased at various times to its present amount of £1000. The present librarian, Mr. Charles Welch, F.S.A., has kindly supplied the writer with the following precise statement. "This amount has to bear some trifling charges (about £40 per annum). The rest is devoted to the increase of the library in about the following proportions :—

> 1. *Fixed Charges*, subscriptions to publishing societies, £70, 5s. Periodicals and newspapers (no daily papers taken), £64. Directories and other annuals, continuations, &c., £139. Binding, £214, 10s. Petty cash, £18. Making a total of £540, 15s.
> 2. *Balance* available for new purchases, about £420."

Mr. Welch also adds: "We are always on the look-out for London rarities, which are getting fewer, however, every year as our collection increases. We also make a feature of genealogy, and to a less extent of British topography, and encourage writers in the former class by subscribing to nearly all parish registers, visitations, &c. &c., which are announced for publication."

The library committee also acts as a publishing committee to the city corporation. Many provincial free libraries have been enriched by grants of valuable works of national importance published by the committee.

In 1855 the ratepayers of the City rejected the Public Libraries Act of Mr. Ewart. In 1861 also the same fate met a similar proposal. Latterly the establishment of free lending libraries at Bishopsgate and Cripplegate, and at the St. Bride's Institute, endowed out of the City charities' funds under a scheme approved by the Charity Commissioners, seems to have confirmed the citizens in their desire not to place themselves under the Public Libraries Acts. Mr. Welch has been very active of late years in advocating a scheme of unification for London free libraries, under which the Guildhall Library would become the premier reference library, with a limited number of reference libraries systematically distributed throughout the metropolis with due regard to public needs, thus leaving free many of the smaller public libraries committees for concentration on lending library work. Much has been said both for and against this proposal. One must confess that the policy of concentration upon a reference library in the City adopted by the committee in no way conflicts with the adoption of the Public Libraries Acts, and it is greatly to be hoped that the citizens of the first city in the world will not long withhold the revenues which a library rate would yield for the further development of this excellent library.

The beautiful Gothic building which contains the library and museum was erected at a cost of £25,000 (exclusive of fittings), and opened on the 5th November 1872 by Lord Chancellor Selborne. During the last year of the use of the old library apartments the attendance of readers and visitors numbered 14,316. In 1874, the first completed year in the new premises, the number had increased to 173,559. In 1893 the library contained 68,369 volumes, besides 38,075 pamphlets.

Under the present admirable management by the committee, with Mr. Edward Lee as chairman, and Mr. Charles Welch, F.S.A., as adviser and librarian, the public have every guarantee of an honourable future to one of the best of the city's institutions.

In Chapter XIII., dealing with Endowed and Voluntary Free Libraries, are some references to London free libraries other than those founded or supported under the Public Libraries Acts.

CHAPTER VIII

LONDON LIBRARIES UNDER THE PUBLIC LIBRARIES ACTS

OF the eighty-two parishes enumerated in schedules A and B of the Metropolis Management Act, 1855, all but thirty-one had been included in adoptions of the Public Libraries Acts by the end of 1896. The fifty-one parishes which are included in Public Library Districts form thirty-six areas of adoption. The only complete Metropolitan Districts of more than one parish covered by a single adoption are those of Whitechapel, Westminster (St. Margaret and St. John), St. Giles, and Holborn, but separate parish adoptions have now covered the whole of the Poplar, Fulham, and St. Saviour's Districts. With the exception of Tooting Graveney parish, all the Wandsworth District is included in separate adoptions. No adoptions have been recorded yet in the Greenwich District, the Plumstead District, and the St. Olave District, and only one in the Strand District, and one in the Hackney District. The following parishes, which are districts to themselves, and most of them very wealthy, have not yet adopted the Public Libraries Acts :—St. Marylebone, St. Pancras, Islington (St. Mary), Paddington,

Bethnal Green (St. Matthew), St. James (Westminster), and St. Luke (Middlesex).

The first adoption in London, that for two parishes in Westminster, took place in 1856, and was not followed by a second until the parish of Wandsworth adopted the Acts in 1883. The progress of the movement in London since that time has been indicated in previous pages. The particular accounts which follow will give a fair idea of the history of typical individual free library organisations.

It is very difficult to state who are the authors most favoured by readers in London free libraries. In fiction, probably Mrs. Wood and Marie Corelli lead the way! but in some parishes, Weyman and Anthony Hope, with the older classical novelists, are first favourites. Of the serious writers, Carlyle, Ruskin, Darwin, and Dean Farrar are much studied. Many librarians say that it is not possible to state the six most popular authors in their libraries.

BATTERSEA

Battersea distinguished itself by adopting the Public Libraries Act in the year of the Queen's jubilee, but during four years an organised committee had been preparing the way for success. Opposition there was, but it was neither extensive nor well organised. The date of adoption was 16th March 1887. In that year a rate of one penny in the pound produced £2300 ; in 1895–96 the revenue from the same source was £3128. At first there were very few donations, but the Vestry in 1891 gave the Commissioners £2500 out of the proceeds of the sale of parish lands, a sum used to reduce the debt. About two hundred volumes of general interest are received by presentation annually, a much larger number than ordinarily is given to a London free library. In 1887 a modest beginning was made with a reading-room in hired premises, and in 1888 a permanent library of 4654 volumes, to be reckoned a branch hereafter, was opened at Lammas Hall, which was hired for the purpose. Here provision was also made for magazine and newspaper readers. The handsome Central Library was opened on 26th March 1890. The ground floor contains a news-room, magazine-room, and lending library, and upstairs there are book stores and a handsome reference library. Three hundred readers at one time can be accommodated on the premises. The cost of site and building was £10,000. On 30th September of the same year the Lurline Gardens branch, which cost £2000, was opened. This is a single storey building, with a large reading-room and a lending library. The reading-rooms are open on week days from 8 A.M. to 10 P.M., and on Sundays from 3 to 9 P.M.; the lending libraries from 10 A.M. to 9 P.M., except on Thursdays, when they close at 1 P.M., and on Sundays, when they are not open. The reference library opens an hour later on week days than the reading-rooms, and closes at the same hours. The average daily issue of works for home reading is 900; for reference, 70. Three thousand visits per day are made to the reading-rooms, and the libraries contain 36,000 volumes, increasing yearly at the rate of 1400 volumes. The materials of local history are collected and cared for. The libraries have always been "well-used in every sense of that expression," and by all classes of people.

CHELSEA

The agitation commenced by Mr. B. W. Findon for the establishment of free libraries for Chelsea, received strong support from two of the local papers, the *West London Press* and the *West Middlesex Advertiser*. There was, however, little opposition, although the Vestry carried a vote adverse to the adoption of the Acts. The Acts were adopted in May 1887, and the first rate was levied in the September of that year. Temporary reading-rooms, lent by the Vestry, were provided in the Town Hall, and opened in November. The full rate was levied, and brought in £2250 at first, but now it yields £3100. Donations in money to be expended on books reached £900, and the freehold of the library site in Manresa Road was the gift of Lord Cadogan, K.G. Other large donations have been received: namely, from Lord Cadogan, £350; and from Sir Charles Dilke, M.P., £500. Chelsea has been particularly fortunate in its occasional gifts of excellent books. In 1895, 508 volumes were so received, the previous year 729 volumes. The permanent Central Library was opened in January 1891; it is a beautiful and well-arranged building, and the casual visitor is struck with the many artistic objects which meet his gaze; for example, Ongania's reproduction of the façade of San Marco at Venice, and examples of statuary by distinguished sculptors long resident in Chelsea.

The library is a well balanced one, with perhaps a little leaning to works on the fine arts and technological text-books. The materials of local history, including election literature and scraps of all kinds, are diligently collected; but the works of resident authors are not specially sought after, owing to the vastness of such an undertaking in a parish where so many authors reside. The friendliest relationship exists between the S.W. London Polytechnic next door and the free library. The latter serves as the library of the former. Both institutions were promoted by the same individuals, though the committees of management are not identical. A special classified catalogue of books for students of science and art has been issued by the librarian. The library is open every week day from 9 A.M. to 9 P.M., and for six hours every Sunday. A boys' reading-room is provided, and volumes were issued more than 40,000 times in this room during 1895-96. In January 1890 a permanent branch library in Kensal Town, which is several miles away from the main part of the parish, was opened, a temporary library having been established earlier. Here, too, there is a boys' reading-room. The libraries in June 1896 numbered altogether 28,561 volumes. Seven hundred and four is the average number of volumes per day issued for home reading, and 101 that for consultation. Visits to the reading-rooms are nearly eighteen hundred per day. The librarian calls attention to a characteristic of Chelsea people, which is said to belong to readers in most London parishes—their dislike to using works of reference on the premises. Each borrower appears to think that every work should be available for home reading. This demand is hardly known in provincial towns. If yielded to, the consequent uncertainty of finding works of reference in the library when wanted would more than nullify any advantage to students.

Clerkenwell

The librarian and commissioners for Clerkenwell have distinguished themselves by a bold innovation in library management—the introduction of the system now generally known as "open access." Clerkenwell is also interesting from another reason. The Acts were adopted in 1887—in celebration of the Queen's jubilee—but the opposition was determined to use every means to render the adoption abortive. The authority which arranged the poll, the method of delivery and collection of voting-papers, and other matters, were objected to, but the objectors were finally overruled by the judgments of Justices Field and Wills in the case Reg. v. Morris.

The first rate was collected in 1888, and a news-room was opened in hired premises on 20th

November of that year, and in the following March a lending library of 8000 volumes. The penny rate at first brought in £1380, now it yields £1550. Donations have been received to the extent of £900 in cash and £300 worth of books. The growth of the library has been gradual, but the management always has been spirited, and the results achieved are of a solid character. The present building was opened on 10th October 1890. The London School Board has in operation a good system of school libraries, and this fact has prevented the Clerkenwell library authority, and probably some other metropolitan authorities, from forming children's libraries. Yet ever since 1893 teachers and scholars applying for them have been allowed extra students' tickets. The materials of local history are industriously collected, including prints, medals, coffin-plates, and "old water-conduits." The prints are exhibited occasionally in frames with false backs. Other special kinds of literature sought after are works on design, clockmaking, art metal work, jewellery. The library now contains 15,500 volumes, issues on an average 360 works per day for home reading, and 91 for reference; while 2010 visits are made daily to the institution. The library is kept well under public notice by means of handbills, press notices, information circulars, paragraphs on the backs of rate-papers, and metal tablets attached to street lamps. A "Quarterly Guide for Readers," which has been copied more or less in more than a score of other free libraries, was started in July 1894. In its pages annotated lists of books on special subjects appear from time to time. Special exhibitions of pictures, bindings, old printing, and art metal work have been held in the library for five or six years past. The help of opticians, watchmakers, and others is sought in the suggestion of technical works for the library. The news-rooms are open from eight in the morning until ten in the evening on week days, and also for six hours on Sunday afternoons. The expenses connected with loans absorb about a quarter of the income, and salaries and wages about one-third.

The system of "open access" introduced in 1893, and now adopted by a number of other libraries, may be briefly described as that of admitting registered borrowers under scrutiny into the library enclosure to select from the shelves the works which they want. It is claimed that this system is economical, reduces the reading of fiction, brings readers and librarians into beneficial personal contact, and is greatly appreciated by the borrowers. The system is not, however, applied to the Clerkenwell Reference Library, except to a comparatively small section. Music scores were introduced into the library in 1893, and since 1891 annotated entries in the catalogues have been frequent.

Hampstead

The adoption of the Public Libraries Acts for Hampstead was first mooted in a thickly-peopled ward of the parish, and its friendly discussion assisted by the offer of Mr. Henry Harben, chairman of the Vestry, to present £2000 to the building fund when the Acts should be adopted. Not much feeling was evoked, but after the usual delays the poll was taken in 1893, and the result announced as favourable. The voting-papers stated no limitations, and a penny in the pound has been levied hitherto. For 1893 only half a year's appropriation was made, but the penny in 1894 brought in £2800, which is now increased by £300 through the last quinquennial re-assessment. Mr. Harben increased his offer to £3500, with the promise of £1500 more if the whole cost of the building were to be covered by £5000, a promise since redeemed. A librarian of experience was appointed, and a hired news-room quickly opened at Stanfield House. A large house in Priory Road was taken and adapted as a branch library, with reference, lending, and news departments, stocked with 6000 books, and opened in November 1894. Another branch library, to be known as the Belsize Branch, and a central library are also in course of erection. The lord of the manor, from whom the central site was purchased, gave a donation of £350. No sooner was the Kilburn (Priory Road) Branch opened than the demand for books was considerable, and so lately as July 1896, with only 7500 volumes in stock, a daily issue of four hundred for home reading and fifteen for consultation on the premises had been reached. A special feature of the work at Hampstead worth a passing note is the open-air reading-stand near Hampstead Heath, on which are posted early every morning the advertisement sheets of daily papers for the information of the unemployed. The children are not forgotten, and books suitable to their years are provided in the library, while special juvenile lists are now being prepared for the press and furnished to the local schools.

All the parochial records are in the hands of the librarian, also the official scrap-book of local cuttings, which until recently was the charge of a sub-committee of the Vestry. The Vestry some years ago contributed towards the expense of publishing some of the local records. When the Central Reference Library is formed, the local collection, towards which some rare books and MSS. have been received, will be a special feature. The library of the late Professor Henry Morley was lately purchased for £806, and now forms part of the Hampstead collections. This is rich in the literature of the sixteenth, seventeenth, and eighteenth centuries, English and foreign classics in first and early editions, and fine Shakespeare editions and commentaries. A selection of the whole will be set apart as the "Morley Memorial Library," and increased from time to time by additions which will not alter the character of the collection. A "Quarterly Guide" is regularly issued and sold to readers; in it are published topical lists, notes, and news, and latest additions to the libraries. There is every reason to believe that when the present plans of the library committee of the Vestry are completed, the Hampstead Public Libraries system will be one of the best in London.

Lambeth

Lambeth is pre-eminent among London library districts in the extent to which it has attracted the gifts of the generous. Money, books, and buildings, to the value of £43,000, have been given to the Commissioners for public libraries and museums. The list of benefactors is a long one, too long to print here, but the principal donors ought to be had ever in remembrance. They were:—

> Mr. Henry Tate, who gave the Tate Central Library Building, Brixton, £16,640, and the Tate Library, South Lambeth Road, £9000.
> Miss J. Durning Smith, £10,000 (for the Kennington Branch Library Building).
> The executors of the late Mr. W. Noble, £4000.
> Mr. F. Nettlefold, £1080.
> Messrs. Crompton-Roberts and J. Rolls Hoare, £1000.
> Miss J. A. Esquilant, £500.
> Mr. H. Brooks Marshall, J.P., works of reference, £500.

There were also six donors of 100 guineas each. The Public Libraries Acts were adopted in December 1886, and at first the rate was limited to a halfpenny in the pound, which brought in £2400 per annum. In 1891, by vote of the ratepayers, stimulated by conditional gifts, the rate limit was increased to one penny in the pound, and in 1895-96 raised £6256 for library expenses. In 1887, in hired rooms, a library with 5000 volumes and news-room was first started. There are now five large libraries, which in 1895 were open on 250 days, and issued on an average 2924 volumes per day. The Tate Central Library contains 25,000 volumes, and each of the others from six to ten thousand. The total is nearly 70,000. In 1888 the West Norwood and South Lambeth branches were opened, in 1889 that at Kennington, in 1893 the North Lambeth branch and the Central Library. An edition of 5000 copies of the catalogue of the Central Library was sold out in six months. Every effort is made to secure the works of local authors, and there is a very fine collection of Surrey topography at the Central Library. The staff of the libraries consists of about thirty-four persons.

Under the management of the Lambeth Commissioners is placed the Minet Library, situated in a portion of Camberwell surrounded on all sides by Lambeth. The building was presented by Mr. Minet, and cost about £10,000. This library was opened in 1890, and in 1895 possessed more than 12,000 volumes, and had an issue of 377 per day. Here, also, is a special room for the use of children from seven to fourteen years of age, which was opened on 2nd October 1893. Before 30th July 1895 volumes had been used by children 69,736 times. Periodicals are also provided for them; and their behaviour has, generally speaking, been admirable. Lectures are also given to children, and the optical lantern is used for illustration. This room is considered by the librarian to be a valuable training ground for readers.

NEWINGTON

The lesson of the defeat which ensued on the first agitation (in 1888) for the adoption of the Acts in Newington was not lost. The poll of October 1890 had been prepared for by the efforts of a vigorous committee, who, even to the extent of holding street processions, had thoroughly permeated Newington society with the knowledge of the question to be decided. In 1891 the first rate was levied, and produced £1700, a sum increased in 1896 to £1830. A few subscriptions were obtained in the beginning, and considerable gifts of books have since been received from the Fishmongers' Company, the University of Cambridge, and a few private donors. The library building, with the site, cost £16,000, and the annual charge connected with the necessary loans absorbs fifty-five per cent. of the income. The lending library, with 9500 volumes, the news-room, and the boys' room, were opened in 1891, and an embarrassing influx of readers immediately ensued. More than 2000 copies of the catalogue were sold in less than five months, and in less than two years and a half the issues amounted to thirty-four times the number of books in the library. The reference library, with 1200 volumes, was opened in April 1895, and a month earlier free popular lectures were commenced. A boys' library was formed in May 1896, and a monthly *Library Chronicle*, ably edited, commenced in April 1896. School children are admitted as ordinary borrowers on the recommendation of their teachers.

Special attention is given to books on the industries in which local residents are most engaged, and the materials of local history are well looked after. Many residents of Newington have been, or are, eminent in literature or art, and books written by them, or relating to their work, are collected. Among them figure the names of Faraday, Browning, Taylor (the Platonist), and Tinworth. The reference library and reading-rooms are open for three hours every Sunday in the winter months only. The boys' room is open three hours each week evening, and practically all day on Saturdays. The expenditure on the staff is very low, only twenty per cent. Seeing that eight persons are wholly employed, and three partially, for less than £450 a year, one is inclined to think hard things of the managing authority, especially as few such authorities are served by such an efficient librarian and secretary. The daily average issue of works for home reading is 613 ; for reference, 51. The number of visits to reading-rooms is about 2500 per day. The volumes on the shelves number nearly 14,000. The librarian reports, "Our difficulty continues to be the want of a much larger stock of books."

POPLAR

Poplar is another working-class constituency where the Acts have been adopted. An ably conducted campaign, in which holding public meetings and canvassing formed the principal methods of action, led to the adoption of the Acts in December 1890 by a majority of 10 to 1 on a poll of more than 3600 votes, and this without a suggestion of less than a penny rate. The rate was first levied in 1891, and realised £1324. In 1895-96 the rate brought in £40 more. A public subscription brought in £1450, 2s. 6d., which was expended on the site. Promises were also made which have not yet been fulfilled. The site of the Central Library in Poplar Terrace, however, cost £2000. While negotiations for a site were pending, the librarian was purchasing, storing, and cataloguing the books that were to form the first library. St. Stephen's Mission Room was also acquired and opened as a temporary reading-room.

During the first year an average of 800 persons per diem used the reading-room, and nearly 17,000 volumes were consulted there. The Local Government Board allowed a loan of £7000, repayable in thirty years, to be raised for the library building. On the 3rd October 1894 the Central Library was formally opened by the chairman of the Commissioners. Two days later the reference and lending departments and the news-room were first used by the public, and a complete catalogue of books for home reading, extending to 317 pages, was on sale. In six months 1600 persons had been registered as borrowers, and the registry was proceeding at the rate of 200 per month. For three months Sunday opening was tried, but so few availed themselves of it that the Commissioners considered that Sunday opening was not required, and closed the library again. An evening branch library at Island Gardens was opened in November 1895. The cost of this branch is about ten per cent. of the total expenditure. The Central Library was opened with 7700 volumes; the Commissioners now possess 10,000 volumes, with an average daily issue of 350 for home reading, and 50 for consultation. The daily visits to the reading-rooms number about 1200. It is intended to pay special attention to the provision of works on shipbuilding, navigation, and chemistry, and a beginning has been made with books about Poplar. The catalogue and its supplement of 1896 are on the dictionary plan, with numerous subject headings, very distinctively printed. The taste of the East End artisan is found in the popularity of Gardiner, Gibbon, and Malleson, Darwin and Huxley, Stanley and Brassey with serious readers; Mrs. Wood, Miss Braddon, "Edna Lyall," Charles Dickens, Rider Haggard, and Conan Doyle among the readers of fiction. Works by these writers are most frequently asked for.

St. George, Hanover Square

The parish of St. George, Hanover Square, is, next to that of Kensington, the richest parish in London. Here a rate of one halfpenny in the pound yields £3900. If anywhere, it is in such a quarter that one would expect opposition to the proposal to establish free libraries, yet the poll taken on 24th June 1890 was carried by a majority of 754 votes, with considerably more than half the voters voting. More than a year before, the Vestry had adopted the report of a committee strongly in favour of this step. This report is a very interesting document, and should be read by all propagandist committees. After a very brief statement of the abstract merits of free libraries, as to which, it is assumed, all agree, the special needs of the parish and the annual expense are discussed. Population and its distribution, assessments, present provision of denominational or sectional libraries, are touched upon, and the best situation for a principal and a subordinate library stated. The balance-sheets and rating of surrounding parishes are cited in support of a contention that a halfpenny rate is all that is needed. The report was carried by 28 votes to 18.

Twelve days before the poll a public meeting was held, at which Sir John Lubbock presided, and the Duke of Westminster and the Right Hon. G. J. Goschen, M.P., spoke in favour of the movement. The Duke of Westminster presented a valuable site in Buckingham Palace Road, and a handsome building in the English Renaissance style was erected and opened. This building was completed and officially opened in April 1894, but books were first issued on 16th July following. The librarian had been appointed in October 1891, and assisted the Commissioners by his experienced advice as to the necessary modifications in the architect's plans, and also in the purchase, temporary storage, cataloguing, and preparation of the books for the new building. The library opened with 18,000 volumes. Of these 11,860 were in the lending department. A beautifully printed catalogue of 406 octavo pages was prepared while the building was in progress, thus justifying the wisdom of the early appointment of the librarian. Long before the principal library was ready for opening, a second library had been begun in South Audley Street for the use of residents in the northern part of the parish. This was opened without ceremony on 1st July 1895. The principal library with fittings cost about £20,000, and the books about £4000; the South Audley Street library cost £10,000 for building, fittings, and books. No free libraries in London are so sumptuously or comfortably furnished. The larger one contains a reading-room, lending library, reference library, ladies' room, and natural history room, with abundant space for storage. The second floor is the librarian's official residence. Two thousand five hundred volumes were received as gifts at the outset, and about 500 volumes annually have since been presented. There are now 26,300 volumes in the two libraries. The Northern Library opened with 7000 volumes, handsomely catalogued in 236 octavo pages. Separate collections of children's books are in both libraries. Local literature is specially collected. The reference library is strong in historical literature and in books on the fine arts. The natural history collection is a special feature here, and serves as an introduction to the British Museum collections at South Kensington.

This collection is under the curatorship of its donor, and the Commissioners have promised to house it for a period of four years, the cost being defrayed by voluntary subscriptions. The principal library costs about 63 per cent. of the whole outlay. Loans, interest, and ground rent consume 30 per cent. of the income. The daily average circulation of books is for home reading 654, for reference 100 volumes. One thousand nine hundred visits per day to the reading-rooms are recorded. The libraries are being increased by 1000 to 1200 volumes yearly.

St. Leonard, Shoreditch

From Hanover Square to Shoreditch is a considerable change ;—from the abode of ease, wealth, and art, to long crowded streets and the homes of clerk and mechanic. A short agitation led to the adoption of the Acts in March 1891, on the understanding that the rate was not to exceed three-farthings in the pound. The Commissioners early determined to build two libraries of about equal importance, one for Hoxton and one for Haggerston. Mr. J. Passmore Edwards has given £8250 to assist the libraries of Shoreditch, besides a large number of books. A building at Haggerston which had been used as gas offices was secured with land for £4250, and adapted and furnished for £1640. With the buildings were obtained a plot, which, at a cost of £250, defrayed by the central governing body of the City Parochial Foundation, was laid out as a public garden. The opening ceremony was performed by the Duke of Devonshire, K.G., on 10th May 1893. One thousand five hundred pounds had been spent on books, and this library opened with 6460 volumes in the lending and 2346 in the reference department. Recently it has been found necessary to extend the building at a cost of £2037, which Mr. Passmore Edwards has undertaken to defray.

On 26th February 1894 the Hoxton Library was opened in temporary premises, hired at a rental of £100, and adapted and furnished with 5000 volumes at a cost of nearly £900. The news and magazine rooms had been open from 27th November preceding. A fine new library for Hoxton is now in course of construction in Pitfield Street, which is to cost £10,250—the site costing £4500 additional. Mr. Passmore Edwards, after whom the library is to be named, has given £2000 towards the cost.

Special attention in the choice of books is paid to the local industries of cabinetmaking and shoemaking. For home reading 337 books per day are issued from the libraries, and for consultation 68. More than twelve hundred visits per day are made to each library. The Haggerston Library contained in July 1896 11,599 volumes, and the Hoxton Library 5482 volumes. Since the adoption of the Acts 3834 volumes have been presented. The number of borrowers' tickets in force in March 1896 was 3048. The catalogues issued by the librarian deserve high praise for their wise originality, clearness, and excellence; the subject headings are very numerous and distinctive.

St. Martin-in-the-Fields, and St. Paul, Covent Garden

St. Martin's is not a large parish as measured by population, but it is in the heart of the activities of London. Its library, within a minute's walk of the National Gallery, is excellently situated to attract attention from the numerous day-time visitors who do not swell the population returns.

The Acts were adopted by the parish on 10th February 1887 with but little opposition, and a penny rate, producing £1833, was levied in the same financial year. The first reading-room—a temporary one—was opened in Long Acre on New Year's Day 1889. To the reading-room was added a reference library of 1000 volumes. No help from generous donors has been forthcoming. In 1892 the parish of St. Paul, Covent Garden, adopted the Acts, and agreed to form one library district with that of St. Martin. The revenue is now for St. Martin's £2243, for St. Paul's parish £415. The permanent library building was opened by Mr. W. E. Gladstone on 12th February 1891. It is excellently adapted for its uses, and is very spacious; nevertheless, for its 3593 visitors per day, more room is needed. "Open access" is in vogue here, but, reversing the Clerkenwell plan, it applies only in the reference department. An ingenious device to acquaint visitors with recent additions to the library is in use: it is known as the "wheel catalogue." This invention of the librarian is placed beneath glazed portions of the counter, and by means of a lever is made to revolve and bring successively into view a long list of book-titles arranged on the circumference of the wheel.

A very valuable collection of prints, maps, &c., relating to the neighbourhood has been got together by the librarian, and the library is rich in books relating to London. A fine catalogue has been published. The lending library is open eight hours per day (four hours on Wednesdays). The news-room is opened from nine o'clock in the morning, the reference department from ten o'clock until ten in the evening of every week day (Bank holidays excepted). The daily issue of books is 251 for home reading, 278 for consultation, and the library contains 27,678 volumes.

Wandsworth

Wandsworth was the second parish in London to adopt the Public Libraries Acts. On 3rd July 1883 what one may call the library Renaissance of London was inaugurated by this south-western parish. The local movement owed its origin to Mr. E. E. Greville, the Vestry clerk, who early in 1881 was pressing the question of adoption on members of the Vestry. Dr. Hooper was early active in the field; and the Wandsworth Free Library owes very much to Dr. Longstaff, who gave the Longstaff Reading-room and £3000 besides. The majority for the adoption of the Acts was 1068 out of 2032 votes. A reading-room was opened in the Commissioners' own building on 21st March, and lending and reference libraries on 1st October of 1885. At the end of 1885 there were 8208, now there are more than 15,000 volumes in the libraries. A thousand visits a day are made to the reading-rooms, and 350 books are issued per day for home reading and consultation. A valuable experiment was commenced in January 1895, when a branch delivery station and evening news-room was opened at Earlsfield.

The importance of gathering the materials of local history is well understood, and a catalogue of local views at the library has been issued. A guide to the contents of the library, intended to supplement the use of the catalogue, was issued in 1885, entitled "Notes on the Contents of Wandsworth Public Library," by Mr. G. B. Longstaff. A similar and improved guide on the same plan was issued by Mr. Ll. W. Longstaff for the Wimbledon Free Public Library, and in 1888 it had gone through three editions. The plan of these guides is worthy of wide imitation. The expenditure for 1895–96 was £1047, of which £126 was in respect of loans, and £222 for books and periodicals.

CHAPTER IX

FREE LIBRARIES UNDER THE ACTS IN SEVEN
FIRST-CLASS TOWNS

IN the free libraries of eight British towns whose population reached 250,000 in 1891, there are gathered considerably more than a million volumes of books. Separate histories of these libraries (with one exception) follow. The public spirit which founded and developed, and which now sustains them in their useful work, can hardly be adequately extolled; while the administrative ability of the librarians, who have helped to secure a popularity represented by an issue to readers of more than seven millions of volumes in a single year, is worthy of public gratitude. Yet there is every reason to believe that the past achievements of these great town libraries will in the near future be far exceeded. The chief obstacle to further progress in Liverpool, Leeds, Hull, Edinburgh, Dublin, and Belfast, is the existence of the penny rate limit in the Acts of Parliament which regulate their management. Several of the towns whose libraries are described already by a local Act have shaken off that encumbrance.

The absence of Glasgow from the list of first-class

towns which have adopted the Acts is much to be regretted, but it must not be assumed from this fact that Glasgow has no free library. The excellent Mitchell Library is described in a later chapter on Endowed and Voluntary Free Libraries.

An attempt to ascertain the names of the half-dozen most popular authors in the free libraries in first-class towns has not been successful, owing probably to the very large number of the issues of books in these towns. Yet some information on the character of the reading may be gleaned in one or two of the brief accounts devoted to particular libraries.

Manchester

A public library organisation, which costs nineteen thousand pounds annually, and circulates more than two millions of volumes in a single city every year, compels respect from the magnitude alone of its operations. Such an organisation is that of the free libraries at Manchester. This city was the fourth to adopt Ewart's Act of 1850, but furnished the earliest instance of the opening of a free library under the authority of that Act. A public subscription was raised to establish a free library. Sir John Potter was indefatigable in collecting, the enthusiasm of all classes was fairly aroused, and sums varying from one shilling to £500 went to make up the total of nearly £13,000, which also included £2000 — accrued interest and small balances — received from the overseers of the township.

The provisional committee purchased the Hall

of Science in Campfield, and there, on 6th September 1852, the library was first opened, and formally conveyed to the corporation, the adoption of the Act having taken place on the 20th August. A halfpenny rate, levied at the time, produced £1951, but the first year's expenditure out of that sum, owing to the preliminary expenses being paid out of subscriptions, came only to £698. The first stock of books, purchased on the advice of Mr. James Crossley, F.S.A., and Edward Edwards, who was appointed the first librarian, amounted to 18,000 volumes, and the first year's use reached 138,312 issues. By the end of the first year the lending and reference libraries contained 25,000 volumes in a single building for the use of a population of somewhat over 300,000 ; now, for a population not much exceeding 500,000 the magnificent number of nearly 270,000 volumes are available at sixteen centres of distribution. The importance of the eleven branch libraries may be judged from the fact that the average expenditure per branch is close upon a thousand pounds. Indeed, any one of these branches may be deemed of as great importance as the free library of the larger of our third-class towns ; and those at Openshaw and Hulme may even rank with many of the free libraries in towns with a population of 100,000. Even the yearly budget for the reading-rooms of Bradford, Harpurhey, Hyde Road, and Chester Road accounts for totals varying from nearly £300 to more than £500 per annum. A large reading-room for newspapers, magazines, and reference books is attached to each of the branch libraries, and a second reading-room, except at Harpurhey, for the special service of boys, for whom there are distinct collections of books especially suited to their tastes and capacities. The interesting pamphlet by Mr. William R. Credland, the deputy chief librarian, on "The Free Library Movement in Manchester" (1895), may be quoted here :—

"There can hardly be a more pleasing and suggestive sight than is presented by any one of those rooms, with its bright lighting, its busy and helpful female attendants, and its crowd of readers eager for amusement or instruction. And the boys themselves are of that age and class which it is most desirable to influence for good. They are for the most part children of parents whose poverty draws them perilously near to the borderland of crime, but they are still too young to have crossed that border themselves. It is just such lads as these whom it is essential to detach from vicious companions, and to surround with every possible influence that can tend to moral and social improvement, if they are to be made into useful men and good citizens, and rescued from absorption into the pauper and criminal classes."

The four reading-rooms referred to above are not provided with lending libraries, but a few hundred books are kept for consultation and reading on the premises, and they have latterly been constituted "delivery stations." Books applied for at any delivery station before ten o'clock in the morning may be called for after noon on the same day, and those applied for at a later hour may be had after noon on the following day. This privilege has not been much used, owing to the easy accessibility of one or other of the branch libraries from any part of the city. The Openshaw Branch Library needs a special description. In 1894 the Openshaw Branch was opened. "The legatees of Sir Joseph Whitworth had undertaken the erection at Openshaw of a range of buildings which should include a public hall, recreation rooms, and a library and reading-room. They offered to present to the corporation land worth £2200 for the site, and £6000 towards the cost of the building. Their gifts were gratefully accepted, and the building was completed for a total cost of about £15,000, the cost to the committee of the library portion being about £4000. . . . The library and news-room form, perhaps, the finest, best appointed, and most extensive of the branch libraries. In addition to these rooms there are a coffee-tavern and chess and billiard rooms (wherein smoking is allowed), which, by the express desire of the legatees, are also under the management of the Libraries Committee." Mr. Credland, from whom we are quoting, continues: "The year which has elapsed since their opening has made it apparent that the coffee-tavern is not a necessity of the neighbourhood; whilst, on the other hand, the games-room and billiard-room are so popular and crowded, as to make it doubtful whether they do not detract from the utility of the more intellectual side of the institution."

Help was also received towards the establishment of the Newton Heath Branch. Here, before the incorporation with the city, the Acts had been adopted by the old Local Board District (in 1887), and a building was in course of construction when the incorporation with Manchester took place. While the corporation were finishing the work thus begun, some residents showed their sympathy with the movement by subscribing £240 for the purchase of books. With this sum a considerable part of the library of 4828 volumes opened on 28th September 1891 was purchased.

Another branch library is in course of formation at Blackley, where land and a building have been acquired. The development of the Manchester branch system may be gathered from the dates of opening of successive establishments : Hulme, 23rd November 1857 ; Ancoats, 7th December 1857 ; Rochdale Road, 4th June 1860 ; Chorlton, 8th October 1866 ; Cheetham, 1872 ; Bradford and Harpurhey Reading-rooms, February 1887 ; Hyde Road Reading-room, 7th May 1888 ; Newton Heath Library, 28th September 1891 ; Rusholme, 30th April 1892 ; Longsight, 23rd July 1892 ; Chester Road Reading-room, 31st March 1894 ; Gorton Library, 5th May 1894 ; Openshaw Library, 7th July 1894. The Deansgate Branch, opened in 1870, may be considered the joint-heritor with the King Street Reference Library of the Campfield establishment.

In 1877, owing to the structural weakness of the Campfield building, it was abruptly closed, and the books were removed to the old Town Hall, in King Street, which had just been vacated by the corporation. After alterations this building was opened as the reference library, and immediately the issue of books went up by leaps and bounds; in one year to thrice that in the latter years at Campfield. In 1878-79 the issue was 170,000; in 1879-80, 203,000; in 1884-85, 283,000; in 1889-90, 308,000; in 1894-95, 416,000; and the lessening room for public use, consequent on increased space used in storing accessions, has at length made impossible the extension of the library in the building as it now stands. One of the most urgent matters now engaging the committee's attention is that of determining what had best be done in the interest of the institution.

Manchester, like Birmingham, is often referred to by the advocates of the Sunday opening of libraries. After much public debate the Manchester Free Libraries were open on a Sunday for the first time in 1878, and the practice has been uninterruptedly continued ever since. In 1878-79 the daily average of Sunday visitors was 2436; in 1894-95, 4551; at no time has it been below 2000. The daily average use of the Manchester libraries (including Sundays) was 18,844 in 1894-95.

A circular calling the attention of schoolmasters to the advantages of the libraries, as continuing their work for the young, was issued in 1890, but was received with remarkable apathy. This conduct of the teaching profession here is in marked contrast to the zeal shown by schoolmasters in some other towns, where they have manifested a laudable desire to direct the reading of the scholars out of school hours.

Manchester, like every forward town, is not

deficient in its collection of local publications and the materials of local history. The writer has had occasion to note the alacrity with which a rare pamphlet or an old file of papers is placed at the disposal of the searcher into local history.

The committee of management has never been niggardly in publishing catalogues. That of the reference library, prepared by Dr. Crestadoro during his librarianship, is regarded with well-merited respect by every practical librarian; and the more recently issued hand-lists on certain special subjects have attracted wide notice, and won high encomiums on the collections. The more important of these numerous lists deal with Lancashire works, architecture, and shorthand. Similar lists on the remarkable Bataillard library of works on the gipsies, lately acquired, and on Carlyle, Emerson, Leigh Hunt, and Hazlitt, are now being prepared. A handbook, historical and descriptive (60 pages small 8vo), was also issued in 1887, which is worthy of being imitated by other libraries. Every effort is put forth to harmonise the work of the public libraries with that of the other educational bodies in the city. Facilities are about to be given for the display of the Home Reading Union circulars, and a scheme for more intimate association with the work of the School of Art and Art Gallery is under consideration. The active interest in educational work of the members of the Manchester committee has been recently honoured by the presidency of the Library Association falling to Mr. Alderman Harry Rawson, its late chairman;

and it is illustrated in the work of Mr. J. W. Southern, chairman, and of Mr. T. C. Abbott, late deputy-chairman of the committee, for that Association, and for other related interests.' Manchester early established lectures in connection with her free libraries, but for some reason these were discontinued for several years. The earlier practice has latterly been revived, occasional lectures being given in the various libraries.

Several small societies concerned in scientific, artistic, and intellectual work have their headquarters at the Manchester Reference Library. The work of the present city librarian, Mr. C. W. Sutton, for the Spenser, Chetham, and other learned societies, as editor and as secretary, is well known in the world of literature.

During 1894–95 nearly £7200 was paid in salaries and wages; nearly £6000 in books, periodicals, and binding; and nearly £1600 for loans and interest thereon. In the same year more than 13,000 volumes were purchased, and more than 2,000,000 books used, or a daily average of 6190 volumes. Add to this the number of visits already stated, and the magnitude of the Manchester Free Libraries system may be dimly realised; but who is to measure its influence or estimate its effect on national character?

LIVERPOOL

The movement for the establishment of a free public library for Liverpool began at about the same time as that for founding the Manchester

Free Library. The introduction into Parliament of Ewârt's first Library Bill in February 1850 had evidently attracted much notice in Liverpool, the city of Ewart's birth, which had formerly been represented by him in Parliament (from 1830 to 1837). In April, long before the bill had become law, Mr. (afterwards Sir) James Picton, a town councillor of less than a year's standing, was in communication with Edward Edwards on the subject dear to his heart, and in the same month moved that the town council appoint a committee "to inquire into and report on the propriety of establishing a free public library in the town of Liverpool." A committee was appointed, and made a favourable report, suggesting that a library and museum should be created by public subscription, and maintained and extended by the town council. A town's committee was formed, with Mr. Thomas B. Horsfall as president, and the Rev. A. Hume, LL.D., F.S.A., an eloquent supporter of the movement, as secretary. The appeal which was issued, under date 18th January 1851, bears ninety-nine signatures, including the names of the most prominent citizens and merchants of Liverpool. Probably the only living survivor of this honoured company is Mr. Alfred Lafone, M.P. for the Southwark division of London. A sum of £1389, 2s. 10d., about one-tenth of the sum raised in Manchester, and 4000 volumes were collected. Meanwhile the town council acquired a building known as the Union News-room, at the corner of Duke Street and Slater Street, and fitted it up for the temporary reception of books, pictures, and specimens, and on 18th October 1852 this building was opened by the Mayor, the late Mr. Thomas Littledale, as a library and reading-room. On 8th March 1853, the centenary of William Roscoe's birth, the museum department and in October of the same year a branch library for the Northern District was made public. A few weeks later, on 1st November, a branch was opened to serve the Southern District, and Mr. Peter Cowell, the dean of public librarians in this country, handed out the first book to the first borrower therefrom. Both these branches were situated in schools maintained by the corporation, and indeed for a time some portion of the library rate was used for the expenses of the schools, it being thought that the penny rate yielded more than was wanted for the libraries and museums, a notion which died away with the expansion of the work of the institutions. The North Branch was removed to Great Nelson Street in December 1854, and the South Branch to Hardy Street in June 1855, and to Upper Parliament Street in 1858, where till lately it was located. The North Branch is now closed, but the Everton Branch has taken over its work.

Liverpool holds a rather peculiar position in regard to the Public Libraries Acts. Certain conditions with regard to a bequest made it necessary to obtain a local Act, and so the Ewart Act was never adopted by the city; but the Museum Act of 1845 had been adopted, and the rate partly employed for maintaining the Botanic Gardens.

The title of the original local Act is "An Act for establishing a Public Library, Museum, and Gallery of Arts at Liverpool, and to make provision for the reception of a Collection of Specimens, illustrative of Natural History, presented by the Earl of Derby for the Benefit of the Inhabitants of the Borough of Liverpool, and the neighbourhood thereof, and others resorting thereto." It is dated 3rd May 1852. Various amendments have been added; thus in 1867 power was obtained to make " bye-laws," and in 1882 to hold art exhibitions; while later a doubt as to the legality of the branch lending libraries having gained currency, authority to establish lending libraries, and to make charges for admission to the Gallery of Arts, was obtained through the Liverpool Corporation Act, 1889.

To Liverpool belongs the honour of establishing the earliest branch library, of first introducing into a free library books for the blind, in 1857, and book-music, in 1859. It is also claimed that popular free lectures were organised by the Library Committee earlier than by any other free library committee, viz., in 1865, from which time there has been an uninterrupted annual series. Five years before the introduction of lectures the reference library was removed from Duke Street to the William Brown Library, which was then ready for occupation. This handsome library and museum cost £35,000, and was built and presented by Sir William Brown, Bart., M.P. for South Lancashire from 1848 to 1858, a wealthy merchant of Liverpool, who early had shown his interest by contributing to the first subscription list, and later made increasing offers, which culminated in this magnificent gift. Mr. Joseph Shipley, of Brandywine, Delaware, U.S.A., a former partner of Sir William Brown's, also gave the handsome donation of £1000, which was expended on specially valuable, rare, and costly works. But putting aside these large benefactions, the Liverpool Free Library has been very little helped by the favours of her wealthy citizens. University College seems to have attracted almost all the educational munificence in the city, notwithstanding the great popularity of the free library.

For more than thirty years the city was served by a central reference library and two lending libraries; and during all this time, under the able chairmanship of Sir James Picton, a magnificent collection of the very finest books was being built up. No temptations to dissipate resources in the multiplication of reading-rooms or lending libraries were heeded during all these years. Other cities have followed a different policy, and can show a different and perhaps equally excellent result; but Liverpool is chiefly interesting to the student of popular libraries for the long concentration of effort on the reference collections. There are limits, however, even to a policy of centralisation, and this the Liverpool committee seem to have realised in 1884, for from the 11th to the 14th of March four evening reading-rooms were opened in various schoolrooms within the city. Each costs the committee from £100 to £120 per annum. A news-room had first been opened at the Brown Library a few months before that time. The relief which the committee's funds experienced by the city's grants from the Exchequer contribution under the Local Taxation (Customs and Excise) Act, 1890, enabled the policy of extension to be carried out still further, and so the East Branch at Kensington came into existence, and was opened on 31st January 1890. Later, the Everton Branch was designed, with a view to serve also as a centre of technical teaching, and to take the place of the North Branch at Great Nelson Street. This branch, which has only been opened in the closing months of 1896, is the most complete yet organised in the city, and affords ample accommodation for a large library and a large following of visitors, both adults and children. A very neat and attractive catalogue of books for the young at the Everton Branch has just been issued.

On 17th June 1895 a central lending library was opened, and it has been exceedingly well used. The staff consists chiefly of lady assistants. In 1895 the city boundaries were very greatly extended, and one condition of the agreement between the outlying districts and the city was that four or five branch libraries and reading-rooms should be established in the extended area; the committee and the staff are therefore likely to be kept busy for some time to come.

The accommodation at the William Brown Library in 1875 had been quite outgrown, and in that year was commenced the Picton Room. This magnificent apartment, named in honour of Sir

James Allanson Picton, chairman of the Library Committee from its foundation until his death, enlarged the seating capacity at the central institution to 800. Its circular form and dome-like roof remind one of the Reading-room at the British Museum. In the evening a centrally placed electric arc lamp lights the huge space, and, whether by daylight or arc-light, the long radiating tables are seldom to be seen without an eager company of earnest students, journalists, professional men, and authors, pursuing their studies with an air of the utmost comfort. The catalogue, in three portly volumes, is worthy of the highest praise for beauty and for utility. The Picton Room is open daily from 10 A.M. to 10 P.M., except that on Fridays after 2 P.M. and during the whole of Sundays it is closed. Two of the branches are open every week day but one from 9 A.M. to 8 P.M., and on Saturdays from 9 A.M. to 3 P.M. Another branch is open from 9 A.M. to 9 P.M., except on two week days, on one of which it is closed at 4 P.M., and on the other at 2 P.M. The cost of each branch is about twelve per cent. of the total expenditure. The reference library now contains 109,642 volumes, and the lending libraries 70,025. For home reading 1883 books daily are issued, and for reference 2340. To the various departments a daily average of not less than 7000 visits must be paid, exclusive of the large numbers attending the winter lectures. The libraries are increasing at the rate of 5000 volumes per annum. Besides possessing special features already named, the library is rich in the materials of local history, which for many years have been collected on a very liberal and extensive scale. Particular attention has been paid to forming a collection of drawings of buildings which are now making way for modern improvements; the Herdman collection of drawings is very extensive; playbills and local obituaries are also well looked after. Indeed, it is to be hoped that a special hand-list of the local historical materials will be undertaken at no distant date. Natural history and the fine arts are represented in the reference library in an altogether sumptuous manner. On 12th December 1892 the accommodation for Patent investigators was much improved, and the specifications are now perhaps as well housed and as convenient for reference as anywhere outside London. A handlist of books on architecture and building construction has attracted wide and surprised attention among architects, not only in Liverpool, but elsewhere; and a subject catalogue of technical literature received high and well-merited praise from the press. Smaller lists on special subjects have also been issued at intervals. Some idea of the extent of the work done at the Liverpool Free Libraries may be gathered from the fact that there are some seventy-seven persons on the staff, and the item of salaries amounts to £2434. For thirty-six years past local societies and science classes have been encouraged to meet on the premises owned by the committee. There is also a very close connection with the Art Gallery, which is a charge on the library rate, and the Museum, which until 1895 was chargeable also, but since then has been supported out of a halfpenny rate raised under the Museums Act. In 1852-53 the penny rate yielded £4000, and of this £3000 was spent on the library; in 1895 the rate produced £13,527, of which £8278 was expended on the libraries and news-rooms. Comparisons have often been made between the libraries of the sister cities of Liverpool and Manchester. The unfairness of most of these comparisons will be evident when it is considered how much smaller has been the income of the Liverpool than that of the Manchester libraries.

BIRMINGHAM

The earliest attempt to establish a free public library in Birmingham was made in 1852, and met with strenuous opposition from the devotees of voluntaryism. Falsehood and ignorance did their best and worst, and secured 363 votes against the adoption of Ewart's first Act. On the other hand, 534 votes were cast by the friends of free libraries, which being some sixty-four votes short of the necessary two-thirds majority, meant defeat. Before the next appeal the Act of 1850 had been greatly altered and improved, and doubtless the temper of the town had improved also. On 16th August 1859 a motion requesting the Mayor to convene the statutory meeting to consider the adoption of the Acts was defeated by an amendment to appoint a committee to inquire into and report on the subject. This committee's report, presented on 3rd January

1860, is an exceedingly interesting document, and may be read in Langford's "Birmingham Free Libraries" (1871). The former non-success is stated, the present regarded as a favourable time to make another appeal, the terms of the Act set forth, the number of adoptions mentioned, and, in considerable detail, the experience of Manchester and Liverpool in the working of the Act related. The report was accepted, the committee reappointed to organise the necessary meeting of burgesses, and on 21st February 1860, in the Town Hall, the Act was adopted in due form by an overwhelming majority in spite of expressed opposition. A committee of sixteen, eight being non-members of the council, was soon appointed, and quickly got to work. They recommended the levying of the full penny rate, the establishment of a reference library, four distinct lending libraries, and a gallery of art. Their estimate for the establishment and maintenance of four lending libraries for the first year was £3252, and the annual cost of maintaining the same afterwards £1480. The council authorised the committee to carry out their plans. The first library organised was in adapted buildings at Constitution Hill, and was designed for the northern part of the city. Early in 1861 Mr. Edward Lings, formerly of the Campfield Library, Manchester, was elected librarian, and on 3rd April this library was formally opened, and the issue of books commencing on 22nd of the same month. "Crowds of persons presented themselves for tickets, and so great was the excitement that for several weeks applicants had to wait upwards of an hour before their turn arrived to be attended to, as many as two hundred applying at one time." The average daily issue in the first year was 376 volumes, and more than 800 volumes had been sent out in a single day. It is strange nowadays to read in the first annual report : "One of the most interesting features of the experience of the past year is the uniform good conduct and order manifested by the thousands who frequent the library."

On the 1st July 1862 the council authorised the erection of the Central Reference Library on land adjoining the Midland Institute, at a cost not exceeding £12,000, and in accordance with Mr. Martin's designs. On 11th January 1864 the Free Library and Museum at Adderley Park was opened. On 11th April 1865 the building of the Central Library was so far advanced that the committee advised the appointment of a librarian, and on 30th May 1865 the council appointed Mr. J. D. Mullins, who still holds the honourable position of chief librarian. The Central Lending Library and Art Gallery were opened with proper pomp and ceremony in presence of many distinguished people on 6th September 1865, during the meeting of the British Association in the town. On the 19th September books were issued, and the demand was overwhelming. On 26th October the reference library was declared open in the presence of the principal inhabitants ; and Mr. George Dawson, M.A., who at every stage of the movement in Birmingham had given his valuable aid, delivered an eloquent and telling address. In purchasing books for the reference library the committee, says Dr. Langford, "were guided by three principles : first, that the library should as far as practicable represent every phase of human thought and every variety of opinion ; second, that books of permanent value and of standard interest should form the principal portion of the library, and that modern and popular books should be added from time to time as they are published ; third, that it should contain those rare and costly works which are generally out of the reach of individual students and collectors, and which are not usually found in provincial or private libraries." At the time of opening, the reference library contained 16,195 volumes, besides 2030 volumes of patents' specifications, and the Central Lending Library contained 11,276 volumes. In 1866—on 26th October—the Deritend Library was opened, and in June 1868 the Gosta Green Library ; a newsroom at the same place having been available since 1st February of the same year. Thus the original scheme of the committee of 1860 was completed, though the cost of carrying on all these institutions and repaying the loans proved a severe strain on the resources accruing from a rate of a penny in the pound. Hence the addition of books to the various branches during the next few years was hardly sufficient for their needs. Nevertheless, at the end of 1870—the year of the passing of Forster's Elementary Education Act—the free libraries of Birmingham contained 56,764 volumes, and the daily issue for home reading exceeded 1000 volumes.

The effect of the improvement in elementary education in these later years may be seen in the 1895 issue of 2663 volumes per diem for home reading, and 1100 in addition for consultation in the reference library. In April 1872 Sunday opening was commenced in the reference library and art gallery. The issue of books to readers on Sundays in 1895 amounted to 414 volumes per diem. A distinguishing feature of the Sunday management at Birmingham is that five Jewish assistants are employed for this work, so as to give the regular staff the usual day of rest. In 1873 Mr. Bragge's unique Cervantes collection was presented; and in 1875 the valuable collection of works illustrative of the history and antiquities of Warwickshire, formed by the father and brother of Mr. John Staunton, J.P., of Longbridge, was acquired for the small sum of £2285, of which £1467 was subscribed by townsmen. The report of the committee for 1875 speaks of this collection as "magnificent." Expensive topographical works, unique drawings, rare incunabula, and manuscripts of immense local importance were alike included in it. Alas! that these precious treasures, with one exception, should be doomed to perish in the fire of 1879, together with great part of the Shakespeare library, which, through long years of judicious purchase and important gifts, had become a collection of first-rate importance. The story of the great fire has been often told with more or less of dramatic effect, but the facts are simple, and may be simply stated. Alterations at the library building were in progress on 11th January 1879, and a workman was engaged in thawing a gas-pipe behind a wooden screen, when the flame suddenly leaped beyond control, caught the shavings near, and ignited the partition, so setting fire to the whole structure. Only 1000 volumes from the reference library of nearly 50,000 were saved. Nearly the whole of the special collections were burnt; some volumes of the Shakespeare library and the " Registerium ffratrum et sororum Gilde Sancte Anne de Knolle in Com : War., 1412-1535," from the Staunton Collection, being nearly all that was rescued. The principal contents of the lending library were also saved. The spirit of the committee might well have been broken by such a calamity, but they were men of mettle ; they immediately sought as far as possible to repair the loss. The Mayor, Mr. Alderman Jesse Collins, called a public meeting, and the chairman of the committee submitted proposals for raising by subscription a sum of not less than £10,000, to add to the £20,000 to be received from the insurance companies. The town responded nobly, and in a short time no less than £15,197 had been subscribed to the Library Restoration Fund. Rich and poor alike helped, societies and individuals. National sympathy was also freely expressed in valuable gifts of books from the Queen, the committees of institutions and free libraries, publishers, and private individuals.

Committees went to work, and early presented to

the council reports on the reconstruction of the buildings and the libraries. As to the former, provision for an increased area of 5900 feet was proposed for the lending library and reading-room. Noble reference apartments 100 feet by 64 feet, and 61 feet 6 inches by 45 feet; a Shakespeare library with 610 feet superficial area, and a suite of workrooms, were also to be provided at a cost of £32,000. As to the re-forming of the libraries, the report urged the importance of a bibliographical collection, including every known book about books, the reformation as far as possible of the Cervantes and Shakespeare collections, the collection of local records and the materials of Birmingham history, and the formation of a county of Warwick collection to take the place of the destroyed Staunton books. While these plans were being carried out, the lending and reference libraries were temporarily located in a suite of rooms in the Council House; the news-room being opened on 10th June, the central lending library, with 12,000 volumes, on 12th September 1879, the year of the great fire.

The restored Central Libraries were opened on 2nd June 1882 by the Right Hon. John Bright, M.P., in the presence of a brilliant representative gathering. The speeches delivered on this historic occasion, and at the banquet which followed, were of high excellence. They are printed at length in the Annual Report of the Committee for the years 1881 and 1882.

The year 1885 is memorable as that in which the

Art Gallery was taken from under the care of the Libraries Committee, who had had charge thereof since 1867. The new permanent Museum and Art Gallery were erected as the result of an offer of £10,000 from Messrs. Tangye Brothers on condition of adequate accommodation being found, and a sum of £5000 being raised by public subscription. The conditions were fulfilled, and the now famous Art Gallery of Birmingham passed out of the fostering care of the Free Libraries Committee of the city. This removal set free a large space for the extension of the reference department.

The Aylesford Collection of Warwickshire drawings and prints was acquired in 1886. It included 174 portraits, 310 drawings of churches, and 422 of country seats. For the next few years steady progress was reported in the filling up of the ugly gaps in the collections caused by the fire.

A step forward was taken in 1889, when the council sanctioned the provision of three additional branches, since increased to five. Their names and dates of opening are as follows :—

Bloomsbury Branch . . News-room opened June	4, 1892
,, ,, . . Library ,, Sept.	29, 1892
Harborne Branch . . News-room ,, Aug.	27, 1892
,, ,, . . . Library ,, Nov.	12, 1892
Spring Hill Branch . . News-room ,, Jan.	7, 1893
,, ,, . . Library ,, April	20, 1893
Small Heath Branch . News-room ,, Dec.	30, 1893
,, ,, . Library ,, Mar.	7, 1894
Balsall Heath Branch . News-room ,, } April	18, 1896
,, ,, . . Library ,, }	

The Harborne and Balsall Heath branches were established to serve areas but recently incorporated in the city.

During 1892 a seventeenth-century library, known as the Thomas Hall Library, was transferred from King's Norton to the Birmingham Reference Library, there to remain for a term of years, renewable from time to time. A MS. catalogue of this collection, with annotations by Mr. W. Salt Brassington, F.S.A., has been prepared.

In the same year the catalogue of the Reference Library, containing 1284 pages quarto size, was completed, a work which must remain a monument to the energy and ability of Mr. J. D. Mullins and the members of his staff. As indicative of the thoroughness of this work, we may mention its index to 5000 plays, and the minute care with which the contents of important serial transactions are set out. Many other catalogues of first-rate importance are issued by the Birmingham committee, notably the catalogue of the Shakespeare Memorial Library, the first part only of which was issued before the great fire. It consists of 344 pages, and is the largest inventory known of English editions of Shakespeare's works, of the separate plays, and of works on, or illustrative of, the great dramatist. A perusal of this publication brings home in a powerful degree the great loss sustained in the fire of 1879, a loss which, through subsequent care and at great expense, it is gratifying to be able to say has been nearly made good in the present Shakespeare collection, with its nearly 10,000 items in twenty-eight different languages. Considerable minor collections, illustrating Byron, Milton, and Cervantes, are also included in the reference library.

Since 1887 a large number of works of reference, now occupying forty-eight shelves, have been freely accessible to the public without formality. The eager use of these is not recorded statistically. In the period 1884-86 a series of lectures on the books in the library was delivered by eminent specialists, the greater part of which have been published as "Books for a Reference Library." Special lists of books suited to children's needs have not yet been issued, but children are accepted as borrowers on the guarantee of their schoolmasters. The staff of the system of libraries is very extensive, and includes sixty assistants and twenty-one cleaners; the total annual cost reaches £4500. Since 1883 the penny limit of the rate has been removed. This was accomplished by the Birmingham Corporation (Consolidation) Act. The expenditure for 1895 for the central libraries and the nine branch libraries reached £9161; books alone cost £1534. The books issued exceeded 1,200,000 volumes, nearly three times the issue of 1870, and more than eleven times that of the year of the establishment of free libraries in Birmingham. The number of volumes in the Birmingham libraries at the end of 1895 was nearly 210,000.

LEEDS

Leeds adopted the Public Libraries Acts at a meeting held in 1868. It is curious to note that one of the opponents of the movement in 1868 is now a member of the Library Committee, and presumably a supporter of free libraries. The rate first levied in 1870 then realised £2500, now it produces £5860. No large donations have been received, but about two hundred volumes of general interest are obtained annually as gifts. A commencement was made by a library and two branches in hired rooms. Including Patent specification volumes, there were 13,137 volumes for consultation and 8000 for home reading at the central establishment, and 4806 volumes at the two branches. The only initial difficulty was that of an overwhelming demand for books. To enumerate the branch establishments now in operation at Leeds would take up too much space. There are thirty-seven school branches, and twenty-one other branches. Mr. James Yates is the librarian.

The Central Library is accommodated in beautiful rooms in the same block with the municipal offices. Here a sub-librarian and thirty-one assistants serve the public. Thirty-four assistants are employed in the branch libraries. Few of the branches are placed in most suitable buildings; as good, say, as that at Hunslet. In 1895-96 the total expenditure for salaries and wages was £2038, from which it is clear that a large number of the assistants are either very young or very ill-paid. Several local societies hold meetings at the Central Library, and a home reading circle meets there. The daily average of works issued for home reading is 3073; for reference, 464. Two thousand two hundred visits per day are paid to the news-rooms, and the libraries contain 191,000 volumes.

Kingston-upon-Hull

This large borough, whose population in 1891 was 260,000, did not easily obtain its free libraries. In 1857, 1872, 1882, 1888, successive efforts were made to secure the adoption of the Public Libraries Acts. In 1882 the opponents had a majority of 1677, and in 1888 the much increased majority of 8294, yet in December 1892 the adoption of the Acts was secured by a majority of 942. What wrought so great a change in public opinion in four years? The first report of the Public Library Committee explains :—

"At this stage [when the 1888 defeat took place] Mr. [now Sir] James Reckitt, with a view of furnishing an object-lesson for the town, undertook to provide the buildings, books, furniture, and the entire cost of maintaining and working a library for the use of the residents in East Hull, offering to subscribe annually an amount equal to a penny rate on the whole of the property in the borough east of the river Hull. The offer was accepted, and an influential committee formed for carrying out the work. A library building was erected and equipped, being opened on the 10th December 1889 by the Marquis of Ripon, and it proved very successful. As an object-lesson it served to show that a public library could be carried on successfully with the income derived from the penny rate."

The James Reckitt Library at the end of its first year's working had a stock of 8422 volumes in the lending department and 1286 volumes for reference; while during 306 open days the average daily issues were 333. The final report of this library as an independent institution showed the stock to be 8758 in the lending and 1550 volumes in the reference department. The nine months' issues ending September 1893 showed an average of 270 volumes per day. On 2nd October 1893, in accordance with the terms of the trust deed under which the library was founded, the books, premises, and furniture were transferred to the mayor, aldermen, and burgesses of the borough, together with stocks and shares valued at about £6300, the interest of which was deemed sufficient for future maintenance. The deed included the transfer of the reference library kindly presented by Mr. Francis Reckitt, J.P., of Highgate, and stipulated that the Reckitt Library should not be removed from East Hull. The cost of managing the Reckitt Library had been strictly limited to the amount that a penny rate would have produced if levied over the limited portion of the borough which it was intended to serve.

The Public Libraries Committee first met on 14th March 1893, and soon devised a scheme by which the northern and western parts of the borough were to be furnished with libraries similar to the Reckitt Library, while the town was to have a Central Library on a large scale, and in close connection with a public hall and technical schools. Until the central part of the scheme could be realised, temporary premises were obtained and made use of, and from 15th October 1894 to 31st March 1895 an average issue of 952 volumes per day was recorded.

The Western Library was opened on the 26th January, and the Northern on the 13th June 1895; and in the year 1895-96 the total issues of books exceeded half a million. The daily averages for 1895-96 were: Central Lending Library, 584; Reckitt Library, 274; Western Branch, 444; Northern Branch, 454; total, 1757. The daily average of visits to reading-rooms was 2250. The number of volumes in the libraries at the end of March 1896 was 52,588, of which 12,830 were in the two reference libraries. The accommodation for consultation of works of reference at the Central Library is not nearly adequate at present, hence the report records an average daily consultation of twenty-five! The proceeds of the penny rate amount to £3037.

Manifestly it is yet too soon to expect that great attention should be given to special collections of books, local or otherwise; but it is very gratifying to find that excellent catalogues of juvenile literature are provided at all the Hull town libraries. All the catalogues, and particularly that of the Central Lending Library, deserve hearty praise for their clearness of typography and handiness of form. Hull has done more wisely in establishing a few really adequate branch libraries conveniently situated than she would have done in multiplying centres, to the weakening of all.

EDINBURGH

Unsuccessful attempts to obtain the adoption of the Public Libraries Acts for Edinburgh were made in 1868 and in 1881. The existence of several metropolitan libraries, some of them free—at least to scholars—and the fear of the rate, seem to have contributed in equal measure to the non-success of these efforts. Large adverse majorities were recorded on both occasions. In 1886, however, the offer of a gift of £50,000 to establish a free library for beautiful Edinburgh from the Scottish-American millionaire, Mr. Andrew Carnegie, turned the scale of popular opinion, and so came to be adopted, on 26th October of that year, with not more than a score of dissentients, the Public Libraries (Scotland) Act.

A halfpenny rate, realising £3560, was levied in 1886; and in the next year increased to a three-farthings rate, bringing in £6800 for library purposes. The city council lost no time in carrying into effect its proposals. A committee visited the principal libraries, and reported on the architectural necessities of such institutions; a book committee, with Professor Masson at its head, and a building and a finance committee, went eagerly to work. A site on George IV. Bridge was chosen, designs were obtained by public advertisement, and Mr. Alfred Waterhouse was made assessor. Eventually Mr. George Washington Browne's design was adjudged the best, and, with alterations in detail, carried out at a cost of £30,000. The lending library provided accommodation for 48,000 volumes, and the reference library for 40,000. The latter department is so designed that it can be increased by the addition of a third tier of shelves when needed. News-rooms and a juveniles' library of ample extent were also provided. A principal librarian was appointed on 28th June 1887, and two experienced sub-librarians in March 1890. Books were bought, and their location settled before the building was ready to receive them. On 9th June 1890 Lord Rosebery—Lord Provost Boyd presiding—declared the library open, and delivered an eloquent address full of allusions to the literary glories of the Northern capital. The lending library opened for the issue of books on 1st July with a stock of 34,000 volumes, the children's library with 4000, while the reference library with 20,000 volumes had been opened a few days earlier. In 1896 the number of volumes had reached 91,000, and it is increasing yearly at the rate of 6000. The catalogue of the juveniles' library was ready on the opening day, and consists of sixty-three pages in double columns; the lending library catalogue extends to 538 pages in double columns; and 10,000 copies were sold in five months. A supplementary catalogue for 1890-92 is now out of print. The reference library catalogue, with its subject index, contained 317 pages, and was published in April 1891. The number of readers on the roll at the end of 1894 was nearly 30,000.

In 1891 and 1892 lectures on the technical books in the library were given to various classes of tradesmen in succession. This had an excellent effect on the use made of certain books which had been bought out of a gift of £1436 voted to the committee by the executive of the Edinburgh International Exhibition of 1886 for the purchase of technical works. At each of these lectures special printed lists of the books on the particular trades were distributed gratis to the artisans and others present. Local history is specially collected, and the literature relating to Burns and Scott. A branch was opened in 1895. The daily use of the libraries is about 2000 volumes for home reading, 380 for reference, and 7000 visits to the reading-rooms.

Dublin

The slow progress of the movement for establishing free libraries in the Irish provinces is not difficult to account for, but the backward condition of the capital of Ireland is not so easily understood. The municipal council on 1st December 1883 appointed a Libraries Committee to carry into effect a recommendation of a special committee on the subject of establishing two free libraries for the city. Dublin, it is true, possessed other large and very much used libraries, but the facilities afforded to the public by these were not deemed sufficient.

A library was opened in Capel Street on 1st October 1884 in a dwelling-house which was specially adapted to library purposes. After a time a new reading-room was added to the house. The use of the 6000 volumes provided here is not very great—a daily average issue of 112 for home reading, and 35 for reference. The news-room is more popular, and is visited by 900 people on an average each day. Every class, without distinction, makes use of this library. Macaulay, Carlyle, and Green are the historians most read here, and in fiction the works of three English ladies, Mrs. Wood, Miss Braddon, and " Edna Lyall," are much sought after. The library is increasing by about 290 volumes per annum, about a dozen of which are gifts.

Another library was opened at Thomas Street on the same day as that in Capel Street. Here also are 6000 volumes, and the use made of the establishment—80 issues per diem for home reading, 30 for reference, with 700 visits to the reading-room—is not very different from that at Capel Street.

Middle-class people, tradesmen, and clerks are said to be the most frequent visitors at Thomas Street. Smiles, Darwin, and Edmund Burke are much in demand among the serious authors, but among the novelists Charles Reade, Conan Doyle, and Mrs. Wood are most in favour. A report on the working of both libraries is being prepared for the Dublin Corporation; it is to be hoped it will end with a strong recommendation to adopt the

Public Libraries (Ireland) Acts, and to enlarge and multiply these excellent but insufficient accommodations for its intelligent artisans and book-loving clerks and tradesmen.[1] Comparisons are proverbially odious, but Dublin ought to feel keenly her condition when she thinks of the free libraries of her northern sister, Belfast.

It is only fair to note that the real free reference library of the city for serious reading is provided as part of a branch establishment of the Science and Art Department, and maintained at the Imperial Government's expense. This, the National Library of Ireland, is housed in a building of beautiful exterior close by Leinster House, the home of the Royal Dublin Society. The members of this renowned Society still have certain rights and privileges connected with the management and use of the library, in virtue of the very considerable part taken in establishing the National Library and furnishing it with its first stock of books, which included the library of the Society collected during a long course of years. An Act of Parliament, passed in 1876, laid, as it were, the foundation of the present institution, which performs in Dublin in a proportionately limited degree the functions of the British Museum in London. The first librarian, Mr. William Archer, F.R.S., deserves the gratitude of all scholars and readers for having established the administration of the library on

[1] This report has just been issued, but it is far too halting in its conclusions. It recommends the building of a fine free library, but puts off practical proposals to a very indefinite future, presumably on account of poverty and high taxation.

sound lines, and for having co-operated with the architect to secure space for vast extension in the collection of books and a right distribution of the presses for the ready service of readers. His successor, by his scholarship and enthusiasm, seems to have caught the mantle of his chief of former days. A few figures from the latest published report (for the year 1895) are added here. It should be remembered that the library is strictly for students' use. The library was open to the public on 294 days; the turnstile recorded 125,500 visits, 6000 more than in 1894. The daily average from 10 A.M. to 6 P.M. was 284, and from 6 P.M. to 10 P.M. 119; also twenty-four ladies per day attended, making a total daily attendance of 427 persons. The volumes catalogued and made available were in number 2451. More than 3000 volumes were lent out to the borrowing members of the Royal Dublin Society and officers of the Science and Art Department. The admirable published catalogues of yearly additions compiled by Mr. Archer are models of most-specific-subject-entry catalogues on the dictionary plan, and when combined into one alphabet will be a bibliographical tool of no mean value to scholars and to all librarians.

Belfast

The possibilities of the free library in Ireland are best exemplified in that of Belfast. Mr. William Gray gathered a few friends about him in 1881, and brought before the Belfast town council the desirability of establishing a free library. This effort did not meet with success, not for want of sympathy, but because the council had its hands full of other work. In the following year a renewal of the appeal met with more consideration; a deputation was received; the council provided for the necessary poll, and the Acts were adopted by 5234 votes in favour to 1425 against the proposal. In 1883 the first library rate was collected, and realised £2211; in 1895 the amount received was £3283. The rate was not collected in 1887. The full penny is levied, but an art gallery and museum, as well as lending and reference libraries and reading-rooms, are supported out of it, with the addition since 1890 of occasional assistance from the Corporation Gas Committee for the purchase of art objects. A library committee of the town council consulted with the members of the committee which first brought the matter before the town as to the course to be taken in giving effect to the vote, and in the main adopted the memorandum drawn up for their guidance by the non-official committee. Up to the present no outsiders have been admitted to the corporation committee, a matter for regret, and contrary to the more usual practice in towns.

A handsome central building was erected and formally opened by the Lord-Lieutenant and Lady Londonderry on 13th October 1888. The librarian had been appointed in the previous spring, and an excellent catalogue of the 7800 volumes in the lending department was speedily prepared. The reference department was not opened until 1890, the year in which the art gallery and museum were opened. In choosing books for the reference library the first lists were submitted to the judgment and criticism of local professors. About twenty-seven per cent. of the total expenditure is accounted for by loan redemptions, and interest. There is a separate curator of the art gallery and museum. In all twenty-three persons are employed on the staff, and a little more than forty per cent. is expended on salaries and wages—not too large a sum for efficient service. The libraries now contain 33,469 volumes, and latterly have been increasing at the rate of 700 volumes per annum. More than three thousand visits per diem are made to the reading-rooms, which are often inconveniently crowded. For home reading 637 works on an average are issued each day, and for reference 168. Fifteen thousand sixpenny catalogues have been sold in eight years, a remarkable proof of the estimation in which the libraries are held by the people. The most popular books are, in fiction, Marryat's "Poor Jack," Lever's "That Boy of Norcott's," Grant's "Jack Manly;" in other classes, Deschanel's "Natural Philosophy," Cassell's "New Popular Educator," Green's "Short History of the English People."

CHAPTER X

FREE LIBRARIES UNDER THE ACTS IN SEVENTEEN
SECOND-CLASS TOWNS

OF the towns and urban districts in Great Britain and Ireland with a population at the last census of between 80,000 and 250,000, there are but three—Burnley, Huddersfield, and Ystradyfodwy—which have not adopted the Public Libraries Acts; and in 1891 each of these places had less than 100,000 inhabitants. The development of the idea of a free library in the different towns has been so various, that a considerable number of types must be studied in order to learn the possibilities of adaptation inherent in this kind of institution. Government organisation and control would doubtless have produced libraries of a uniform kind; the absence, therefore, of centralisation in the early days of the movement has been of great service to the free library as an institution. In the following brief histories, variation in endowment and sources of revenue, in concentration or distribution of effort, in association with other educational institutions, in aim and character, may be studied better perhaps than in any earlier chapter of this work.

In a dozen representative free libraries of second-class towns, answers by the librarians to a request for the names of the most popular authors included the following :—Mrs. Henry Wood (in eight lists), " Marie Corelli " (in seven), Rider Haggard (in four), Charles Dickens (in four), Stanley Weyman and Miss Braddon (each in two); and of the serious authors, Ruskin (in five), Carlyle (in three), Shakespeare, J. R. Green, Froude, and Dean Farrar (each in two). Names which appear in one list only are R. L. Stevenson, Conan Doyle, Sir Walter Scott, Thackeray, Henty, W. H. G. Kingston, Miss Worboise, " Edna Lyall," S. R. Crockett; also Drummond, Lang, Balfour, Slatin Pasha, Tennyson, Charles Kingsley, Smiles, Sir R. Ball, Captain Lugard. It would be easy to deduce wrong conclusions from such a chance list, but it at least proves a varied and, on the whole, healthy taste in the readers.

BRISTOL

Bristol claims the honour of possessing the record of the earliest public library in Britain, that of the religious guild of the Kalendars, a library which was destroyed by fire in 1466. Furthermore, it is claimed for this city that the first public library in the United Kingdom after the Reformation was established and opened here in the year 1615, an honour which properly belongs to the city of Norwich. The interesting history of this old City Library has been adequately related by Mr. Charles Tovey in "The Bristol City Library: its

Founders and Benefactors" (1853), and with greater brevity by Mr. E. R. Norris Mathews, the present city librarian, in his " History of the Public Library at Bristol" (1896). Tobias Mathews, a native of Bristol and sometime Archbishop of York, and Robert Redwood were the founders of the old City Library; but the corporation had exclusive management thereof until 1773, when a private subscription library company, under the title of the Bristol Library Society, induced the city fathers to allow them the free use of the rooms and the management of the City Library. Henceforward until 1855 the library seems to have lost its public character, although it is doubtful if any citizen was ever refused access to the city's books. The society from time to time obtained valuable grants and privileges from the corporation, and eventually these became so much a matter of course, that when resumption of management by the city council was being advocated the members of the society began to talk of rights and compensation. That the city did, however, hold by its own there is ample proof in the fact that in 1855 the society relinquished its valuable corporation privileges and went into private rooms. The precipitation of this event was doubtless due in great measure to the publication of Mr. Councillor Tovey's booklet above-mentioned, and the considerable, though apparently fruitless, agitation in the local press in 1853-55 for the adoption of the Public Libraries Acts.

The character of the old City Library may be gathered from a catalogue of the books published by Mr. Tovey. This catalogue appears to have been made in 1815, when for forty years prior to that time there had been no new accessions to the City Library. The books numbered about 2000, half of them works of theology. Thirteen works printed in the fifteenth century are mentioned, several from Venetian presses and a Pynson of 1499. There are a large number of sixteenth-century tomes, including the Complutensian Polyglot Bible; and nearly a score manuscripts. The theology includes, besides many editions of the Scriptures, works of the principal Fathers of the Church, Greek, Latin, Scholastic, Catholic, Protestant, and Puritan, many of them in very early editions. French and Italian books of a theological kind are numerous. Bossuet, Calvin, Fénelon, Flechier, Guion, Pascal, may be mentioned among others. The general literature shows signs of ripe scholarship and good taste in the collectors who gave or bequeathed the books. Altogether, it is matter of great satisfaction to know that a special catalogue of these works is in course of preparation by the librarian.

After the exit of the Library Society in 1855, and with the appointment of Mr. George Pryce in 1856 as city librarian, the institution rapidly revived. This devoted officer obtained no fewer than 1500 volumes and pamphlets relating to Bristol history for the library, thus forming the nucleus of the present valuable local collection. Mr. Pryce's successors have likewise shown considerable zeal in this department, but to Mr. Pryce certainly belongs the credit of a pioneer in the work of collecting the materials of local history for storage and use in a public town library, a duty, as the pages of this book sufficiently demonstrate, now generally regarded as imperative by every efficient public librarian. The good seed sown by Mr. Tovey and Mr. Pryce germinated in 1874 in the adoption of the Public Libraries Acts by the city of Bristol, six years after Mr. Pryce's death.

The penny rate was levied in 1875, and the famous old City Library became the central establishment around which has grown up the present system of free libraries in Bristol. The process of reorganisation of the Central Library was completed, and the library re-opened with reference and lending departments and a news-room on 9th October 1876. Three months earlier the St. Philip's Branch Library had been opened, namely, on 8th July, in the premises of the St. Philip's Literary Institute, purchased during the previous years. A new and more worthy building for this large district will have been opened before these lines are published. In 1877 two other branches were established for the North District and for Bedminster, on 24th March and 29th September respectively. On 8th June 1885 the Redlands Branch Library was opened, and on 25th January 1888 the Hotwells Branch. The circulation of books at these libraries varies between an average of 262 and one of 480 per day, while the Central Library reaches only 195 per day. The total daily issues are about 2000. The books at the Central

Library were, in June 1895, 15,000 in the reference department and 13,000 in the lending department, while the stock at a branch varied between 9000 and 14,000. The total stock (exclusive of the Museum reference library of 60,000 volumes) in July 1896 was 90,000 volumes. The Bristol Museum and Library had been transferred to the city in 1894. The library is valuable, and includes the books of the old Bristol Library Society. The Public Libraries Committee have not yet acquired the control of this collection, but as a new Central Library is urgently needed, and is being talked of, it is to be hoped that this collection and the Central Library books may find a home together in a commodious building worthy of the city and the past history of both collections. The museum and its library are supported out of a halfpenny rate raised under the Museums Act.

The premises of the Central Library, built in 1740, and enlarged by a new wing in 1785, hallowed as they are by historic memories, and by literary association with Coleridge, Southey, Landor, and Sir Humphry Davy, though totally inadequate for their present purpose of a central free library, might well serve as a repository of special treasures, or a historical museum of Bristol antiquities.

To illustrate the development of the use of the public libraries, the total issues of books in 1876 numbered 74,000, in 1895 nearly 500,000, exclusive of students' use of the museum library; and the aggregate attendances in the reading-rooms went up from 100,000 to close upon 2,000,000. The last annual report contains a very interesting list, compiled from readers' application forms, of some of the books read or consulted in the reference and reading-rooms during the year. There are several hundred titles in the list, but the following consecutive twelve taken from it, being free from suspicion of selection, fairly represent the kinds of work asked for in the Bristol library, and, one might add, in other public reference libraries :—

>Robertson's " Reign of Charles V."
>Robson's " The Lord's Supper."
>Roebuck's " Proverbs."
>Roscoe's " Elementary Chemistry."
>Rosebery's " Life of Pitt."
>Ross's " Arctic Expedition."
>Rossetti's " Ballads."
>Rossetti's " Memoirs of Shelley."
>Rousseau's " La Nouvelle Héloïse."
>Routledge's " Discoveries and Inventions."
>Ruskin's " Modern Painters."
>Ruskin's " Stones of Venice."

A classification of the issues of books according to the occupations of readers, shows that of the 106,000 readers on the premises nearly 13,000 were artisans, 8000 clerks, 3400 labourers, 4000 professional men, 41,000 juvenile readers, 9600 students. Of the 385,000 issues for home reading, 32,000 were to artisans, 35,000 to clerks, 2400 to labourers, 16,000 to professional men, 67,000 to juvenile readers, and 15,000 to students.

Excluding salaries and repayment of loans, the cost of each branch averages 6.4 per cent., and of the central establishment 9 per cent. of the total expenditure. Salaries amount to £2200, being 47.5 per cent., and repayment of loans with interest to 11.5 per cent. The penny rate produces £4412.

The staff consists of eleven junior assistants, five senior assistants, five branch sub-librarians, five branch librarians, all of whom are women, with eight male assistants, a binder and two assistants, six porters and six cleaners. Admission to the library service is by examination. Vacancies in the higher are supplied by promotion from the lower grades. The hours of service for the staff are forty-four per week.

West Ham

The extensive industrial borough of West Ham —the forest of homes continuous with our great capital on its Essex side—did not get its free public library without an effort. The movement begun in 1887 resulted in a defeat at the poll, but the year 1890 brought a revived interest and a more energetic and united effort to obtain the desired boon. The local press, the town council, Mansfield House University Settlement, the local elementary school teachers, the ministers of all denominations took up the cause, and so won over public opinion that by a majority of nearly 3 to 1 on a poll of nearly 13,500 voters the Acts were adopted. This was in November 1890. In October 1891 an experienced librarian was engaged, and by 30th July 1892 a temporary news-room and reference library at Rokeby House, Stratford, was opened. Twelve days earlier the foundation stone of the Canning Town Branch Library was laid, a building to cost £8800 exclusive of the site. Whilst this building was being erected the library staff were collecting, preparing, and cataloguing books, to be ready for the inaugural ceremony. Mr. J. Passmore Edwards, on the 28th September 1893, formally opened the building, and presented 1000 volumes to the library. The news-room was thrown open a few days later, and the reference library made available on 9th October. The lending library was ready on 1st June 1894.

The catalogue is a monument of patient work, its subject entries remarkably numerous and instructive. The corporation have now entered upon the erection of a large central library and technical institute, the cost of which, £50,000, is to be defrayed out of the coal and wine dues. The rate of one penny in the pound produces £3519, already £839 more than four years ago, yet the greatest economy is necessary to keep up two large libraries, each with a reference department and a large staff. The reference library issues amount to 142 per day, and the use for home reading (with a single lending library) is 567 volumes daily. Each day more than 2000 visits are made to the reading-rooms. At present the central establishment located at Rokeby House takes forty per cent. of the income, and the branch library the remaining sixty per cent. A useful quarterly guide is published at Rokeby House, entitled "West Ham Library Notes." A juvenile catalogue of 140 pages has also been published lately.

Salford

To Salford belongs the honour of establishing the second free public library in Britain under the powers of the Museums Act of 1845. The resolution of the council to this end was passed on the 13th June 1849. By the Salford Improvement Act, 1893, the Public Libraries Act of 1855 is deemed to have been in force in the borough from the date of its passing into law. In the year ending August 1849 the expenditure on the library amounted to £9, 1s. 9d., and in the following year the museum and library cost £651, 16s. 9d. A commencement was made with a reading-room and reference library and museum; but an Act passed in 1890-91 increased the rating limit on museums and libraries in Salford to three-halfpence in the pound, and the Museums and Gymnasiums Act, 1891, gave power to expend an additional halfpenny. In 1895-96 the amount of rate levied was 1.26d. in the pound. The principal library is situated in Peel Park, and the same committee manages the public parks and the museum and libraries. The curator of the museum is also the librarian. Donations and public subscriptions were forthcoming for the purchase of Peel Park and House, and the adaptation of the House to its present purposes of a museum and library. Mr.

E. R. Langworthy, who died in 1874, greatly benefited the institution by bequeathing £10,000, which was used for building the Langworthy wing, containing an art gallery and reading-room, and for the purchase of books and works of art to furnish it. Every alternate year the library receives £16 for the purchase of books out of the "Brotherton Memorial Fund." Mr. Brotherton's early advocacy of the library movement is thus fittingly kept in mind. Once in four years, also, the trustees of the Pendleton Mechanics' Institute contribute £20 towards the cost of lectures. Four branch libraries were established as under: Greengate, November 1870; Regent Road, October 1873; Pendleton, April 1878; Albert Park, December 1890; and two branch reading-rooms, namely, Charlestown, July 1892, and Weaste, September 1892. The last-named serves also as a delivery station for books from the Regent Road Library. The number of books in a branch library varies from six to twelve thousand. The total stock in all the libraries is 81,556. The issues of books per day amount to 3500. The following figures form an instructive contrast :—

Year.	Issues in Reference Library.	Issues in Lending Libraries.	Readers in Rooms.
1870	52,199	64,192	87,107
1895	63,327	368,741	796,401

Books for children in the lending libraries are seldom asked for, but books for boys are much issued in the reading-rooms after five o'clock in the evening. Files of local newspapers and reports are kept. A complete library of specifications of Patents is much used by patentees. The heavy expenditure on branches necessarily keeps down the revenue available for book purchases; the present net rate of increase in the stock is under 700 volumes per annum. The museum is widely known; the geological collection is valuable and well arranged. Every winter an admirable series of free lectures is given at the central institution. The first course was held in 1881-82. Of the expenditure on the library side of the committee's work, the small proportion of 27.3 per cent. is on account of the central reference and lending libraries. The expenditure on branches varies from 6.5 to 15.4 per cent. of the total expenditure. Loan repayments and interest account for from one-sixth to one-third of the expenditure of each branch. The total staff of the Salford libraries is thirty-five persons.

Bradford

Bradford furnishes an excellent example of a northern town of the second-class doing useful work over a large area in every rank, from the unpolished though shrewd labourer or artisan to the journalist and professional man. The Acts were adopted in 1871, but the movement which led to this was initiated by several gentlemen four years earlier, and the opposition of two or three prominent representatives of the artisan class had to be borne down before the cause was victorious. The exact date of adoption was 15th March. The rate was levied forthwith, and a lending library and news-room in hired premises opened on 15th June 1872, and on the 17th February following the reference library. There were 13,400 volumes to begin with; now there are 43,335 in the Central Library, and 81,621 in the entire service of libraries. One penny in the pound brought in at first close upon £1800, but now £4075 is available from the same rate. There were few generous benefactors to help on the cause in its beginning, and almost the only important donation Bradford has had for its town libraries is the "James Hanson" library of 12,000 volumes, which was purchased and presented by Mr. Jacob Moser in July 1895. The gifts of volumes of interest do not often exceed a hundred in one year. Here, as in many other important English towns, municipal funds and municipal energy have built up the whole system and service, and the result is rightly regarded with pride by the townsmen. An art gallery and museum are under the same management, and £1018 is received out of the borough fund for its maintenance. Much might be said in praise of the artistic side of the committee's work if it came within the scope of this book. The museum, however, is not allowed to be a serious charge on the library's resources. In 1892, £1000 was voted from the Exchequer Contribution Account, and £300 year by year since towards the committee's funds, while a farthing rate, levied under the Museums Act in 1895, produced an additional income of £1000. At quite an early period the Bradford Committee began to bring its libraries to the doors of its burgesses. The following is a list of the branch libraries, their dates of establishment, number of volumes, and issues in the year 1895-96 :—

Branch.	Date.	Volumes.	Issues.
Great Horton	Dec. 27, 1875	4529	23,547
Girlington	Feb. 9, 1880	4083	22,509
Bradford Moor	May 1, 1882	3929	22,323
Otley Road	Nov. 20, 1882	3770	46,910
Bowling	April 4, 1883	4013	21,167
Manningham	Oct. 24, 1883	8555	117,116
Manchester Road	Jan. 18, 1887	5117	61,021
Allerton	Aug. 29, 1889	2237	8,584
Listerhills	Oct. 7, 1895	2053	34,873
Total			358,050

All the administrative work for the branches is done at the Central Library, hence any estimate of their cost would involve an analysis of the services of the central staff, and is therefore omitted. Happily Bradford has no loans to pay off for its libraries; the cost of salaries is about twenty-eight per cent. on the total income, and the total staff numbers thirty-four persons (including cleaners). Local literature is most assiduously collected—all matter printed in Bradford, about Bradford, or by authors of Bradford connections, and anything bearing on local history and topography. The excellent quarto catalogue contains many pages of entries in small type relating to this class of books, and even Yorkshire books of a wider range are extensively represented. Works relating to the local textile industries are provided, and a "Hand-list of Works on Technical Subjects in the Reference Department" has been published. The more recently published hand-lists of accessions and catalogues of branches are published in a peculiar elongated form, resembling a quarto in height and a 12mo in width; it is a very convenient form for the pocket; a somewhat similar form is in use at the Paris Municipal Libraries. A reading-room for the special use of ladies is provided at the central establishment, and a special portion of the counter partitioned off for them as an issue desk. This latter arrangement has, after six months' working, trebled the issues of books to women. The central lending department issues 328 books, the branch libraries 1196, and the reference department 213 per diem. The number of visits made to the rooms is a million and a half in one year. It is noticeable that the lending department of the Central Library closes at eight in the evening. The Central Library at different times has cradled local societies, some of which have grown beyond the accommodation, and have left for more convenient premises. Several societies still meet at the library, and the committee aim to provide here a home for much of the intellectual activity of the town.

NOTTINGHAM

The borough of Nottingham has acquired a good name for educational enterprise. The corporation was the earliest to provide and maintain a University

College, and the School Board has long been noted for its progressive policy. But earlier than the School Board, or than the municipal committees for higher school and college instruction, the Committee of the Free Library and Museum was at work. The Acts were adopted on the 29th May 1867, and a librarian shortly afterwards appointed. An old artisan's library was bought and made the nucleus of the town's collection, but the office premises in Thurland Street first occupied were almost immediately too small for satisfactory use. Here for about thirteen years a lending library, a small reference library, and a single-table news-room did their useful work. In 1868 the daily average issues were 430, in 1879–80 555 per day. Then came a period of closure, and the transfer of the books to a wing of the handsome suite of buildings erected at the cost of £80,000 to accommodate the new University College, the Free Public Library, and the Free Public Museum. About the middle of 1881 these buildings were opened by H.R.H. the late Prince Leopold, and the library straightway renewed its usefulness, and increased it. In the first two years in these premises the issues of books went up to 913 volumes per diem. At the re-opening the libraries contained about 30,000 volumes, but in March 1896 they held (including branches) 81,436 volumes, and the daily average issues had increased to 1380. For the past six years the yearly issues have averaged more than 400,000, and the attendances at libraries and reading-rooms 2,000,000 per annum.

At an early date branch libraries and reading-rooms began to be established. There are now thirteen branch reading-rooms and four lending libraries, one of which is a children's library, towards the establishment of which the late Mr. S. Morley, M.P., gave £500. It was the first separately housed free library for children's sole use under the Acts. A branch delivery was established at Bulwell so long ago as 1879, but, since the recent revival of interest in the delivery system, Nottingham has arranged for periodical deliveries at most of the news-rooms. The librarian, Mr. J. Potter Briscoe, introduced six years ago a system of Half-Hour Talks with readers about books and book-writers; eighteen of these were delivered in the winter of 1895–96. These brief lectures are given in the reading-rooms after due announcement, and are designed for introduction to, and guidance in, the reading of good books. Many towns in different parts of the country have followed Nottingham's example. Some of the bibliographical curiosities and special books in the reference library are exhibited in a glazed case, and the exhibits are frequently changed. Portraits or autographs of celebrated authors are exhibited on the walls and landing of the reference library. Selected books have also been lent to the police stations and to the fire brigade. Frequently published catalogues and supplements keep the public well acquainted with the contents of each library. Few libraries can show so long a list of publications. In the choice of books for the reference library specialists' advice in most departments of knowledge has been sought and obtained. One scholar only — Mr. Herbert Spencer—declined his aid on the ground that free libraries were Socialistic institutions. The free libraries and museum are supported by the product of the penny rate and a grant of £2000 annually out of surplus funds of the corporation, derived from profit on municipal gas and water undertakings.

NEWCASTLE-UPON-TYNE

As far back as 1854 a resolution was passed in the Newcastle town council appointing a committee to consider the propriety of, and report upon the measures necessary for the formation of a free library, but no practical result followed. The son of the proposer of the 1854 resolution, Mr. Councillor H. W. Newton, revived the subject by a similar resolution on 2nd February 1870. In December 1871 the committee recommended "that the Mayor be requested to convene a public meeting in accordance with the requirements of the Public Libraries Acts, with a view to their adoption in this borough." The report was adopted, and the meeting held on 28th May 1872; the statutory resolution was carried by forty-eight to thirty votes, but a poll was demanded by opponents, and refused. Questions as to the legality of the adoption being raised, the matter was allowed to rest for a time; but in February 1874 another town's meeting was called, and adoption carried by a large majority. The first committee was appointed in the May following. Further delay was occasioned by the search for a suitable site for a library building, but in September 1878 an agreement between the trustees of the Mechanics' Institute and the Public Libraries Committee was effected, whereby the mechanics' building and library were to be handed over to the corporation on condition that the liabilities about (£2000) be paid, and that the art and science classes be continued and extended under the style and title of the Educational Department Mechanics' Institution Section of the Public Library, while nine members of the committee of the institution were to be selected to serve on the Public Library Committee for seven years. This agreement was opposed in the town council, but on a vote ratified. A project to erect a new building in extension of the Mechanics' Institute premises was opposed vigorously, on the ground that it involved the demolition of an antique tower situated on the town wall; yet on 4th February 1880 a contract was signed for the work at the price of £10,513, a sum eventually exceeded by more than £1500. The late Mr. W. J. Haggerston, an experienced librarian from South Shields, and a gentleman of singular energy and organising ability, was appointed librarian, and continued in this office until his death in 1894. The reports of thirteen years bear witness to Mr. Haggerston's enthusiasm for his work. The first library rate collected in 1877 produced £2760, that of 1896 yielded £3976.

Power, presumably under a local Act, is possessed to levy a halfpenny rate for branch libraries, but this power has not yet been exercised. Three branch reading-rooms, open during the winter evenings, were established in Board School premises in 1884, but in the following year, owing to the scanty attendance, they were abandoned. The new central building was finished in 1884, and opened by H.R.H. the Prince of Wales on the 20th August.

In November 1884 occurred a disastrous fire in the libraries, from the overheating of a ventilation flue and ignition of a joist. The damage done, though covered by insurances, necessitated fifty-two days' closing of the lending library and twenty-one weeks' of the reference library. As the result of negotiations with the trustees of the "Thomlinson" Library—a collection rich in seventeenth century theology—an order of the Charity Commissioners was obtained on 1st April 1884, providing for the transfer of the books to the mayor, aldermen, and citizens, an annual payment of £25 to a librarian to be nominated by trustees named, and the balance of the revenue (declared under £50) to be spent in the purchase of additions to the Thomlinson Library. This transfer was completed in January 1885; the books were found to number 4365, and the city council made a special grant for the re-binding and shelving of the collection. The free library also contains a valuable collection of books on India, bequeathed by the late Mr. H. P. A. B. Riddell, C.S.I., J.P., in January 1889. About 900 volumes are in "the Riddell Bequest Library."

The report for 1888-89 describes an arrangement by which the care of the science and art classes was transferred to another authority, and the classes were to be held in another building.

A juvenile library has been provided here from the first; it now contains about 3500 volumes, and its catalogue extends to eighty-two very large and closely printed pages. Works by local men on local history or local industries receive proper attention; and special lists of blue-books, musical works, books for the blind, architectural works, and an anglers' list have been lately issued, and widely and freely circulated. A list of the principal books purchased out of the Technical Instruction Grants (1892-95) was also issued in 1895. It is satisfactory to see a departure in the later publications from the small and crowded type at one time in vogue in the catalogues of the Newcastle Free Libraries. The daily average of works issued from the library is for home reading 628, for reference 231. Nearly three thousand visits to the reading-rooms are counted daily. The books now number 84,000. About twenty-two per cent. of the total income is expended on account of loans, and about a quarter of the total expenditure goes in salaries.

NORWICH

To Norwich belongs the honour of having established in 1608 the first municipal free library, with a continuous history to the present time; and though the trust was for a time—as at Bristol—

alienated from the corporation, in later days it has been resumed, and to-day the Norwich Free Library can claim to be the oldest free library in the country, containing, as it does, 1772 distinct works of the ancient City Library. A loan of these books may be had by using a special form of application on any week day but Thursday between the hours of 11 A.M. and 4 P.M. The books may also be consulted on the premises during the ordinary working hours of the library. Norwich was also the first municipality to adopt Ewart's Act of 1850, which it did by 150 votes to 7 on 27th September 1850. At that time £364, 4s. was received in subscription to buy books. The new library, however, was not opened until 16th March 1857, although, before that, two annual rates of a halfpenny in the pound had been levied, producing the sum of £500. A halfpenny annual rate was continued to 1881, when, for the first time, a penny library rate was levied. The committee unfortunately mortgaged a considerable part of their small rate for a long period by erecting a costly building, with a second floor devoted to an art school, consequently for years the library was starved and inadequate. The penny rate in 1896 realised £1245, and the libraries now contain 31,250 volumes, and have a daily issue of 382 works. Norwich, too, has eagerly taken up the provision of books for the libraries of elementary schools, and in this way 2790 yearly are lent to be issued by the teachers in twenty-four board and voluntary schools. Last year 43,000 out of the

138,000 total issues were thus accounted for. In 1890 subscriptions amounting to £300 were received to start the juvenile libraries. A donation of £150 has also been received for the purchase of works of a technical character. The collection of local literature contains 300 volumes and 4300 pamphlets, besides views, maps, portraits, &c. University Extension lectures are given on the premises, and home reading circles held. Gilchrist Trust and other lectures are also delivered here. The library is open for six hours on Sundays.

BIRKENHEAD

Birkenhead was much smaller both in population and in area when the Public Libraries Act was adopted for the township at a meeting of ratepayers held 16th February 1856. Unanimous was the vote, and striking was the success of the new movement. Hired rooms were obtained, and on the 13th of December 1856 a lending library of 3132 volumes was opened. A few weeks of actual use proved the inadequacy of the premises, and it was resolved to move to the upper rooms of the old post-office in Conway Street. On the 1st May 1857 these convenient rooms were opened. Still success grew apace, and the present library building had to be commenced in good earnest early. On 23rd April 1864, the tercentenary of Shakespeare's birth, the new library was opened. This building, which still serves as the Central Library, after various small extensions and adaptations to meet latter-day pressing needs, cost £3400. Three hundred and fifty pounds of the sum was raised by public subscription for providing an ornamental façade, and the rest was raised by a loan recently paid off. The rate of a penny in the pound on the property of Birkenhead and Claughton brought in at first about £422. In time the inhabitants of the out-townships of Tranmere, Oxton, and Rock Ferry found the convenience of the open doors to the valuable reference library and reading-rooms of their neighbour township; accordingly the 1868–69 report contains a gentle suggestion that they too should adopt the Public Libraries Acts. The hint was not taken; but in 1877 the extension of the borough put an end to these inequalities, and the enlarged area of assessment provided more adequately for the development of the free libraries. In 1879 the report states that "the reference library is making rapid progress in the collection of the best county histories, chronicles, antiquarian researches, also in botany, ethnology, ornithology, heraldry, dictionaries, encyclopædias, art and science, the drama, poetry, societies' transactions, history, biography, &c." Undoubtedly the librarian of that day, Mr. Richard Hinton, wisely directed the committee in their purchases of books. The same report contains special thanks to the Shakespeare Club of Birkenhead for a handsome present of thirty-four volumes of Shakespeare texts, apparatus, and criticism. Whether this gift has aught to do with the fact or not, the free library of Birkenhead is worthy of wider fame for its fine collection of Shakespeare study-books, a collection to which the present librarian has given great attention and care. At a time when children's wants were hardly considered, Mr. Hinton made special provision of juvenile books; in 1865, 743 were issued; in 1870, 2608. In 1881 the juvenile section reached the number of 2000 volumes, and the report announces a separate catalogue of the "children's library" in preparation, to be sold at one penny. This is probably the earliest children's list published by a free library committee. Many years later the present librarian brought out a dainty and much improved catalogue, which has been largely copied elsewhere.

A movement for establishing branch libraries began with the extension of the borough boundaries in 1877, and with varying persistency continued until quite a recent date. In 1890 an attempt was made to introduce an extra rating clause into a local Act to enable the committee to provide branches, but from adventitious causes this did not succeed. Grants from the funds accruing under the Local Taxation Act a little later enabled the committee to achieve their desire, and the north and south branch libraries were opened in August 1894. The committee have been ever zealous to extend the knowledge of the benefits of the library, and a "Circular of Information," issued in 1889-90, and widely distributed, together with the posting of an attractive wall-placard, inaugurated a period of greatly increased use of the Central Library. Special lists are frequently issued on important topics of the day and industries of local concern. An excellent collection of books on dialects, and a magnificent series of county histories, are now accumulated, while the catalogue which Mr. May is now preparing for early publication may be expected, from his known reputation as an expert cataloguer, to prove singularly interesting to all book-lovers. The branch libraries have a unique character, from the manner in which the majority of the books of solid information are displayed within view of the readers, thus forming their own indicator. This method of shelving books is the invention of the librarian. It has many advantages in a small library. The cost of each branch is about $12\frac{1}{2}$ per cent. of the total expenditure. The present revenue of the committee, from a penny rate, is £1854, and the daily average of books issued for home reading is 880, and for reference 353. No statistics of the visits to reading-rooms are taken, but they probably amount to more than 2000 per day. The stock of books now reaches 61,530 volumes. Birkenhead is one of the towns where Sunday opening has been tried and abandoned as a failure.

Plymouth

In the year 1871 considerable interest in the free library movement was shown by the people of Plymouth, and on 6th October the mayor of that time, Mr. R. C. Servell, received a numerously signed requisition to summon a meeting to consider the desirability of establishing a free library for the town. The meeting was held, and a little later—at a statutory meeting on 3rd November—the Acts were adopted by a unanimous vote. A public subscription which was started raised £1100 towards the initial expenses of a library; and on the removal of the corporation from the old municipal buildings in 1874, a successful movement for appropriating the old Guildhall to library purposes was set on foot. The first public library committee met early in 1876 and appointed a librarian, and by 30th August 1876 all was ready for the official opening. The library began with about 8000 volumes, on which about £1200 had been expended; and at the very beginning it is noticeable that a "Devon and Cornwall" section was provided, in which, wrote Mr. W. H. K. Wright, the zealous librarian, "I propose from time to time to include the works of all authors of the two counties and all works relating to the same. . . . I hope that my little 'Devon and Cornwall library' may one day expand, and be of considerable importance. It already contains several hundred volumes." The catalogue of this section now occupies more than 230 closely printed large octavo pages, and the Devon and Cornwall library has certainly realised the hopes of its originator, for it numbers 8000 items, and is housed in a special room. Additional rooms were added to the Plymouth Library in August 1879, and an extension of the building was opened in November 1884. Branch evening reading-rooms were established in February 1892 and in October 1893, and a large extension and thorough renovation of the central building has only lately been effected. The reports, however, still urge upon the attention of the town council the necessity of better accommodation, and it is clear that a new building must be provided ere long for the needs of Plymouth readers. From the Central Library selections of books to form suitable children's libraries are made, and these are despatched to the elementary schools of the town for loan to scholars. It is claimed that this system, which has been followed elsewhere, was inaugurated at Plymouth in the year 1887. The committee's report for 1888-89 shows that 1719 volumes had been deposited in twelve schools or departments of schools. On 31st March 1896 in the elementary schools and branch libraries 3236 volumes were located out of a total of more than 40,000 volumes belonging to the town. The number of schools served is not stated in the report, but mention is made of a police library and of two evening reading-rooms, already referred to. The year's use of these branch and school libraries amounted to 128,705. A large extension and thorough renovation of the central premises caused their closing from June to December 1895, consequently the use for that year cannot be considered normal, but in the previous year a daily average issue of 1026 volumes was attained, a large increase on the figure 347, which represents the daily average seventeen years earlier. The added accommodation has already produced fruit in increased use ; for the daily average issue in all departments for March 1896 was 1499 volumes, an exemplification of the principle easily demonstrable from library statistics that supply creates demand. The Plymouth Free Libraries now contain 42,000 volumes, and have increased during the past five years at the rate of nearly 2000 volumes per annum. The visits to reading-rooms number about 2500 daily. The rate at one penny in the pound produces £1300, about double the amount in 1876.

Derby

May 1870 saw the adoption of the Public Libraries Acts in Derby. The local member of Parliament of that day, Mr. (afterwards Sir) Michael Thomas Bass, presented the town with a handsome building, handsomely furnished; while a later donation of £400 added to the burgesses' indebtedness. Sir W. Evans also gave £500 to the same cause; and other donations (two of £100) have been received in money and in books. Of the latter, the Duke of Devonshire's gift of his local collection is the most notable instance. A beginning in the committee's own building, which later was pulled down for the erection of the present buildings, was made in March 1871 by the opening of a reading-room and lending and reference libraries of 8625 and 4060 volumes respectively in October of the same year. The rate levied for that year brought in £540. Twenty-five years later the produce of the same rate was £1700. In 1895 a children's library and also a branch reading-room was opened. The libraries now contain 30,100 volumes, and the additions for five years past have been at the rate of more than 1100 volumes per annum. The daily use for home reading averages 608, and for reference 50. One thousand five hundred visits per day are made to the reading-rooms. University lectures, and classes, and an excellent art gallery and museum are associated in the same institution. Picture exhibitions and promenade concerts in the art gallery do much to popularise the work of the committee and their librarian.

Wolverhampton

The work of the free public library at Wolverhampton is so incorporated with the work of instruction in science and art classes, popular lectures, and a museum, that it is difficult to think of any portion of this work of adult education apart from the rest. Stimulated by the example of Birmingham in 1861, and by earlier examples at Manchester, Liverpool, and elsewhere, the movement for a free library was taken up with earnestness, and after one failure, through the opposition of small property owners and others, the adoption of the Acts was secured on 8th February 1869. In 1870 a penny in the pound was collected, and produced £830; but by an Improvement Act of 1887, powers of levying an additional penny for free library, art school, and art gallery purposes were acquired, and now, in 1896, one penny and one-eighth, realising £1200, is available for the institutions here described. The art gallery is under a separate committee. At the beginning the "Athenæum" turned over a library of 2000 volumes and a few shares in the building, where, on 30th September 1869, the reading-room and, on 1st January ensuing, the library was installed. The removal to the present building took place in 1873; the museum was opened and the popular lectures commenced in 1874. Educational classes were begun in 1873. Twelve hundred entries of students are registered in these classes every winter, and about 500 people usually attend the popular lectures. About 1100 persons visit the reading-rooms daily; 330 volumes are daily lent for home reading, and 39 for reference. The lending library now contains 27,900, and the reference library 7000 volumes. Ladies' tables are provided in the reference library, and a students' library in the laboratory. Two general and one special course of Gilchrist Lectures have been delivered here. The Gilchrist Trust is an endowment for the delivery of lectures for the stimulation of interest in educational classes in places where means are limited. The charge for rent, or rent equivalent, is only 1.4 per cent., and salaries in the library 33 per cent. of the expenditure. A sum of £300 has been annually voted by the council out of the Exchequer Contribution Account in support of the work; this sum is only sufficient to pay the salary of the science master, though of course there are fees and Government grants as a set-off. The librarian, Mr. John Elliott, is well known as the inventor of the Elliott Indicator, which was introduced to notice in 1869, and has perhaps not had full justice done to it as a forerunner of forms now more in vogue. Mr. Elliott is also an ardent geologist, and perhaps this accounts for the fact that a naturalist and archæological department of the free library was inaugurated in 1876, for the purpose of organising excursions, to supplement, by the study of nature, the reading of books and hearing of lectures. A volume of interesting papers read at the excursions was published in 1877 at cost price by the committee. Undoubtedly the Wolverhampton Free Library is a centre of considerable intellectual activity. The population in 1891 was about 83,000.

Brighton

Brighton has not adopted the Public Libraries Acts, but supports its free public library out of funds received under the special Royal Pavilion Act, 1850. A reading-room and a reference library were first established on 12th September 1873. The backbone of the reference library consisted of 7000 volumes, presented by the Royal Literary and Scientific Institution, and 3000 volumes of the library of the late Rev. H. V. Elliott, presented by his children. Many valuable donations were added in subsequent years, among the donors being the well-known Shakespearean scholar, Mr. J. O. Halliwell-Phillips, and the classical editor,

Mr. George Long. Sixteen years later a lending department was added to the library. The inhabitants had petitioned the committee to establish one so far back as 1878; but the movement smouldered until 1886, when it was revived and a scheme designed for carrying into effect the earlier suggestion. The Queen's jubilee celebration of 1887 gave birth to a motion at a town's meeting, "That a free lending library be established for the borough as the form of the local memorial of her Majesty's jubilee which will be most beneficial to all classes of the community." Town subscriptions towards a lending library produced £1100, Mr. D. P. Hack gave £500, and Mr. W. D. Hack £1000. The scheme for a separate building had to be abandoned for want of funds, but the Victoria Lending Library was accommodated finally in the Pavilion Rooms, and opened by the Mayor of Brighton (Mr. Alderman Sendall) on 16th October 1889. At the present time there are in the reference library 15,000 and in the lending library 29,000 volumes. The daily average issue in the lending library is 402 volumes, in the reference library 152. The museum and art gallery, though under a separate management, are closely associated with the library, and the local Natural History Society has meetings on the premises. Brighton and Surrey books are collected. The work of the libraries is greatly cramped for lack of space.

Preston

Preston, with its population of 108,000 (in 1891), is as to a public library far and away the best endowed place of the size in England; but in spite of this fact and its seventeen years of history, the library cannot yet be said to have achieved an average place among those in towns of similar size. The Acts were adopted by public meeting in 1878, and the solitary dissentient on that occasion became a regular borrower, and continued eagerly to use the institution until his death! From the first, Preston had rating power up to three-halfpence in the pound for its library, but did not avail itself of its right to the full until 1895, when the rate received reached £2000. In 1879 the product of the rate was half that sum. In the beginning, public subscriptions to the amount of £600 were received; and for £150 the local Literary and Philosophical Institution made over to the committee its books, pictures, and museum objects. In later years the Newsham bequest of pictures, valued at £40,000, was received from a townsman. For the first fourteen years the corporation granted premises free of rent. A lending library of 6000 volumes and a reading-room were opened on 1st January 1879. The reference library and patents' library and the museum were at first installed in other premises some five minutes' walk away.

The Harris bequest of £105,000 enabled the committee to build a princely home for the library and museum. The style of the building is modelled on classic Greek architecture, but with a very clever adaptation to modern necessities as to lighting from side windows, and the addition of a lanterne. The severity of the Greek style has also been avoided, and an appearance of elegance and solidity obtained, which it would be difficult to parallel in English public buildings. The cost of the work was £80,000, while the site provided by the Preston corporation is worth £30,000. The building has long been completed, and it is supposed that the library of reference books is somehow being got together. Certain it is that the committee have a grand opportunity here of distinguishing their borough among the towns of England, and it would be a thousand pities if they should fail for lack of proper advice in the spending of the large sum of money placed in their hands. The present stock of books reaches 40,000, and the daily average issue of volumes for home reading 371, and for reference 120. The library is increasing at the rate of six hundred to eight hundred volumes annually. Local literature and the needs of children do not seem to be as well looked after as they might, but works on the staple trade and on topography are collected. In the proposal of books for purchase the librarian has received very little help from persons of special knowledge. The staff consists of eight adults, and its cost is under thirty per cent. of the total expenditure. Doubtless there are local circumstances which account for the present slow development of the Harris Library which time may be trusted to alter; and doubtless all Lancashire ere long will be gladdened to see a great library worthy of that fair fane of the Muses which has been prepared for it in the city by the Ribble.

Cardiff

The rapid development of the coal trade in South Wales has had the effect of transforming Cardiff into the most important town in the Principality. At the last census the population reached 129,000, but it is far greater now. The history of the free libraries of Cardiff was for years a history of difficulties and slow progress, but since 1885 it may be described as that of a triumphal advance. An attempt to adopt the Acts on 30th October 1860 was frustrated by a majority of one, but the two years of correspondence in the local press which led to the effort were not wasted. Before the meeting which had rejected the Acts dispersed £60 had been subscribed for a voluntary free library, and in a little time a sum of nearly £200 was obtained. A reading-room was opened on 15th June 1861, and the attendance was so large that the opponents of the Acts veered round; the statutory meeting convened on 22nd September 1862 in the Town Hall was very largely attended, and the Acts adopted with but one dissentient. The voluntary library, thereafter taken over by the corporation, with its small collection of 400 books, had recorded 4343 loans in ten months, while the visits to the reading-room in one year had reached nearly a hundred thousand. A lending library with 1076 volumes was opened on 13th October 1863; and on 1st January 1864 more commodious premises, rented from the Y.M.C.A., were entered upon. About the same time a museum was commenced in a back room on the top storey, and in 1865 science and art schools were added to the committee's enterprising programme. In 1867 " Phil Robinson," whose articles and books on the literary aspects of natural history are well known, became librarian, and the museum increased rapidly in value under the fostering care of the Cardiff Naturalists' Society, which he started. The necessity for still larger premises became urgent, and the committee spent years in debating the question of sites and plans. Agreement was secured at length, and a building erected which cost £11,000, and was to serve for the library, museum, and school of science and art. This was opened in 1882, but three years later it had become too small. Meanwhile the distant wards were clamouring for branch reading-rooms, and, unable longer to resist the pressure, the committee, in 1889, voted £30 per annum to each of five districts for the establishment, with outside help, of district reading-rooms. Let it be remembered that with this extent of operations the income of the committee for the first and several subsequent years was only £450, out of which, from 1864, £100 had to go for rent; and that in 1882 the grant from the council was £1510 only, from which more than £400 had to be deducted for loans ; and it will be seen that little was left wherewith to buy books. Indeed, for the first twenty years the average expenditure on books and binding amounted to less than £150, whereas the average for the next ten years reached no less than £524, and for the ensuing two years nearly £850 per annum. The change for the better was occasioned by a more liberal policy on the part of the council, and by the rapid increases in the assessment after 1885; but even more by the adoption of the Technical Instruction Act, soon after its passing in 1889 ; the transfer of the science and art school to a new authority in 1890 ; and the subsequent adoption of the Museums and Gymnasiums Act in 1893, involving the transfer of museum charges from the library rate.

In 1893, too, the committee were able to take over the full charge of the branch libraries, and about the same time to commence the work of extending the library. The extension building has cost £15,000, exclusive of furniture ; it is a beautiful stone structure, with handsome frontages to a public square and on two other sides. Very commodious it is, and beautifully furnished. The news-room and magazine-room contain 450 superficial yards of floor space, and will accommodate adequately 280 persons at a time. The ladies' room provides for 43, and the reference library for 143 readers. Thus, at one time, 466 readers may be comfortably seated in this people's palace. The old part of the building will continue to be used as a lending library and for storage, and in a year or two the museum, which for the present is housed there, will find a home in a special building in another part of the town, thus leaving further room for library expansion. The lending library accommodation is ample for 150 borrowers at a time, and must be added to that mentioned above. Each of the branch libraries is well supplied with newspapers and periodicals, and has from 300 to 1500 volumes for reading on the premises. At four of the branches these are in open book-cases, to which readers have free access. The books in these four branches were given by various donors, and some of the gifts were conditional on a trial of the "open access" method of issue. Unfortunately the plan has been abused by systematic book thieves. Now that the Central Library is completed, the committee will be free to give more attention to the improvement of the branches. The Central Library has benefited by gifts of 2000 volumes from Judge Falconer; of sets of *Challenger* Reports, Ray Society, Royal Society, Linnean Society, and Zoological Society publications, and other books from Mr. H. M. Thompson; and by many gifts from the Marquis of Bute and Colonel Page. From 200 to 300 volumes of general interest annually are received by way of presentation. Magnificent collections of Welsh books and books relating to Wales find their home here. In 1891 the collection made by the Rees family of Llandovery, the well-known printers of the "Liber Landavensis" and the "Mabinogion," was purchased. It contained 7000 volumes of printed books, 100 volumes of MSS., and a large number of local maps and prints. A portion of the cost was subscribed. The additions to this department have brought up the collection of manuscripts to 1000 items, and that of prints, photographs, drawings, &c., from 6000 to 7000 items. Books on coal-mining, engineering, iron and steel receive special attention, and a children's library has been established. The libraries are increasing at the rate of 3000 volumes per annum, and in June 1896 included 63,000 volumes. The libraries of two local societies are also in charge of the committee. The daily average of works issued for home reading is 533, for reference 101 volumes, and the visits to the reading-rooms reach an average of 7500 per diem. These figures, being for a period of transition and expansion into the new premises, may reasonably be expected to be greatly exceeded very soon. Among the benefactions mention has not yet been made of a surplus fund of £1300, derived from an industrial exhibition, and spent on decorations, pictures, books, and apparatus, shortly after the erection of the 1882 building; nor of the munificent gifts to the very fine art gallery and museum. The total annual cost of the staff is under £1000, a very moderate sum for so large and active a system. Loans absorb £1238 per annum, and the rate yielded in 1895-96, £3600. Many of the foregoing facts are derived from the pamphlet by Mr. John Ballinger, the librarian, entitled "The Cardiff Free Libraries," 1896.

Swansea

The Acts were adopted in Swansea in 1870, and an ambitious project of providing for a central library and four branch reading-rooms out of an annual grant from the council of £650 was launched. The lending library was opened with 3500 volumes in hired premises on 1st May 1876, but in the previous year three branch reading-rooms had been already established. A fourth branch was added, but one of these branches was subsequently closed. Swansea has been fortunate in the gifts to its library. The Rev. Rowland Williams, D.D., of "Essays and Reviews" fame, bequeathed his books; the executors of Mr. T. J. Margrave, Llangenech, contributed 1230 volumes of French, German, Italian, and Spanish classics; and Mr. J. H. Rowlands, of Neath, a miscellaneous collection of 1142 volumes. The annual presentation of books of general interest varies between three and four hundred volumes. The most conspicuous gifts, however, have been those of Mr. J. Deffett Francis, of Swansea, who has created the art museum of the town, and presented a very choice collection of 2500 engravings, prints, and drawings chiefly illustrating the English School from Hogarth onwards, and carefully selected for their fine condition, local interest, or educational value. Seven thousand volumes of reference relating to the fine arts—kept together as the Deffett-Francis Collection—are also the gift of the Honorary Curator, who has thus devoted his purse, his knowledge, and his services to the promotion of a high standard of taste in his native town. For years the library and museum struggled on in adversity, but towards 1884 the prospects of the institution greatly improved, and in the June of the Queen's jubilee year a fine central building, purposely designed and erected at the cost of £20,000, was formally opened amid unbounded enthusiasm by the Right Hon. W. E. Gladstone, M.P. The new building provided accommodation for science classes as well as for the ampler carrying on of all the previous work. Now ensued great financial difficulties, but these were happily ended by the powers conceded in the Swansea Improvement Act of 1889, which allows the appropriation of twopence in the pound to library and museum expenses. The maintenance of the science and art classes is provided for by a special grant of £150 per year from the town council. As far as possible the librarian collects local printed matter relating to the Principality, and the library possesses a fine collection of books, portraits, views, maps, &c., relating to Wales in general and the immediate locality in particular. Works relating to the copper-smelting, tin-plate, and coal-mining industries are sought after. A special nook is also reserved for Shakespearean literature. Free lectures on Saturday evenings are held in the winter, and the *Cymrodorion Abertawe* (Welsh Society) holds fortnightly lectures on the premises. A branch of the National Home Reading Society is also accommodated with a room. For home reading 235 books per diem are issued on an average, and for reference 460. Daily visits to the reading-rooms, which between 1889 and 1892 were increased in number to six, amount to 2350. The library now contains 35,000 volumes, and has latterly increased at the rate of 760 volumes per annum. The expenditure for 1894-95 amounted to £2350; of this sum £826 was on account of loans. The expenditure on the art gallery is about £52 per annum, on the Central Library under £1000, and on each branch from £62 to £72 per annum.

DUNDEE

A desire to perpetuate the memory of the late Prince Consort and the wish to have a free library for Dundee were both satisfied in the establishment of the Albert Institute of Literature, Science, and Art. Prior to this, in 1866, the Public Libraries Acts were adopted, and the subscriptions towards an Albert Memorial went to provide the building fund. The rate was first collected in 1867-68, and produced £1452; in 1895-96 it produced £3018. The libraries and reading-room were opened in 1869. Classes for art instruction, an art gallery with annual loan exhibitions, a museum and public lecture courses are parts of the Institute. In 1874 the great hall, used as a reference library, was opened. The museum and art gallery were opened in 1874, the first exhibition held in 1877. A branch library was begun in 1873, and a second and larger one in 1896. A subscription library was commenced in 1876. Gifts have poured in upon this popular institution. Mr. J. M. Keiller gave in 1887 £10,500 to pay off the debt incurred in building the art gallery and museum. He also gave £1000 worth of books. The same year £15,000 was raised by subscription to further extend the museum and galleries. Dr. J. Boyd Barter bequeathed £500 and a library of 3000 volumes. Other bequests of libraries have been received from time to time, and Sir W. Ogilvie Dalgleish gave £1000 to instal the electric light. In 1888 a gigantic bazaar was organised to raise funds for building purposes, and a profit of £5000 was made. In connection with this a beautiful bazaar book, illustrated by numerous excellent pictures and designs, was published. The libraries commenced with a stock of 20,722, and now contain 71,000 volumes. The daily issue of works for home reading is 864, for consultation 194. Visits to the reading-rooms are estimated at nearly 700 daily. The Geographical Society, the Shakespeare Society, the Graphic Arts Association, and other educational societies are allowed to meet rent free at the Institute. Local literature is the especial care of Mr. A. C. Lamb, the author of one of the largest and most sumptuous town histories ever published, who takes great interest in the free library collections. Books bearing on the local industry—the jute trade—are sought after and added to the library. The publications of the committee are deserving of special attention, the fine catalogue of the lending department, 1891 especially so; and next to it the catalogue of the Lochee Branch Library, a library founded by the bequest of the late Mr. T. H. Cox. Frequent finding lists bring the catalogue up to date. No one can examine these thorough pieces of work without an emotion of wonder and surprise. The subject entries are particularly well done, and journalists and literary men would find the Dundee catalogues unlock new stores of special knowledge even to the best informed. Whether the thoroughness of the work is explained by the generosity of the people, or the generosity explains the thoroughness, it is perhaps difficult to say; but certain it is that such work implies both men and means.

Aberdeen

When a few citizens interested themselves in the free library movement and procured a statutory meeting on 7th May 1872, their effort to secure the adoption of the Public Libraries Acts was defeated by 488 votes against 134 in favour of their motion. Twelve years later opinion had veered quite round, and doubtless the offer of the directors of the Mechanics' Institute to transfer the building and library, on condition of the town's adopting the Acts and taking over certain financial burdens, amounting to £2500, led to a reversal of the former decision. This was on 25th March 1884, the votes being 891 for, 264 against adoption. A penny rate was levied in the same year, and produced £1511. In 1894-95 the penny brought in no less than £2098. A part of the building taken over was opened as a reading-room on 25th August 1894, and the work of overhauling the library stock and adding suitable new books was completed by 12th March 1886, when the lending library of 14,525 volumes was thrown open. Success was almost too great; borrowers were registered rapidly, and in a very short time had reached in number 8000; the space occupied as a reading-room had to be drawn upon and new premises sought. Eventually a new building was erected on the Rose Mount Viaduct, at a cost exceeding £10,000. Towards that sum nearly £4000 was collected by subscriptions, headed by the town council £1000, Mr. Andrew Carnegie £1000, Lord Provost Henderson £250, the trustees of Mr. Robert Donaldson £250, and six sums between £100 and £200 each. The new library was opened in 1892, and by recent special gifts it has been entirely freed from debt.

Local literature, always a considerable quantity in an ancient university town, is adequately represented in the library. Juvenile literature is also supplied. The last report shows a daily average issue for home reading of 850, for reference 65. The library contains 41,750 volumes. A number of books, as in many other libraries, are accessible without formality, and no record of these "open access" issues is kept. A small branch reading-room for Old Aberdeen was opened on 17th March 1894. Mr. H. W. Robertson, M.A., the librarian, has invented a special form of indicator for the Aberdeen Library. In this indicator the titles of the books available for borrowers are visible, and the absence of a title indicates that the book bearing it is in use. Catalogues and "Indicator Lists" are published at the library, the entries in both species of entry list being more or less annotated for the guidance of readers. Out of the eleven assistants on the staff of the library, seven are women and girls. The cost of the staff clearly indicates that this is not a mere matter of economy, as it is in many other libraries.

CHAPTER XI

FREE LIBRARIES UNDER THE ACTS IN SIXTEEN THIRD-CLASS TOWNS

IN the larger towns the public library is sometimes overshadowed by a more splendid or more pretentious institution, but in towns with a population between, say, 10,000 and 80,000, the public library is not seldom the "cynosure of all eyes," and a centre of intellectual life.

The difference of revenue from the rate has little relation to population, but in many of the smaller towns there has been lacking neither resource nor generosity. Would that this could be said of all! Munificence, like the wind, bloweth where it listeth, or the financial climate would be more equable in the regions about to be described. In towns with a population exceeding 30,000 there has usually been a sufficient income to engage competent librarians trained in one or other of the large libraries, and consequently the most has been made of every resource, and the institution has developed rapidly; but in every lesser town, unless a local Mæcenas or Midas has given the assistance of his purse, either the soul of the institution (the library) has had to be put under lock and key for considerable portions of the week, or its opportunities for enlargement have been impaired. The popular cry for reading-rooms has often led library committees to establish small branches prematurely. No town of 80,000 inhabitants or less is able to support creditably a branch reading-room within the first twelve years of its library's history, unless indeed large gifts or bequests have been received, or rooms and service are supplied for a nominal sum. Many of the public libraries in our third-class towns benefit by gifts from local worthies, from the Clarendon Press, Oxford, from the University Press, Cambridge, from the Trustees of the British Museum, and from the Comptroller of H.M. Stationery Office, nevertheless the number of volumes of general interest received as presents varies greatly in the towns here mentioned. Dundalk obtains only six, but Southampton and Wigan each receive about two hundred volumes per annum as gifts. The rapid growth in the amount of the assessment in many of the towns instanced is a favourable augury for the future of public libraries, as it is a sure sign of the present prosperity of our country.

But what do the people in our small and moderate-sized towns read ? . Answers received from fifteen libraries seem to show that the most popular authors in fiction are Mrs. Wood, who was named in eight lists; Miss Braddon, "Marie Corelli," each named in four lists; Crockett, Henty, Weyman (3); Dickens, Scott, Haggard, Stevenson, Hall Caine, Worboise, "Edna Lyall," and Charles Lever (2). Names on one list only are omitted. Among non-fictional writers Carlyle and Ruskin lead the van, Macaulay comes next, Darwin and Froude, Green and—shall we say it ?—Smiles follow abreast.

Another answer to the question is furnished in certain library reports, showing the number of times particular books have been asked for in the libraries. The following are taken at random from the Southampton report of 1894-95 :—

Balfour's " Defence of Philosophic Doubt," issued 14 times.
Balfour's " Foundation of Belief,"   „ 11 „
Brooke's " Tennyson,"   „ 19 „
Darwin's " Descent of Man,"   „ 20 „
Drummond's " Ascent of Man,"   „ 14 „
Gore's " Lux Mundi,"   „ 16 „
Mill's " Political Economy,"   „ 12 „
Oliphant's " Jerusalem,"   „ 29 „
Ruskin's " Sesame and Lilies,"   „ 28 „
Traill's " Social England,"   „ 18 „
Scott's " Ivanhoe,"   „ 27 „
George Eliot's " Adam Bede,"   „ 28 „
" Q.'s " " Dead Man's Rock,"   „ 33 „

To take an example from Ireland: the Second Annual Report of the Cork Library (1894) states that—

Carlyle's " Life " by Froude (4 vols.), was issued 37 times.
Darwin's " Origin of Species " (1 vol.),   „ 19 „
Green's " Short History " (1 vol.),   „ 19 „
Dickens's Works (40 vols.),   „ 1077 „
Lever's Works (29 vols.),   „ 934 „

The Cork report gives the occupations of the people who borrowed various books in one year ; here is an interesting example : Carlyle's " French Revolution," borrowed by an accountant, by a bar assistant (twice), by a carpenter, by eight clerks, by a grocer's apprentice, by a housekeeper, by a medical attendant, by a saleswoman, by a scholar (four times), and by almost as many other people. Local works also came out well in such lists; for instance, at South Shields, Lawson's "Tyneside Celebrities" was borrowed sixteen times in a year. Who can read these by no means exceptional facts and not be proud of an institution that is quietly effecting so much good? Turn now to the record of particular libraries.

South Shields

has a population of 78,000, and is a busy hive of industry, the forms taken by its activities bringing out the mental force and skill of its population. In 1871 it had a large Mechanics' Institution in full and successful operation, though in the opinion of many its resources were insufficient to meet the growing demands of the inhabitants. Hence arose a movement to hand over the property to the town, on condition of the adoption of the Public Libraries Acts. Opposition voices were also heard decrying the proposal, but a public meeting held on 24th April 1871 adopted the Acts, and on 28th October 1873 the Mechanics' Institution, building, and contents were, by a deed in Chancery, vested in the new library authority. Many of the books were found to be too much worn for use, and about 2000 had to be cast aside; but with the aid of the donations presently to be mentioned, assisted by the rate, more than 5000 volumes were purchased, and the library was re-opened as a free library, with about 8000 volumes. Mr. J. B. Stevenson, M.P. (the borough member), gave £500, Mr. Alderman Williamson £500, Mr. Archibald Stevenson £500, Mr. J. J. Stevenson £100, and Mr. Edward Moore 100 guineas, to contribute to this result. The rate was first levied in 1874, and produced £608; in 1894-95 it yielded £1052. The rents obtained for the Mechanics' Hall and rooms have always been an important item of revenue at South Shields, and up to 1892 as large a sum as £5120 had been thus received; but since 1885 the amount realised from that source of income has greatly declined; in 1895 it was £168, but ten years earlier it had been £320. The committee in this Tyneside borough has all through maintained science and art classes as part of its work, but the accounts for 1894-95 show that the charge on that score is met by a grant from the Local Taxation (Customs and Excise) Residue Fund. A branch reading-room was opened in 1874, and another in 1893. These are very cheaply maintained, the cost of both not amounting to ten per cent. of the total expenditure. For several years past the managers have been complaining of want of room, and considerable alterations are now in progress at the central institution to increase the accommodation. A room was early set apart as a museum, and Roman remains from the locality are a chief item of interest in the exhibits, though natural history also receives attention. The library also collects local publications, and the catalogue shows a large number of bound volumes of pamphlets on local matters. It is to be hoped that the covers of these pamphlets are also bound in the volumes. About 670 volumes are added each year, and the library now contains 20,100 volumes. The daily average of works issued for home reading, according to the last received report, was 371, and 58 for reference; 12,100 visits per week are made to the reading-room.

Most of the English examples in this chapter are taken from Northern and Midland towns, but the South also can show very good instances of successful free libraries.

SOUTHAMPTON

The council of the Hartley Institution and the members of the local Parliamentary Debating Society took steps to obtain the statutory public meeting in the Queen's jubilee year. This meeting was held on 13th June, and the Acts were unanimously adopted. Organisation, for local reasons, was deferred until the following year, but the first rate was made in November 1887. The rate, at one penny in the pound, produced £953; last year (1896) it produced £1144; this year, owing to the enlargement of the borough boundaries, it is expected to produce £1433. In the beginning money donations exceeded £100, and about 2500 volumes were presented, Mr. Passmore Edwards giving 1000 volumes. The library opened in

January 1889 in hired premises, and with 5000 volumes, and an overwhelming demand for books at once ensued. A new and excellently designed building was opened four years later—July 1893—a branch reading-room in December 1895, and before this book is published there will be open another library, with reading and news-rooms, for the advantage of dwellers in the added area of the borough. Among the presentations may be mentioned a gift by Miss Gordon of a number of books which had belonged to her brother, General Gordon, of Chinese and Soudanese fame. Hampshire books and the materials of local history are diligently collected. The friendliest relations with the Hartley (Scientific) Institution, with University Extension lecturers, and with the local press are cultivated; and the library is much used by students. The local library has also been of use to authors. The public appreciation may be measured by the fact that 412 volumes per day are given out for home reading and 46 for reference, besides which 1300 visits are made to the reading-rooms. The library now includes 19,400 volumes. The librarian considers "that education has made great progress in [the] town since the establishment of the library, and the institution has done a great deal to supply [the] local Literary Societies with good books."

Aston Manor

The progressive urban district of Aston Manor is itself suburban to progressive Birmingham, and in earlier years, like its sister local board districts, was impressed by the free library system of the neighbouring city. Smethwick and Handsworth adopted the Public Libraries Acts in 1876, and at a public meeting held on 15th May 1877 Aston also decided, without opposition, to have a free library. The rate was first levied in 1877, and yielded at a penny in the pound £457. The same rate in 1895-96 produced £680. Without a great flourish of trumpets or the aid of large donations a beginning was made, and a temporary lending library opened in a room which was approached through a coach-house. This was on 4th February 1878. Four years later a suitable permanent home was entered—part of new premises devoted to public official work. The success which has followed has twice necessitated an additional room being allotted to the public library, and even now there is much need of greater space. There are few libraries with the same limitation of resources that have accomplished more than Aston. Greater numerical results can be shown. In the character of the books that have been gathered together, the guiding of a wise and well-trained librarian is evident. In the very first published report the committee declared their intention of placing in the lending library "standard works in every department of knowledge, including a few expensive books usually found only in reference libraries," a declaration amply carried out. The reference department has not been neglected in the pursuit of this policy, but has been gradually enlarged to its present stock of 6587 volumes by additions, of which the following are reasonable examples :—

Ruskin's "Examples of the Architecture of Venice."
Planché's "Cyclopædia of Costume" (2 vols.).
Bloxam's "Principles of Gothic Architecture."
Redgrave's "Dictionary of English Artists."
Bradley's "Dictionary of Miniaturists."
Eissler's "Metallurgy of Gold and Silver" (2 vols.).
Toulmin Smith's "English Gilds."
Henry Irving Edition of Shakespeare (8 vols.).
Shelley's and Keats's Complete Works, edited by Buxton Forman.
The Salt Society Staffordshire Collections.
Sir W. Stirling Maxwell's Works.
Dugdale's "Antiquities of Warwickshire."

These are examples of about 140 volumes purchased out of the residue of a special Victorian Jubilee Fund amounting to £50, increased by other gifts to £110, and handed over for the purpose in 1891. Special attention is paid to the provision of books on design and industrial art, owing to the nature of the local industries. The materials for local history are also very carefully collected. The librarian firmly believes "that this is one of the most important duties of a librarian outside of the general routine of his library. But for him a large amount of ephemeral matter, which can be had for the asking, would perish, and the materials for local history would thereby be lost." So thoroughly is this duty discharged at Aston, that occasionally photographs of the advertising stations are taken for preservation in the library.

The lending library began with 2700 volumes, and now numbers 9146. The total possessions in volumes now number 15,733. In the twelfth year the issues of books had passed one million. The daily average of works issued is for home reading 283, for reference 40 to 50, and daily visits to the reading-rooms, 500. A branch reading-room was opened in 1883, and is very economically conducted; the cost of management in 1895-96 was under £57. Aston has always been well supplied with catalogues and class-lists. A fifth edition of the lending library catalogue was issued in 1894, and a second edition of the reference library catalogue is now being printed. A special and attractively printed catalogue of books for the young was published in 1892, and a catalogue of musical works in 1893. Free popular lectures have been a special feature in the work of the committee since 1883, and have done much to increase the use made of the library.

WIGAN

is a typical Lancashire mining-town, with much more of historic interest than is usual in a mining locality. The population at the last census was 55,000, and with the outlying parishes, where dwell many of the borrowers at its public library, the district must have near upon 200,000 inhabitants. The adoption of the Acts at Wigan in 1876 was brought about by the munificence of two local gentlemen. The late Mr. Thomas Taylor, J.P., gave the building and fittings (£12,000), and the late Mr. Joseph Winnard, surgeon, bequeathed £12,000 to be spent on the purchase of books. By the Winnard bequest, with the addition of a special subscription of £1000, collected in 1878, a total of 15,000 volumes was purchased, and housed in a building worthily designed by Mr. A. Waterhouse, R.A.

The principal adviser in expending the Winnard bequest, Mr. G. Finch, had been senior wrangler in 1857, hence one need not be surprised that the foundation of a scholarly library of high excellence was laid, and a character stamped upon the library which subsequent additions have suitably sustained. Valuable county histories, richly illustrated galleries of art, learned societies' publications, the Bollandist Fathers' "Acta Sanctorum," Dugdale's "Monasticon Anglicanum," the Patrologia of Migné, magnificent bibles, manuscript and printed, Piranesi's "Rome" (original issues), Hakluyt's "Collections of Early Voyages"—these items sufficiently indicate to the scholar and student the character of the Wigan collection. Right worthily, too, has the recording of these treasures been done. A complete MS. catalogue of the reference library exists, and is now being printed and issued in parts, eight of which, forming two quarto volumes, and reaching to the end of letter H, have been issued. To enable this to be done the town council voted a special sum of £500 for the expenses of printing. The fulness of the entries is extraordinary; thousands of articles hidden away in journals and transactions have been brought to light and ranged under each author's name and under the proper subject entries: the article Bible occupies eleven pages; bibliography, forty-five pages; engineering and engineers, eight pages; England and the English, twenty-three pages. But this is not all: several special subject catalogues have been published by the committee, chief among which is Mr. H. T. Folkard's " Index Catalogue of Books and Papers relating to Mining, Metallurgy, and Manufactures," issued in 1880, and filling 152 large octavo pages—a work copies of which have been sold all over the world, and one that has made the Wigan Public Library famous with mining experts. The more prosaic everyday work of a public library is not in the least neglected on account of these achievements. Besides 33,000 volumes now in the reference library, there are 14,200 in the lending library, and 500 openly accessible for reference at the branch boys' library. More than a hundred volumes a day are issued for reference, and 300 for home reading. Public lecture courses are established in connection with the library work, and partly through the generosity of Sir Francis S. Powell, M.P. for Wigan, who is contributing £50 per annum towards its support, the Powell Boys' Reading-room and Juvenile Library has been opened. In the first eight months nearly 30,000 attendances of boys and girls were recorded, and nearly 45,000 loans of books. The reading-rooms have been open on Sundays from 2 to 9 P.M. from the first; the average attendances in 1882 were under 200, in 1896 nearly 400. The committee have not always been free from financial troubles, for in 1878 the rate produced only £505 at one penny in the pound, but in 1889 a clause allowing a twopenny rate was inserted in a local Act, and the rate now levied realises £1489. An affiliated subscription library—passing on its books to the free library after twelve months' use in return for housing and service—and a voluntary halfpenny additional rate, were extraneous sources of income from 1879 to 1889. During this period, also, the corporation did not charge the committee with gas, cleaning, or repairs. The library opened with 22,108 volumes, and separate news-room, lending library, and reference library; a second news-room and magazine-room was added in 1890, and the Powell Boys' Reading-room in 1896.

WARRINGTON

To Warrington is due the honour of establishing the earliest English town library assisted by a special rate and under municipal management; and the steps which led to the founding of its library are narrated in the first part of this work. In 1848 the halfpenny rate realised less than £78, and in the succeeding year the total expenditure amounted only to £236, but local generosity supplied liberally both books and specimens, and a very fair beginning was made with nearly 12,000 volumes. The museum and the library for reference, which alone was free and open to the people—at first on three days and later on two days per

WARRINGTON 255

week—were established in hired premises, and the annual average consultation of books for the first five years was 548 volumes. A subscriber of half a guinea, however, was admitted every day of the week, and could borrow for home reading besides, while family subscriptions of a guinea were also received. The average annual issue to subscribers in the same period was 956 volumes, and the average annual subscriptions amounted to about £76. From seven thousand to twelve thousand visits were made to the museum in each of these early years, and the institution was very popular. As early as 1852 a science class in zoology and physiology was commenced with fifty-three students.

The subscription system side by side with free reference was maintained until 1887, when an alternative method of allowing the loan of a book for the payment of a penny to any guaranteed borrower resident in the town commenced, and for three years had considerable success. But to hark back again. In 1854 was given the site for a building, which was completed and opened in 1857, the subscriptions received towards the cost thereof amounting to £1100. In 1875 a building for an art gallery was added, and again a sum of £1000 in subscriptions was collected. In 1875 weekly papers were first supplied to the reading-room; an art gallery was established in 1877. The lending department was made free in 1891, through the powers given by a local Act of 1889, which also permitted a three-halfpenny library rate. Three years later daily papers were provided. Besides the gifts referred to, the first chairman of the committee left a bequest of £450. Compare the present use of the library with that of the early years—237 works issued per diem, with 956 per annum; nearly as many books lent now in four days as then in a whole year! The library now contains 29,000 articles, including 4000 pamphlets. Here is an unusually complete and excellent collection of Warrington books, tracts, pamphlets, and chap-books, and all are kept in a condition allowing of ready and rapid reference. Many considerable writers have been connected with Warrington, notably Joseph Priestley and the Aikins, and the works of these writers are collected here. The library is increasing at the rate of about 725 volumes a year, of which about 150 are presented. Public lecture courses are organised in connection with the institution, and the librarian is also local secretary for the technical instruction classes held in the library, museum, and school of art buildings. It is questionable if any free library has had a more honourable career.

BOOTLE

furnishes a conspicuous instance of the rapid up-building of a corporate town out of the increase of a great city. Though the history of the place goes back to the Doomsday Book record, the borough is essentially modern. The greater docks of the port of Liverpool are within its limits, and this fact determines the assessment of nearly half a million pounds, and explains why the yield of the rate is between two- and three-fold that of a penny at Warrington, a town of similar size in the same county. The scope of the work centred in the free library at Bootle is very comprehensive. These are the main facts in its development. In January 1884 a resolution was passed by the General Purposes Committee, and in the following month was confirmed by the town council, requesting the mayor to call a town's meeting to consider the adoption of the Libraries Acts. The meeting was held on the 19th March; there was no opposition, and the Acts were adopted. In the ensuing July Mr. R. Tudor, a medical gentleman of retiring habits, who had lived over half a century in the town, bequeathed his library of 1500 volumes, including many valuable works. The books were received in the following year, and also a gift of £360 from the executors of the doctor's friend, Mr. T. P. Danson, who died in that year. The late Earl of Derby also gave £250 to be spent on specimens for the museum, and an equal sum to complete the purchase was taken from the Danson bequest, leaving £110 for library purposes. The town council at once proceeded to erect a home for the new institution. This building cost near upon £8000, and provides ample accommodation on the ground floor for two large reading-rooms and a library, and in three large upper rooms for a museum and art gallery. Besides, the very large basement six years ago was altered to form class-rooms for the technical school, which had been developed out of classes meeting in the private rooms of the library and museum. As the building approached completion the residue collections of the Liverpool Royal Institution were purchased and transferred to their new home, and afterwards—a week before the opening of the institution—the librarian and curator was appointed, and began his work. No rate had been levied during the erection of the building, so that the fund available for book purchases out of the rate of 1887-88 was very restricted, yet with gifts, about 2100 volumes, and bequests and purchases a beginning with a library of 4800 volumes, fully catalogued, was made in February 1888. But before then much had been done : a reading-room and a loan exhibition of pictures were opened on 22nd June 1887, a second loan exhibition on 15th October, science classes were commenced in the same month, while books were first issued for reference, and a course of illustrated weekly popular lectures was inaugurated in November of that year. Besides this, good work had been undertaken in the museum, particularly in the delivery of regular museum addresses by the curator. All the work (with the exception of occasional art exhibitions) has been continued and developed to a large degree, with the result that the institution is one of the most popular in the town, and a centre of local intellectual life. A second reading-room was opened in 1889 ; special facilities for children and a children's catalogue were added in 1891 ; and in

December 1894 a branch delivery station for the children in one of the large Board Schools commenced its operations. Until 1895 it had been usual to close the institution for one afternoon and evening per week for cleaning purposes, but in the April of that year the open hours were extended to the whole of every week day.

The library now numbers about 16,600 volumes, of which the reference library contains about 5000. The issue of books has never been phenomenally high, but it has steadily grown from a daily average in the first few months of 139, to 338 in the period covered by the report for 1896-97. In less than eight years the issues reached half a million; and at the present time the daily average of readers in the news-room is 570. The scope of this book precludes comment on the large amount of instruction in the science, art, and technological classes carried on in close association with the library and museum. More than 800 students attend in about thirty technical school classes. As Bootle is a county borough, complete control of the Local Taxation Residue Fund rests with the town council, and a grant of about £300 per annum has been made for several years towards the cost of museum maintenance and technical books. For a library of its size very many are the costly books, especially on technology, contained therein; and a catalogue of nearly three hundred large octavo pages, including several hundred subject lists, and published last year, unlocks its treasures to the students, journalists, preachers, and teachers, who largely make use of the library. The population of Bootle was 49,000 in 1891, and the penny rate now realises £1900.

CHELTENHAM

did not obtain a free library without a prolonged struggle. First a meeting held in the Town Hall in 1856 rejected the proposal to adopt the Act, again in 1878 a poll of the burgesses decided negatively—1030 against, 702 for—and not till 18th July 1883, after a newspaper correspondence war of more than three months and a vigorous campaign by public meetings for and against, did victory crown the efforts of the rector and the other friends of free libraries. The penny rate at first yielded £1037, and now yields about £90 more. The library was opened on 13th October 1884 in all its departments in a private hired dwelling-house; it had then 2600 volumes for home reading, and 1000 volumes of reference; now these two departments include nearly 24,000 volumes, and are excellently catalogued in a well printed volume and supplementary pamphlets. The daily average issue reaches 500 for the lending, and 35 for the reference department. The latter department includes the library of the famous Cheltenham naturalist and ichthyologist, the late Mr. Francis Day, C.I.E., which was presented by the Misses Day, and the Buchanan Collection, purchased out of a bequest of £500 from the late Miss Grace Isabella Buchanan. Much importance is attached to the local collection, and a popular exhibition of Gloucestershire books, maps, and engravings has been held; there is also a good juvenile library. The committee are much embarrassed by heavy charges for repayment of loans; and have few extraneous sources of income. A grant of £100 per year is obtained for the purchase of technological books, and this is very well expended. An appeal for aid in conjunction with the school of art and the school of science realised £1152—£900 of it from three donors—and a further sum of £837 for a jubilee tower. The three institutions work in complete harmony under the same roof, and the local press and the local schoolmasters very much aid the work of these institutions.

Newark-on-Trent

is a town of similar rate-yielding capacity to Runcorn (see below), but much more fortunate in the possession of a handsome and excellently designed library and reading-rooms and an endowment for the librarian's salary, presented to the town, which had produced much of his wealth, by the late Sir William Gilstrap, Bart. The gift was valued at £10,000, and has been increased by a later sum of £2000. The original offer led to the adoption of the Acts in 1882, and in 1883 the first rate was levied, and realised £210—the sum that a penny rate still produces. There are 7000 volumes in the library, which possesses lending, reference, and children's departments. About two hundred books are bought and twelve presented each year. The institution is continuously open from ten in the morning to nine in the evening of every week day. Two hundred persons use the reading-room, 150 books are borrowed and 30 consulted on the average every day. It is doubtful if another town of its size in England is as well off for library privileges as this historic Nottinghamshire market-town.

Runcorn

furnishes a typical instance of what may be accomplished in a small town of 20,000 inhabitants, without any very special gifts, and in hired premises. The adoption of the Acts by a large majority at a public meeting held on the 19th December 1881 was the crowning of a two years' press advocacy, which had been inaugurated by a paper read before the Literary Institute on the 8th December 1879. The books (800 volumes) and book-cases of the Institute were generously transferred to the free library, and with gifts of 460 volumes from sundry donors and the purchase of 470 others, by the end of the first year a good library had been formed. The rate produced £171; donations of money amounting to £36 were also received, and the year ended with a balance of £60 to carry forward and render possible the opening of a reading-room in 1883. The product of the penny rate had increased by about £22 in 1896, the fourteenth year of the library's existence. A beginning was made in the Board Room of the old Commissioners, but afterwards accommodation was found at the Town Hall, where the library and two small reading-rooms are now located. The total annual cost to the committee for lighting, heating, and cleaning is £36. The librarian, an intelligent and enthusiastic official, is allowed to hold a second corporate post, and thereby valuable services are retained for the moderate sum available as salary. The library is open for two hours on five evenings a week, and also twice a week in the afternoons. The reading-rooms are open during several hours of each week day. About five hundred volumes are annually added to the library, and of these about fifty are presented. Lectures on the books in the library are given every winter in the Technical School hard by, the reading-room having been found too small for the purpose. About ninety volumes per diem are lent out, and the present stock of books is nearly eight thousand. The library is very popular, and the chief difficulty experienced has been an overwhelming demand for books in the early days of the library's existence.

Truro

was the first town in Cornwall to adopt the Public Libraries Acts, and the first by a long interval. In 1885 the city council's interest was aroused by the late Mr. Norton, and though there was much opposition—opposition strong enough to unseat

Mr. Norton from the council in the following November—a public meeting, held on 7th May 1885, carried the adoption of the Acts. The penny rate brings in £117, but money, books, and furniture were subscribed, a librarian obtained for the modest salary of £20, and, in hired premises, a reading-room and library of 2000 volumes established. The latter was open for one hour each day. Fortune has been kind since then. The late Mr. Octavius Ferris, in 1893, left his estate to several Cornish towns for free library purposes, and Truro benefits by the interest of £2000 and a number of books. Later Mr. J. Passmore Edwards has presented the town with a handsome building, at a cost of £2000. This was opened on 30th April 1896, and is to be open every week day, Fridays excepted, from 8 A.M. to 10 P.M., and for the lending and consultation of books for five hours of five days a week; but on Fridays the institution will close at one o'clock. The librarian is now more nearly adequately paid. The cost of staff is £82 per annum; with no rent, and a present income of £150 a year, this library should have a very useful future. The population of Truro in 1891 was about 11,000.

WREXHAM

The smaller towns in Wales have not adopted the Public Libraries Acts to the extent one would anticipate from the enthusiasm for literature characteristic of Welshmen, but of the few that have,

Wrexham may be considered a type. The population of this town in 1891 was about 12,000. The Acts were adopted in July 1878, and the rate of a penny in the pound collected the same year. This amounted then to £207; in 1896 it reached £228. Donations and subscriptions have not been wanting here. The National Eisteddfod Committee have given £390, and the Wrexham Working Men's Hall Trust Fund about £25, the latter sum annually. These gifts made possible the establishment of lending and reference libraries in October 1889, but a news-room had been hired from the first at a rental of £37. Children under fourteen are not allowed to borrow, nor have local works to any extent been collected. The local press is friendly, and the institution popular with all classes. The funds are assisted by profits from occasional lectures and entertainments. The reference library is open all day, and the lending library in the mornings and evenings. The librarian is also the caretaker, but he has one assistant. About 120 works per diem are lent for home reading, and 10 issued for reference. Visits to the reading-room average 340 per day. There are close upon 4000 volumes in the library, of which 56 are local in character.

Paisley

is the largest town in Scotland coming under the denomination at the head of this chapter. Here the Acts were adopted without much opposition on 25th March 1867. The promise of 12,000 volumes and a considerable collection of local natural history objects as a present from the Paisley Philosophical Association led up to that result. The rate was first levied in 1871, and then realised about £500 ; it now brings in twice as much. The late Sir Peter Coats, who was a very considerable employer of labour in Paisley, built and presented a large museum, library, reading-room, and lecture-hall, which was opened in 1871, and in 1882 he added another museum, a picture-gallery, and a reference library to his former munificent donation. The old Paisley Library contained about 9000 volumes, and the new free library commenced with 12,000. It does not appear that any annual report is published, nor is the present number of books stated ; but according to the curator, about 500 works on an average are issued for home reading. Public lecture courses, exhibitions of pictures, and a museum are happily combined in this institution, but no special care seems to be exercised in the collection of local literature and the materials of local history ; neither is there any evidence of special attention to the needs of children.

Hawick

At Hawick, a busy Scotch town of 19,000 people, a few gentlemen formed themselves into a committee, collected £1200 in subscriptions, requisitioned the council, and secured the adoption of the Acts by public meeting in 1877 ; a reading-room was opened in hired premises in November

1878, and a library in March 1879, and a beginning made with 2250 volumes. The issues of the first year were as many as 30,000. A recreation-room for chess and games was also opened, but later it was discontinued. Nine hundred pounds of the subscribed funds were lent to the council, and the interest thereon paid the rent until such time as a new Town Hall was built, when the town council discharged the debt by providing suitable accommodation for the library. Among the original subscriptions were amounts of £500, £200, and two of £100. The committee are aiming at acquiring a good collection of Scotch topographical and historical works. Teachers in the local Science and Art School hang up in their class-rooms lists of helpful books in the free library. The reading-room is open all day long every week day, and the library three hours every week day morning, and two or three hours almost every week evening. The rate yielded £260 in 1895, yet in 1878 it only brought in £176; there is no rent or loan charge, and the expenditure for salaries is about thirty per cent. of the income. The library now contains 13,000 volumes, and issues 115 works each day for home reading.

Cork

The city of Cork has a population of 75,000, and furnishes an example of energy and effectiveness in the application of the Public Libraries Acts worthy of further imitation in Ireland. The then existing Act had been adopted in 1855, but apparently with the object of using the rate for aiding schools of art in the city; at least until 1877 the amount of a halfpenny in the pound was allocated by the town council to that purpose. In the latter year an Amending Act applying only to Ireland extended the application of the rate to include schools of music, and an additional halfpenny was then levied by the corporation for carrying out that purpose. Thus was the whole amount leviable appropriated, to the exclusion of a free library; nevertheless the question of providing one was often mooted, and on the 12th February 1892 a special committee of the council was appointed to consider and report what steps should be taken to that desired end. This committee advised the adoption of the Technical Instruction Act, 1889, which empowers the levying of a rate of one penny in the pound for purposes comprehended in the aims of the schools of science and art, and the setting free of the rates levied under the Public Libraries Act for the establishment and support of a free library. Their recommendations were adopted by the corporation, and a sub-committee was appointed to report on the necessary practical steps towards starting the library. In the end the mayor, four aldermen and councillors, and ten other gentlemen were appointed a library committee. This was on 22nd July. The present librarian was engaged in October 1892; the first stock of books, 4174 volumes, was housed by 20th March 1893, and an admirably printed catalogue of 162 pages issued by 30th May of the same year. The library now numbers 6000 volumes, has a daily average issue of 245 for home reading, and of 10 for reference, besides 570 visits are made per diem to the reading-room. A second edition of the catalogue, with 100 additional pages, has been published, and this in spite of an embarrassing demand for books, totally inadequate and unsuitable rooms, and an income limited to less than £440—three-farthings in the pound — with an almost complete absence of large donations. The borrowers are principally clerks, students, and artisans, and there is a juvenile section. The books have been admirably selected, and the grouping under subject headings in the catalogue shows more than ordinary intelligence and skill. The library is regarded as a local centre of intellectual life, and most local societies meet in the building where it is installed.

DUNDALK

In Ireland the difficulties of carrying on a free public library are very great, owing to the small yield of the penny rate in most of the towns. Dundalk, with a population of 13,000, may be taken as the type of many towns. Here the rate amounts to less than £94. When the rate was first levied the product did not equal £59. The date of adoption was 17th December 1856, and the want of a good library in the town and district is alleged as the determining cause. The library is only free for reference, as the limited resources do not allow of a free lending library.

Books are lent to borrowers, who pay one penny per week for the privilege—a questionably legal proceeding. The Literary and Scientific Institute of the town dissolved and handed over its 1600 volumes to the Free Library Committee, who in hired premises established a combined library and reading-room in January 1858. No generous donations or bequests have followed, and the yearly presentations of books of general interest amount to the small average of six. In 1865 the committee secured three rooms in the Town Hall, and the library has steadily progressed ever since. The average additions of books for the past five years have been about 100; about 50 books per day are lent out, and 20 consulted in the room, and the stock has gradually grown to 7000. The rooms are open for four hours every week evening. The librarian has one assistant, but the total annual charge for staff only amounts to £35. The income is about £130.

Douglas

In 1885 the legislature in the Isle of Man passed its first Public Library Act, and in February 1886, in consequence of letters and articles in the papers, on the motion of a member of the Douglas Town Board a plebiscite was taken, and the Act adopted by a majority of nearly two to one. A penny rate was levied, and produced £373. The managers of the Douglas and Isle of Man Savings Bank gave £800 towards the establishment, and donations of books were also received. A commencement was made with 3000 works in a hired room, which served as reading-room and lending and reference library. The library now contains 11,250 volumes, issues 146 works per day for home reading, and 43 for reading on the premises. Nearly 300 visits per day are made to the reading-room. Isle of Man local literature is collected. The local press is very friendly, and the *Manx Sun* has recently published some really valuable guides to historical reading prepared by the librarian, and unlocking to the general reader the valuable series of books published by the Master of the Rolls. The library is growing at the rate of 500 volumes per year. The librarian and his assistant have attended the meetings of local societies to read papers on the books in the public library. The rate now produces £480 per year, and the town council is considering a project for building new municipal buildings and a public library.

CHAPTER XII

FREE LIBRARIES UNDER THE ACTS IN SMALL TOWNS (UNDER 10,000 POPULATION) AND VILLAGES

SIXTY-SEVEN places with a population approximating at the highest to 10,000 have adopted the Public Libraries Acts. Possibly the number is greater, for the English Act which gives local authorities the power of adoption does not compel registration of the fact of adoption. The first of these places to adopt the Acts was Hertford in 1855. In 1860 Ennis furnished an instance for Ireland. The first small place in Scotland—the fourth in the kingdom—to put itself under the Acts was Thurso, with a population still under 4000. Aberystwith adopted in 1874, and Welshpool and Bideford in 1877. In the decade 1880-89, 16 small communities took the same course; and from the beginning of 1890 to the end of 1896 there were 45 more adoptions which must be added to the list. Ashton-on-Mersey has united its fortunes with the Sale library authority, and so exemplifies the advantage of the co-operation clauses in the Public Libraries Acts. Millom, in Cumberland, with a population of 9000, seems to have the highest income from the rate, namely, £279, as reported in 1890. This income is much in excess of that of the average place of its size. The very small municipal borough of Queenborough, with its population of about a thousand, has £10 of free library income, and the rural parish of Middle Claydon has to manage on even less than that sum. Buxton, Falmouth, and Middle Claydon fairly well represent what has been done in small places in England and Wales; and Brechin, Thurso, Tarves, and Drumoak stand in a like position for Scotland. Ireland has practically no result to show as yet, though four adoptions — at Banbridge, Nenagh, Dalkey, Newtonards—during the last six years give ground for hope.

BUXTON

At Buxton a scheme for the erection of a new Town Hall on the site of a burnt-out market-house became associated with a proposal to include accommodation for a free library, a petition for the establishment of one having about that time been signed by a number of ratepayers. The Acts were adopted in 1886, and the penny rate forthwith levied and allowed to accumulate a year or two. The first year's product was £200; in 1895-96 the rate yielded £238. About £400 of accumulated rate was spent in the purchase of books, so that when the building was ready in November 1889, the reading-room and library were opened with a stock of 2729 volumes. There had been some slight opposition to the adoption of the Acts, but the proposal to put up a handsome building had a great effect in subduing it. The library now contains 3780 volumes, and is increasing at the rate of 200 volumes per year; it is used by all classes, including the visitors to this bracing town; about 85 volumes per day are taken home for reading, and 3 or 4 works of reference consulted, while 300 to 400 visitors enter the reading-room daily. The nucleus of a museum exists in association therewith, and the library is the centre of much intellectual activity, lectures on nursing, cookery, ambulance work, and geology, having been held on the premises, besides an art school. A sum of £25 a year under the Museums Act is voted by the urban district council in addition to the penny rate. In 1895–96, £128 was paid for interest and repayment of loans and sinking-fund, £55 for salaries, £97 for books, £30 for periodicals and newspapers, and £18 for other purposes. Excluding balances, the total income for that year was £300. The library is open seven hours on each week day excepting Thursdays, when it is open three hours in the morning only. The population of Buxton was about eight thousand in 1891.

Falmouth,

with a population of 5000, adopted the Acts so recently as January 1893, being stimulated thereto by the bequest of £2000 from the late Mr. Octavius Allen Ferris, who left a like sum to several other Cornish towns on the same condition of the adoption of the Public Libraries Acts. The first rate was collected in 1894, and brought in, at one penny, £130; in 1895 the penny realised £143. Mr. Passmore Edwards, the munificent, also included Falmouth in his schemes for the establishment of Cornish free libraries, and built a home for the institution at a cost of £2000, besides presenting more than a thousand volumes. The library was commenced in a hired room with 1200 volumes, but now contains 3000 volumes. Books on local history and local industries receive special attention, and a technical and science and art school is housed in the same building. The library is open for three hours about mid-day three times a week, and three hours of five week evenings. The new building was opened on May day 1896. The balance-sheet for 1895-96 shows total receipts £186, of which sum £27 came from the use of spare rooms. The expenditure has not yet become normal, but the salary of the single paid officer is £65. There is every prospect of a fine future before the free library of Falmouth and its sister institutions at Bodmin, Liskeard, St. Austell, and St. Ives, towns not dissimilar in size.

Middle Claydon

To the rural parish of Middle Claydon, in Buckinghamshire, belongs the credit of pointing the way to the successful application of the Public Libraries Acts to village conditions in England. Certain villages in Scotland had successfully grappled with the village library problem, but their population and their income from the rate had been much larger. The villagers of Middle Claydon, headed by their enthusiastic librarian, Miss Ellin Verney, and by Sir Edmund and Lady Verney, have shown the rest of England that small resources do not necessarily entail mean results. The adoption of the Act of 1892 was carried by 23 votes to 3 in September 1893, and during the next month a library of 120 volumes was opened in a hired schoolroom. Subscriptions provided the first stock of books, and about a hundred volumes of general interest have been given annually. The library now numbers 1100 volumes, and has a branch, which was opened in October 1895. In winter the library is open every evening from 6 to 9.30, and in summer on Wednesday and Saturday evenings. A rent of £8 pays for room, fire, and light. The library provides special books for children, and all books on Bucks charities. The latter are referred to by people from a long distance. A local paper is bound and filed. The library is greatly used and appreciated by labourers. The rate brings in £9 per annum. A paper contributed by Miss Ellin Verney to the Cardiff Conference of the Library Association gives an enthusiastic account of her work (see "The Library," vol. vii. p. 353).

Brechin

At Brechin, a Forfarshire town of 9000 inhabitants, a beautiful, commodious, and well-planned building was opened as a public library in 1893.

The penny rate realises £120, but happily the building is a gift, and there is an endowment bringing in £60 or £70 per annum in addition. The donor, who prefers to be anonymous, offered £5000 on condition of the adoption of the Acts by the town and the collecting of 6000 volumes wherewith to commence the library. The Acts were adopted on the 1st of March 1890, and the "common good," that excellent Scottish institution and municipal reserve fund, provided means for the purchase of the stipulated number of volumes. The news-room and magazine-room were opened on the 6th July 1893, and on the 3rd October following the lending and reference libraries. Three days before the opening of the libraries Mr. R. W. Alexander Gardiner's bequest of 1000 works of reference was received, and sundry smaller subscriptions and donations since have helped to increase the stock of books. Borrowers from eleven to fourteen years of age are admitted under certain restrictions. The reading-room is open from 9 A.M. to 1 P.M. and from 6 P.M. to 10 P.M. every week day; the reference library is open for eight hours, and the lending library for five hours daily, except on Thursdays, when they are open four hours and three hours respectively. The building cost, including fittings, about £3000. In 1893 a grant of £29 was obtained from the funds available in the town for technical instruction, and an application for similar help is lodged yearly. Lectures have been tried as a means of supplementing the income, but they have not been a financial success. The librarian reports that to take full advantage of the space at disposal three times the income is required. About 120 volumes are issued daily for home reading, but no account is kept of consultations in the reference library. Readers may handle and examine books at the counter before making their choice. There is only one official on the staff and a cleaner, and the resources of the institution are too much taxed to make advertising desirable. A recent count showed that 356 persons visited the reading-rooms in one day. Several members of the Books Committee are graduates. Here, surely, is a case where additional private bequests or Government grants might be well bestowed.

Thurso

The population of Thurso in 1891 was, roughly speaking, four thousand, yet this small community adopted the Acts so far back as 1872. In 1873 the first rate was collected, and the public library from 1875 continued and perfected the service to the community previously performed by certain private libraries, which about that time ceased to exist. The penny rate yields £38, but at different times the Library Committee have received extraneous help. In 1876, from an industrial exhibition £100 was received; an anonymous donor gave £300 of North British Railway stock, bringing in, say, £7 per year, and 600 volumes; Mr. Andrew Carnegie, the American millionaire, also gave £325;

and a bazaar realised £508 for building a museum and reading-room. A reading-room and reference library combined were opened so recently as January 1896. The lending library has from the first been housed free of rent in the Town Hall buildings. It commenced with 900 volumes, and now, with the reference library, the institution contains 5620 volumes. The library is open on Wednesdays from six to eight in the evening, and on Saturdays from two to four and seven to nine o'clock each open day. An average of 104 volumes for home reading is attained, 40 are referred to, and 64 visits made to the reading-room. The reading-room appears to be open from 10 A.M. to 9 P.M., presumably every week day. The annual cost of staff is £24.

Tarves

claims to be the first purely rural parish in the kingdom to adopt the Public Libraries Acts. The population is about 2200, and the only aggregated part of it is at Kirktown, where about 150 people live. Yet here the adoption of the Acts was carried by a 6 to 1 majority in December 1883. The library work is continuous with that of an earlier library established in 1878. Two-fifths of a penny in the pound at first was levied, and brought in £22, 10s., now a halfpenny rate realises £29. The nucleus of the library was the bequest of Mr. Melvin, an old schoolmaster, and Mr. Carnegie gave £100 for building a room. Until a room was built the books were deposited in a side room of a public hall. There are now 3250 volumes in the collection, which is growing at the rate of 100 volumes a year. Books are exchanged during three hours of every Saturday. The librarian is paid £3 per annum for his services. There is a small branch five miles from Kirktown, looked after by members of the committee residing in that neighbourhood. A literary society meets on the premises twice a month in winter. It is interesting to know that the most popular authors in this district are Matthew Arnold, J. A. Froude, Smiles, Crockett, "Rolph Boldrewood," and Annie Swan.

Drumoak

On 18th March 1893 the parish of Drumoak adopted the Acts, and in 1894 levied a halfpenny rate, producing £15. Subscriptions and donations for building and books were received, Mr. Carnegie, of New York, giving £25. A lending library was commenced with 452 volumes, and now numbers 601; 41 volumes are issued weekly among a population of 860 persons, which is about one volume to every fourth family. In winter the library hours are from seven to nine every Tuesday evening, in summer, the same hours once a month. The librarian is paid £5 for his services. The free library grew out of the previous existence of a parish church library and a society library. About ten volumes per year are presented, and the stock is increasing at the rate of fifty per annum.

A word or two may be said regarding the possibilities of the Public Libraries Acts in villages and rural places. Instances have been given of the adoption of the Acts to support a circulating library alone, but it should also be noted that the Public Libraries Acts may be adopted to hire and furnish an evening reading-room. Probably there are villages where this course would be the better one to pursue. Rent is low in villages, papers and periodicals are cheap, lighting and fire need not be very expensive, and a cheerful warm room furnished with papers and a few reference books would be an admirable corrective to the village inn. There are few villages where the legal rate would amount to less than that at Middle Claydon, but with even less than £9 something could be done on the lines suggested. Where an enthusiastic and popular person is willing to undertake a crusade of several neighbouring parishes to obtain a simultaneous adoption of the Acts and a common management, much more might be accomplished. From a common stock of books boxes might be sent out regularly to the several villages for issue, or the same end might be served by an agreement between the committee of the co-operating villages and the nearest town centre having a public library, in which latter case a greater variety of choice and a more efficient management of details would be secured.

With greater elasticity in the law, much more might be done. Why cannot every county be divided into library districts—just as many counties in England are divided into technical instruction districts—and each district be allowed to adopt the Acts for itself, and establish its own library authority? Such a district would then be able to have its common fund of books—a library of no mean pretensions—with a skilled and trained officer at its head, and a proper distributing agency reaching every corner of its area at least once a week. Various detailed plans have been suggested to accomplish this scheme. Mr. J. D. Brown, librarian of the Clerkenwell Public Library, has proposed (1) travelling library vans on a similar principle to the travelling dairy school vans of certain counties; the present writer has suggested (2) combinations of a permanent and a movable section of a library at each of certain fixed stations, forming a "circuit" under one control; Mr. W. R. Credland, deputy chief librarian of the Manchester Free Libraries, has suggested (3) county control, and working in conjunction with county technical instruction committees. Surely what has been excellently done for Paris by its central control and its district committees of the municipal libraries of its numerous arrondissements, or for New York State by its country delivery system, or for New South Wales by the Sydney Central Library distributing agency, may teach the United Kingdom a way to solve the pressing library problem of the hour, How best to furnish our villages with a regular service of wholesome and stimulating reading?

It is undoubtedly true that many villages already

have pleasant reading-rooms and libraries. Unfortunately most of these are under a strong suspicion of religious or political bias, and are not governed by a publicly elected body. The history of the Bray Parochial Libraries, referred to in the first chapter of this work, is a standing warning against management by the village parson uncontrolled by representative trustees, even when the parson is under a bond to perform the duty of maintaining free access to a library under his charge. At present there are in operation several co-operative ventures for the provision of villagers with books. In Cambridgeshire the Technical Instruction Committee of the county council possesses some fifty or sixty circulating boxes of books, each containing about fifty volumes of an instructive character and of high authority, which are circulated among the villages. A box usually remains for twelve months in each village, and the books are, under suitable regulations, gratuitously at the service of any villager. Here, then, is something very like Mr. Credland's plan in actual operation. The Union of Lancashire and Cheshire Institutes and the Yorkshire Union of Mechanics' Institutes have similar plans in operation, but in each of these cases a subscription is demanded from the village committee for the quarterly rotation of the boxes of books. The literature provided is, of course, not limited to subjects of science and the useful arts, as in Cambridgeshire. In Lancashire and Cheshire a circular of information supplied to each village suggests the propriety of adopting the Public Libraries Acts, and of using a part of the rate for subscription to the Union of Institutes Village Library Scheme, so as to secure a regular supply of reading, with great variety of choice, on the cheapest possible terms.

There is now every reason to believe that the opening years of the twentieth century will see a considerable development in this phase of public library work.

CHAPTER XIII

ENDOWED AND VOLUNTARY FREE LIBRARIES

THE subject of endowed free public libraries is only of very subordinate importance in the plan of this work, though it certainly deserves fuller treatment elsewhere. At least one of these libraries, the Mitchell Library at Glasgow, is of first-rate practical importance; others have an antiquarian character, like Dr. Shepheard's Library at Preston, founded in 1759, and now housed in the free public library of that town, or the Thomlinson Library, founded in 1741, similarly housed in the Newcastle Free Library; others again, whilst free to all comers by the conditions of their establishment, leave themselves open to a strong suspicion of partisanship in their management, as, for instance, the Hadley and Barnet Library, established in 1888 by a bequest of £10,000 from Mrs. Julia Hyde, the former lady of the manor, a condition of the bequest being that the trustees were to be the rector and churchwardens of the two parishes. Of course there is nothing to be objected to this last-named class of endowed library beyond its inherent deficiency as compared with a library whose trust is of a more generally representative character. Libraries restricted in their use to academic students are beyond the main scope of this work.

Humphrey Chetham, citizen of Manchester, founded a celebrated free library in 1653, which has been uninterruptedly open to public use ever since. This delightful library contains most important original texts of old English writers and monkish chroniclers, and is also rich in other works of antiquarian and historical interest. It was long regarded as the first free library established in the kingdom. In this library Harrison Ainsworth wrote several of his historical romances. With all its excellences, and apart from sentiment, we must place Chetham's Library in a class much inferior to that which would include the King Street Free Reference Library in the same city.

Archbishop Tenison's Library, established in 1685 for the free use of the inhabitants of certain Westminster parishes, had departed far from the intentions of its founder by the middle of this century.

Dr. Williams's Library is well known to Nonconformist ministers, who appreciate its present facilities as a lending library, but few know that this library originated in an endowment of the founder's in 1716 and from the bequest of his library.

Some other old endowments have been incidentally mentioned in the first chapter, and it is not necessary to dwell upon them here. The age of the endowment of public libraries has not yet passed. Recent years have seen several such established. In November 1874, at a town's meeting held at High Wycombe, Mr. J. V. Griffits, Q.C., the Recorder of Reading, offered to provide a library and maintain it for three years, and if at the end of that time a sufficient subscription could be raised to endow it, promised to hand it over to the corporation for public use for ever. Mr. Griffits bought the old British schools, altered and enlarged them, and was able to see his scheme successfully launched.

At Otley, in Yorkshire, on 2nd August 1892, a library and free school, built, furnished, and endowed at the sole cost of Mr. Robinson Gill, stone merchant of New York, was opened.

At Horwich, in Lancashire, accumulated ground-rents belonging to the parish have been utilised in the establishment of a public free library, without recourse to a rate.

Out of city charity funds the Charity Commissioners have not only erected Polytechnics, but three fine endowed libraries in the City of London, namely, the St. Bride's Institute, near Fleet Street, the Bishopsgate Institute, and the Cripplegate Institute. It is contended that these institutes, which are well provided with reading-rooms and lending libraries, abolish the need of the adoption of the Public Libraries Acts within the city area. This contention is unworthy of the great city corporation, seeing that its Guildhall Library could be vastly increased in size and usefulness by a more liberal supply of funds.

Our plan allows only of a detailed description of two of these endowed libraries.

GLASGOW—THE MITCHELL LIBRARY

The largest of modern endowed free libraries in the United Kingdom is undoubtedly the Mitchell Library at Glasgow. The founder, the late Mr. Stephen Mitchell, was born on 19th September 1789 at Linlithgow, and was educated in the Burgh Grammar School. At sixteen he was apprenticed to a firm of merchants. His father dying in 1820, he became a co-partner with his younger brother in the business at Linlithgow. In 1825 the business was transferred to Glasgow. Here the firm —Stephen Mitchell & Son—built up a large trade in tobacco. Mr. Stephen Mitchell took great interest in his work-people, and encouraged them to attend the mechanics' classes at the Andersonian Institution, and even established night schools at the works for the boys and girls in his employ. In 1869 he retired from the business, and chose to spend his later days at Moffat. Here some of his happiest hours were spent in the back-room of a bookseller's shop, where a subscription library was housed. (This library had been started in the year of Mr. Mitchell's birth, at the suggestion of Robert Burns.) Mr. Mitchell died suddenly on the 21st April 1874 while taking a walk to the "Wells." His will contained a bequest of a sum amounting to £66,998, 10s. 6d., which was to be put out to interest until it reached £70,000 and then used for the establishment of a free library for the city of Glasgow, managed by a committee of the town council. The constitution and early history of the library are briefly summarised by Mr. F. T. Barrett in his excellent "Concise Guide to the Mitchell Library," second edition, 1894:—

"It must be *one* large public library. It must be accessible to the public for purposes of reference and consultation. It must be general and comprehensive in character, so as to be of value to readers of every class and occupation; and should aim at representing every phase of human thought and every variety of human opinion. It should acquire such books as from their rarity and value cannot generally be procured by private persons. No book was to be refused admission merely because it controverted present views in religion or politics.

"The library was opened in temporary premises in Ingram Street in November 1877 with 14,432 volumes, and remained there till May 1890.

"The intervening period witnessed a remarkable development, both in the library itself and in the use made of it by the public. The 14,000 volumes at the opening had increased to 89,000; and the number of volumes consulted by readers amounted to 4,680,000, a number, it is believed, much greater than had ever before been issued during the first twelve and a half years in any other reference library."

The library has been formed on broad and generous principles. The purchases include the whole of or selections from the libraries of the following well-known scholars : Professor Innes, editor of many Bannatyne, Maitland, and Spalding Club publications; Mr. James Maidment, the antiquary; the Rev. W. Stevenson, erstwhile a Professor of Church History in Edinburgh University; Mr. William Euing, founder of the Euing Musical Library in Anderson's University; and the Rev. Principal Morison, D.D.

Very important gifts and supplementary bequests have also been received. Mr. Richard Chalmers in 1880 bequeathed 1000 volumes, chiefly of an educational and philological character. In the following year Bailie Moir bequeathed his well-chosen library of 2420 books and nearly 1000 pamphlets, with permission to exchange duplicates, besides £11,500, which at present yields £100 per annum, after payment of an annuity with which it is temporarily charged. In 1880 and in 1882 Mr. J. Wyllie Guild added more than a hundred early productions of the Glasgow press, and these have become the nucleus of a fine library of Glasgow printing; while in 1883 the library received a large gift of Scottish literature, chiefly poetical, from Mr. Alexander Gardyne, of London, in all about 2250 books and booklets. The "Poets' Corner" in 1895 had grown to 6075 volumes, of which about 1151 relate to the poet Burns. Important bequests have also been received from Mr. Councillor David Logan (£500), Mr. Donald M'Pherson (£500), and Mr. Louis Edward Campbell (£4000), while the University of Glasgow has presented 2000 volumes of duplicates. A fully-equipped magazine-room has always been a part of the Mitchell Library establishment, and as the daily average issue of works has been for years close upon 1700, it is obvious that the expenses of maintenance must be very large. These were met without undue strain until 1889, when the reduction of the rate of interest from 4¼ to 3 per cent. plunged the committee into difficulties on the capital endowment. Temporary relief was obtained in 1891, when the town council voted a sum of £2000 per annum out of moneys received from Government under the Local Taxation (Customs and Excise) Act, 1890. It is thought that this source of revenue may cease at any time, after short notice. Quite recently the library committee submitted to the town council a report, suggesting among other steps the propriety of considering the adoption of the Public Libraries Acts, but this proposal was opposed in the town council, and by a small majority disapproved.

The library now contains 123,000 volumes, and is of a very high level as to quality. The only publications of the library are a series of general reports and two editions of the "Concise Guide." A catalogue in book form has been for some time in preparation, but its progress has been greatly impeded by the rapid growth of the library, and by the necessity of maintaining the temporary printed catalogues for the use of the readers.

There are in Glasgow two other excellent but much smaller free consulting libraries, namely,

Baillie's Institution and Stirling's Library, the latter of which has passed its centenary. These institutions are situated in the same street with the Mitchell Library.

The following proposals for a scheme of free public libraries for Glasgow is prefixed to Mr. F. T. Barrett's "Concise Guide"; it is clearly based upon proposals of Mr. Barrett's own, made as far back as 1888. Why such reasonable proposals have not been adopted and a penny rate levied to carry them out is a perpetual puzzle to the English municipalities, which in so many matters have learned, and are still learning, from this forward and enterprising Scottish city.

The Scheme

I. A large central library, including—
  (*a*) The principal reference or consulting library, to be developed and made as complete as possible.
  (*b*) Central news-room, with a large collection of newspapers and periodicals, representing all localities, trades, opinions, and interests, with a selection of American and Continental serials.
  (*c*) Central lending library, with large collection of books for home reading.

(It does not necessarily follow that the several departments of the central library must be in the same building, but they should be conveniently placed within the central area of the city.)

II. A series of branch or district libraries, not less than six or seven in number, and so distributed throughout the several quarters of the city as to secure that every inhabitant will have one within a convenient distance of his dwelling. Each of the branch libraries would have the same features, in a smaller scale, as the central library, namely, a collection of reference books for consultation at the library only; a lending, or circulating department, from which books would be drawn for home reading; and a news-room, with a selection of the papers of the day and of the week, and a number of magazines and other periodicals.

Subject to the necessary rules and regulations, all the inhabitants of the city would be entitled to the enjoyment of all the privileges furnished by such a series of public libraries without any payment beyond the rate of one penny in the pound of rental (one shilling a year on a £12 house), which is the largest sum leviable under the Act.

In order to extend the value of the libraries to the utmost, borrowers would have liberty to draw books from any or from all of the lending departments. By means of a daily express service books could be brought from branches for the use of readers in other districts, thus placing the resources of all the libraries at the disposal of borrowers, in whatever part of the city resident.

The Mayer Library, Bebington

Mr. Joseph Mayer, F.S.A., once the owner of a prosperous jewellery business in the city of Liverpool, was ever a lover of the curious, the antiquarian, and the artistic. All his life he was a collector. To what purpose may be seen by a walk through the Mayer Museum at Liverpool, with its fine pottery, select manuscripts, and Egyptian remains. Mr. Mayer did not, however, content himself by enriching the city where his business lay; he benefited the village of his residence and retirement also. For years he kept open a valuable library, and made it free to all comers. This he opened in January 1866. The library, the museum, the lecture-hall, and the beautiful little park attached thereto, were managed by himself until his death in 1886. He added thousands of books to the 8794 volumes in the library after he made it free to the public, increased the museum collections, and improved the property; but he left no clue to the cost of all this. On 18th June 1878 he conveyed the property to the churchwardens of Lower Bebington and their successors, to be held in trust for public use, and appointed joint managers of the institution. The deed provided, that, upon the death of these managers, the churchwardens for the time being, the chairman of the sanitary authority for the district, and one or two persons residing within a radius of three miles from the recreation grounds, and appointed by the sanitary authority, should be their successors. The effect of Mr. Mayer's will was, that subject to the payment of debts, funeral and testamentary expenses, and of legacies and annuities given to various persons, the nett proceeds of the whole estate were to be handed over by the executors of the will to the managers for the support and maintenance of the institutions. Mr. Mayer seems to have thought that the sale of his collections, other than the objects in his village museum, would have realised a very large sum, but the nett cash result of the sale was only £5601.

Until recently the accounts of the executors were not closed, but little more can now be expected for the increase of the endowment.

The Public Libraries Acts, however, were adopted by the urban district council of Lower Bebington in January 1894, in response to the unanimous vote of a public meeting of ratepayers, and the Mayer Free Library is soon to be transferred to the local authority to receive a new lease of vigorous life as an institution under the Public Libraries Act. At the present time the number of volumes in the library is 19,400, but since Mr. Mayer's death very few new books have been added, and in consequence the number of readers has considerably diminished, and the volumes issued have become less in proportion; yet in 1896, 13,154 volumes were lent out, the library being open on three evenings and one afternoon—in all seven hours—per week. There were 538 readers registered in 1895. Besides the lending library there is a reference library, containing a strong element of historical literature and some rare things, particularly chap-books, Napoleon caricatures, and early printed books. The museum is not of much value, but reflects the eccentric taste of its founder. A scheme of free lectures which Mr. Mayer projected has not been carried out on account of scarcity of funds. An approximate statement drawn up in 1893 shows an average annual expenditure of £242, 17s., and a deficiency of income amounting to £108, 3s.; but this statement takes no account of the Mayer Hall, containing the museum. The buildings are of an attractive character, and have two towers, one of them provided with a public clock. The situation of the library is an exceedingly pleasant one.

Voluntary Free Libraries

The friends of free public libraries under the Acts have in many places sought to bring home their advantages by establishing voluntary free libraries, in the belief that they would be succeeded by rate-supported libraries. At Hull such a library was established by Mr. James Reckitt, at his sole expense, as has been already related. At Bath, during 1877-80, a library of this kind existed, but after the fourth rejection of the Acts in 1880 it was closed. At Paddington, at Marylebone, and at St. Pancras, such libraries have long been maintained. The history of that at Marylebone may be taken as typical, though the People's Palace Library and the Bethnal Green Free Library have attracted more public attention by their greater size, and a larger share of public beneficence by their position in the East of London.

The Marylebone Free Public Library Association was formed in 1887. It proposed at first to raise money sufficient to build a large central free library, to be offered to the borough on condition of its maintenance under the Public Libraries Acts and extension by branches. Conditional promises up to nearly £8000 were obtained, but the poll of the ratepayers in 1888 resulted in the rejection of the Acts. The committee of the Association then altered their policy, and sought to demonstrate the advantages of free public libraries by establishing a voluntary one in a very poor part of Marylebone. This was opened in Lisson Grove by Lord Charles Beresford on 12th August 1889. The success of the effort was such that a second library and news-room was provided by a special effort in Mortimer Street. One thousand pounds was raised for this purpose, and of that sum Lady Howard de Walden gave £500. The Mortimer Street room was opened on 1st May 1890 by H.R.H. the Duke of Fife, President of the Association. The work accomplished at these two centres may be briefly tabulated here :—

Books Issued.	Report Terminating in					
	1890.	1891.	1892.	1893.	1894.	1895.
For home reading . . .	6,340	36,922	52,001	49,341	18,423	15,630
For reference .	6,204	21,276	19,229	19,475	7,212	5,952
Readers in news-rooms	112,191	336,711	369,002	418,472	164,060	151,241

The great falling off noticeable in 1894, and after, was due to a very decisive rejection of the Public Libraries Acts in June 1893, and the subsequent falling off in the funds. The Association closed for a time both the libraries, a little later to reopen only one of them. The polls of 1891 and 1892 had shown so favourable a progress that hopes of success ran high, but it happened that the local rates in that year had been much increased, and doubtless led to the fifth rejection of the Acts at Marylebone. The Association has now recovered from that stunning blow, so the sixth report speaks cheerfully of yet another attempt at an early date to secure the adoption of the Public Libraries Acts. "'Tis not in mortals to command success, but [they've] done more, deserved it." Some items from the second annual report may fitly close this chapter. The issues of works by the principal novelists were as under:—

Austen (5 vols.)	86 times.
Brontë (8 vols.).	181 ,,
Dickens (50 vols.)	703 ,,
"George Eliot" (29 vols.).	573 ,,
Gaskell (13 vols.)	219 ,,
Henty (25 vols.)	496 ,,
C. Kingsley (19 vols.)	343 ,,
Marryat (21 vols.)	302 ,,
Oliphant (32 vols.)	413 ,,
Scott (53 vols.).	436 ,,
Thackeray (30 vols.).	471 ,,
Ward's "Robert Elsmere" (3 copies)	71 ,,
Yonge (31 vols.)	486 ,,

The following non-fictional issues are very instructive:—

Booth's "Darkest England" (4 copies)	281 times.
Dean Farrar's. "Life of Christ," &c. (7 vols.)	146 ,,
Smiles's "Duty," "Character," &c. (9 vols.)	137 ,,
Herbert Spencer's Works (9 vols.)	106 ,,
Darwin's Works	152 ,,
Works on Electricity (24 vols.)	167 ,,
Musical Works (30 vols.).	210 ,,

Ruskin's Works (24 vols.)	237 times.
Wood's Natural History Works (16 vols.)	125 ,,
Froude's "History of England"	116 ,,
Volumes from Story of the Nations Series	132 ,,
Volumes from English Men of Letters Series	112 ,,
The *Encyclopædia Britannica*	137 ,,
Carlyle's Works (25 vols.)	112 ,,

The Association is still in need of funds; the Rev. Canon Barker is the chairman of the executive committee, and Mr. Frank Debenham is the honorary secretary. Both these gentlemen have been indefatigable in their efforts for the good of the Marylebone Free Library movement.

EPILOGUE

The reader who has followed the writer thus far will have perceived, it is hoped, the national importance of the free library, the variety of its manifestations, the limitations of its resources, the devoted service and generosity it has called forth. Lack of space has precluded any treatment of the free library in the Colonies or abroad, but it may confidently be said, that the history of the free library in the United States, though strikingly different, is no less remarkable; that the more settled parts of Australia and South Africa do not lag far behind the mother-country; and that in France, in Germany, in Italy, in Denmark, the progress of recent years in British and American libraries has excited considerable interest, and may be expected to lead to a healthy rivalry in the near future.

APPENDIX

STATISTICS

RELATING TO FREE PUBLIC LIBRARIES IN THE UNITED KINGDOM

COLLECTED AND ARRANGED BY JOHN J. OGLE

(*July–December* 1896)

STATISTICS RELATING TO LONDON

A. Name of place. B. Population in thousands (1891). C. Date of adoption of Public Libraries Acts. D. Date of opening of first reading-room or library. E. Rate per pound of assessment, and product in the first year. F. Rate per pound of assessment and product in 1895-96. G. Important donations and bequests.

A.	B.	C.	D.	E.		F.		G.
Wandsworth (one branch)	47	3/7/83	21/3/85	..	£..	1d.	£1195	Dr. Longstaff gave a reading-room and £3000
Lambeth (five branches)	275	14/12/86	1887	½d.	2400	1d.	6256	About £43,000 in buildings, books, and money
St. Martin-in-the-Fields	15	10/2/87	1/1/89	1d.	1833	1d.	2243	....
St. Paul, Covent Garden	2	3/8/92		1d.	..	1d.	415	Added to St. Martin's Library District
Battersea (two branches)	150	16/3/87	1887	1d.	2300	1d.	3128	£2500 from sale of parish lands
Putney	18	28/3/87	7/4/88	..	..	1d.	623	Say about £150; some books
Chelsea (one branch)	96	-/5/87	-/11/87	1d.	2250	1d.	3100	£900 for books. Earl Cadogan, £350 and a site; Sir C. W. Dilke, £500
Kensington . .	166	-/6/87	2/1/88	½d.	3270	½d.	3953	Mr. J. Heywood presented 4000 volumes. Public subscriptions, £900. Sir Richard and Lady Burton left 2000 volumes
Clapham . . .	44	7/7/87	1889	1d.	950	1d.	1060	£2000 for building, £180 for books
Bermondsey . .	85	-/11/87	-/11/91	1d.	1460	1d.	1622	£500 for books
Rotherhithe (one branch)	39	-/11/87	-/10/90	1d.	680	1d.	820	....
Clerkenwell . .	66	13/12/87	20/11/88	1d.	1380	1d.	1550	£900 cash, £300 worth of books
Hammersmith (one branch)	98	-/12/87	-/8/89	..	..	½d.	850	A site for Shepherd's Bush Branch. A building from Mr. J. Passmore Edwards
Christ Church, Southwark	13	22/2/88	1/10/89	1d.	420	1d.	480	£20 for books
Camberwell (four branches)	235	1889	-/3/90	..	..	..	..	£13,500 in gifts from Mr. J. Passmore Edwards

FREE PUBLIC LIBRARIES.

H. The result of special efforts to raise funds. J. Number of hours per week the central institution is open—figures in brackets hours for issue of books (R. L. means in the reference library, L. L. in the lending library). K. Percentage annual cost (*a*) of central establishment, (*b*) of branches, (*c*) of loans and rent. L. Daily average issue of books (*a*) in lending libraries, (*b*) in reference libraries. M. Daily average number of visits to reading-rooms. N. Present number of books in libraries. O. Librarian's or other informant's name.

H.	J.	K.			L.		M.	N.	O.
		a.	*b.*	*c.*	*a.*	*b.*			
	78 (66)	..	Slight	11	350	..	1000	15,000	Cecil T. Davis.
Nil	84 (65)	?	?	?	2692	232	?	69,907	[F. J. Burgoyne.]
Nil	78 (R. L. 72, L. L. 44)	..	Nil	28	251	278	3593	27,678	Thomas Mason.
Nil	92 (R. L. 78, L. L. 58)	75	..	25	900	70	3000	36,000	Lawrence Inkster.
Little	75	..	..	50	260	?	..	7,000	C. F. St. Helier Tweney.
Nil	84	70	30	30	704	101	1769	28,561	J. Henry Quinn.
..	82	?	?	25	784	100	2904	38,000	Herbert Jones.
Lectures realised £1	84 (R. L. 66, L. L. 60)	..	Nil	28	359	15	?	8,000	J. Reed Welch.
Nil	75 (66½)	..	Nil	50	400	50	1500	12,500	John Frowde.
Nil	78	..	Slight	25	125	21	1200	5,185	Herbert A. Shuttleworth.
Circular appeal, small success	84 (R. L. 84, L. L. 63)	..	Nil	25	360	91	2010	15,500	James D. Brown.
Nil	78 (52½)	?	?	?	450	12	1600	22,800	S. Martin.
Nil	78 (60)	..	Nil	?	71	23	600	4,320	Henry Wm. Bull.
..	?	?	?	?	2040	..	..		Edward Foskett.

STATISTICS RELATING TO LONDON

A.	B.	C.	D.	E.		F.		G.
					£		£	
Whitechapel ..	32	14/12/89	6/5/90	1d.	1544	..	1289	Mr. S. Montague, M.P., £700, others bringing up to £5000
Streatham ...	43	21/12/89	—/4/91	1d.	1100	1d.	1478	Mr. H. Tate gave a site and building = £8000
Stoke Newington	31	5/2/90	12/10/91	..	..	1d.	738	About £150
St. George, Hanover Square (one branch)	78	24/6/90	1894	½d.	3503	½d.	3900	Site given by the Duke of Westminster; donations for books. Natural history collection
Newington ..	116	—/10/90	1891	1d.	1700	1d.	1830	Books and money to about £300 value
Poplar (one branch)	56	—/12/90	5/12/92	1d.	1324	1d.	1363	£1450 subscribed for site
St. Leonard's, Shoreditch (one branch)	124	—/3/91	10/5/93	¾d.	..	¾d.	1972	From Mr. J. Passmore Edwards, £8250 and 1000 books. Land valued at £720 from the Lawrence family
St. Giles's District	40	12/5/91	1892	½d.	796	1d.	1898	Duke of Bedford, £600; about £157 besides
Holborn District	34	13/5/91	—/1/93	½d.	681	1d.	771	About £35
Penge	20	9/9/91	18/6/92	1d.	528	1d.	551	A few books
St. Saviour's, Southwark	14	7/11/91	2/11/94	..	870	..	900	About £2000
Hampstead (one branch)	68	1893	Spring, 1894	..	..	1d.	2800	Mr. Harben gave £5000 for a building. The Lord of the Manor, £350

Returns were not supplied by the following library districts; the year of adoption is given after each name, and the population in thousands enclosed in brackets:—Westminster (St. Margaret and St. John), 1856(56); Fulham, 1886(92); Lewisham, 1890(72); Bromley by

FREE PUBLIC LIBRARIES (*Continued*).

H.	J.	K. a.	K. b.	K. c.	L. a.	L. b.	M.	N.	O.
	?	..	..	23	248	91	3000	11,560	W. E. Williams.
Nil	78 (52½)	..	Nil	Nil	?	0	1350	16,000	Thomas Everatt.
Nil	..	..	?	22	360	32	1050	11,016	George Preece.
Nil	78	63	37	30	654	100	1900	26,300	Frank Pacy.
Projected bazaar resulted in some donations	78 (L. L. 55½, R. L. 72)	..	Nil	55	613	51	2500	13,756	Richard W. Mould.
Nil	78 (L. L. 66, R. L. 72)	90	10	20	350	50	1200	10,000	H. Rowlatt.
From non-residents' subscriptions, small	78 (72)	?	?	?	337	68	2450	17,081	W. C. Plant.
Nil	78	..	Nil	44	166	39	1530	6,700	W. A. Taylor.
	78 (R. L. 72, L. L. 35)	..	Nil	20	200	17	930	7,244	H. Hawkes.
..	81	..	Nil	6	220	..	200	4,521	William Bridle.
A box in the library produces 15s. per week	90 (58)	..	Nil	56	185	4	1300	9,484	H. D. Roberts.
Nil	84 (R. L. 69, L. L. 52½)	?	?	?	400	15	700	7,500	W. E. Doubleday.

Bow, 1891 (70); Woolwich, 1895 (41); Ratcliff, 1895 (15); Mile End, 1896 (108); St. George the Martyr, 1896 (60); St. George in the East, 1896 (46); Bow, 1896 (40).

STATISTICS RELATING TO FREE PUBLIC

A. Name of place. B. Population in thousands (1891). C. Date of adoption of Public Libraries Acts. D. Date of opening of first reading-room or library. E. Rate per pound of assessment, and product in the first year. F. Rate per pound of assessment, and product in 1895–96. G. Important donations and bequests.

A.	B.	C.	D.	E.		F.		G.
England—				£		£		
Liverpool (seven branches)	518	Local Act dated 3/5/52	18/10/52	1d.	4000	1d.	13,527	Subscriptions, £1389; 4000 books. Brown Library = £35,000. J. Shipley, £1000
Manchester (fifteen branches)	505	20/8/52	6/9/52	½d.	1951	..	18,857	£13,000 before the opening. A large part of the cost of the Openshaw branch was paid by the Whitworth legatees. £240 subscriptions towards the Newton Heath branch
Sheffield (four branches)	324	6/10/53	–/2/56	..	1368	1d.	5,580	Mr. Samuel Bailey gave 1983 volumes
Birmingham (eight branches)	478	21/2/60	3/4/61	..	4000 in 1868	1¼d.	13,722	£15,000 collected after the fire
Leeds (twenty-one branches)	367	12/3/68	..	1d.	2500	1d.	5,858	....
Hull (three branches)	260	10/12/92	2/10/93	1d.	3032	1d.	3,037	The Reckitt Library (building, books, and endowment)
Scotland—								
Edinburgh (one branch)	261	26/10/86	9/6/90	½d.	3560	¾d.	6,800	Mr. Carnegie gave building = £50,000. £1436 from Edinburgh 1886 exhibition profits
Ireland—								
Belfast	256	–/11/82	13/10/88	1d.	2212	1d.	3,283	....
Dublin	270	Not yet formally adopted						
Thomas Street .	..	..	1884	..	..	..	500	
Capel Street .	..	..	1884	..	..	..	500	....

LIBRARIES IN FIRST-CLASS TOWNS.

H. The result of special efforts to raise funds. J. Number of hours per week the central institution is open—figures in brackets hours for issue of books (K. L. means in the reference library, L. L. in the lending library). K. Percentage annual cost (*a*) of central establishment, (*b*) of branches, (*c*) of loans and rent. L. Daily average issue of books (*a*) in lending libraries, (*b*) in reference libraries. M. Daily average number of visits to reading-rooms. N. Present number of books in libraries. O. Librarian's or other informant's name.

H.	J.	K.			L.		M.	N.	O.
		a.	b.	c.	a.	b.			
Very slight	67½ (64)	54	46	?	1883	2340	1687 (central only)	179,667	Peter Cowell.
Nil	..	24	76	12	5070	1120	12,000	266,514	Charles W. Sutton.
	69 (R.L. 69, L.L. 59)	?	?	21	1469	158		108,417	[Samuel Smith.]
	78 (R.L. 78, L.L. 66)	64	36	31	2663	1100		209,497	J. D. Mullins.
Nil	81 (R.L. 69, L.L. 63)	39	61	3	3073	464	2200 (central only)	191,096	James Yates.
Nil	81 (R.L. 69, L.L. 66)	44	56	16	1760	25	2250	52,588	William F. Lawton.
Nil	78 (72)	?	?	Nil	2000	380	7000	91,000	Hew Morrison.
Nil	71 (60)	..	Nil	27	673	168	3059	33,469	George H. Elliott.
	86	..	..	?	80	30	700	6,000	N. Rice.
	83 (74)	..	..	?	112	35	900	6,000	Patrick Grogan.

STATISTICS RELATING TO FREE PUBLIC

A. Name of place. B. Population in thousands (1891). C. Date of adoption of Public Libraries Acts. D. Date of opening of first reading-room or library. E. Rate per pound of assessment, and product in the first year. F. Rate per pound of assessment, and product in 1895-96. G. Important donations and bequests.

A.	B.	C.	D.	E.		F.		G.
				£		£		
England— Salford (six branches)	198	Under Museums Act '45 1893	1849	..	652	1.26d.	..	Donations and subscriptions for purchase, adaptation, and extension of premises. Langworthy bequest = £10,000. Extensive gifts of books
Norwich ..	101	27/9/50	1857	½d.	400	1d.	1245	£300 for books; £300 for juvenile library; £150 for technical books
Bolton (three branches)	115	26/3/52	1854	½d.	..	1d.	..	....
Birkenhead (two branches)	100	16/2/56	1856	1d.	450	1d.	1854	£343, 10s. for ornamenting building
Blackburn ..	120	15/9/53	1862	½d.	263	1d.	.1840	£400 from working-men; about £700 in other money gifts. Dodgson bequest of pictures; Ainsworth bequest of books = 700 volumes
Wolverhampton	82	8/2/69	30/9/69	1d.	830	1½d.	1200	The "Athenæum," with 2000 volumes, given
Leicester (five branches)	142	Under Museums Act	10/4/71	½d.	..	1¾d.	2848 (library portion)	Old Mechanics' Institution books. Mr. C. Clifton, £250; Mr. H. Rice, £676. Garendon Street branch complete from Alderman Sir Israel Hart
Derby (one branch)	94	–/5/70	–/3/71	1d.	540	1d.	1700	Building and fittings from Mr. M. T. Bass; £400; £500; two gifts of £100. The Devonshire local books
Rochdale ..	71	25/5/70	18/9/72	1d.	520	1d.	1066	10,404 volumes presented up to 1896
Bradford (nine branches)	216	15/3/71	15/6/72	1d.	1799	1d.	4062	The Hanson Library, 12,000 volumes
Plymouth (two branches)	84	3/11/71	1876	1d.	600	1d.	1300	"Jubilee" subscription, £1100. Council grant for furniture, £300

LIBRARIES IN SECOND-CLASS TOWNS.

H. The result of special efforts to raise funds. J. Number of hours per week the central institution is open—figures in brackets hours for issue of books (R. L. means in the reference library, L. L. in the lending library). K. Percentage annual cost (*a*) of central establishment, (*b*) of branches, (*c*) of loans and rent. L. Daily average issue of books (*a*) in lending libraries, (*b*) in reference libraries. M. Daily average number of visits to reading-rooms. N. Present number of books in libraries. O. Librarian's or other informant's name.

H.	J.	K.			L.		M.	N.	O.
		a.	*b.*	*c.*	*a.*	*b.*			
Nil	79 (70)	?	?	?	2600	905	?	81,556	Ben. H. Mullen, M.A.
Nil	78 (50)	?	Nil	?	382	20	?	31,251	George Easter.
Nil	72	40	60	?	?	?	?	85,000	J. K. Waite.
Nil	71½	75	25	6	881	353	?	61,530	W. May.
Nil	70½ (58)	..	Nil	26	280	75	?	50,117	R. Ashton.
Nil	78 (66)	..	Nil	33	330	39	1100	36,900	John Elliot.
Nil	75 (59)	50	50	?	1269	72	2000	67,816	C. V. Kirkby.
Nil	58	?	?	Nil	608	50	1500	30,100	W. Crowther.
Advts. in catalogues	81 (60)	..	Nil	23	453	250	600	49,407	George Hanson.
Nil	75 (R.L. 69, L.L. 60)	?	?	Nil	604	221	?	77,693	Butler Wood.
Nil	78 (R.L. 72, L.L. 66)	?	?	?	1533	189	2500	42,000	W. H. K. Wright.

STATISTICS RELATING TO FREE PUBLIC

A.	B.	C.	D.	E.	F.		G.
Newcastle-on-Tyne (one branch)	186	—/3/74	1880	1d.	2761	1d. 3977	Riddell Library = 820 vols. Elswick branch library complete by Alderman Stephenson
Bristol (five branches)	221	13/5/74	1876	1d.	..	1d. 4413	The Old City Library and building
Portsmouth (two branches)	159	1876	1883	½d.	1176	½d. 2692	Rev. R. Hawkes's Library (= £200)
Preston . . .	108	29/1/78	1/1/79	1d.	1000	1½d. 2000	Harris bequest = £105,000. £600 subscribed. Newsham pictures = £40,000
Gateshead . .	86	10/12/80	..	1d.	762	1d. 1095	....
Halifax (one branch)	90	1881	20/3/82	..	..	1d. 1400	....
Croydon (two branches)	103	21/11/88	31/3/90	1d.	2100	1d. 2600	Subscriptions, £512; two gifts of £100; many donations of books
West Ham . .	205	—/11/90	1892	1d.	2680	1d. 3519	Site from the Corporation. Cost of central library is to be paid out of coal and wine dues
Brighton . .	116	Under local Act	12/9/73	..	..	.. ..	Considerable gifts of books and money
Oldham . . .	131	Under local Act	..	?	1406	? 2098	Building for North Moor branch given
Wales— Cardiff (six branches)	129	22/9/62	..	?	450	1d. 3600	Considerable gifts to the museum, less to the library
Swansea (six branches)	90	1870	1875	?	650	? 1350	Considerable gifts of objects and books
Scotland— Dundee (one branch)	153	1866	1869	..	1453	.. 3018	Very considerable (see page 238)
Aberdeen (one branch)	121	25/3/84	25/8/84	1d.	1511	1d. 2098	Nearly £4000 subscribed. Building and library from the old Mechanics' Institution

Sunderland (under a local Act) and Nottingham (which adopted the Acts in 1867) have not supplied returns. Sunderland has a population of 124,000, Nottingham of 214,000. The first

LIBRARIES IN SECOND-CLASS TOWNS (*Continued*).

H.	J.	K.			L.		M.	N.	O.
		a.	*b.*	*c.*	*a.*	*b.*			
Nil	82 (R.L. 66, L.L. 58)	?	?	22	628	231	2957	84,000	Basil Anderton, B.A.
..		68	32	11½	2000	..	?	90,000	E. R. Norris Mathews, F.R.H.S.
Nil	72 (40½)	?	?	?	724	110	2500	36,000	Tweed D. A. Jewers.
Nil	66	..	Nil	Nil	371	120	1600	40,000	W. S. Bramwell.
Nil	75 (58)	..	Nil	32	250	..	950	10,119	Henry E. Johnston.
Nil	53	76½	23½	25	484	..	..	46,214	J. Whiteley.
Nil	78 (58)	43	57	26	990	9	2000	32,353	Thos. Johnston.
Slight	78 (R.L. 66, L.L. 55)	40	60	14	567	142	2058	38,000	A. Cotgreave.
	R.L. 72, L.L. 66	..	Nil	..	402	152	?	44,000	F. W. Madden, M.R.A.S.
Nil	66 (62)	?	?	?	465	78	2145	43,707	Thomas W. Hand.
£1300 from exhibition fund	78 (R.L. 72, L.L. (6)	?	?	34	533	101	7500	63,000	John Ballinger.
..	75	84	16	36	225	460	2350	35,000	S. E. Thompson.
See article, p. 238	69 (59)	90	10	Nil	864	194	700	71,000	John Maclauchlan.
Nil	78 (47)	..	Slight	..	850	65	..	41,750	A. W. Robertson, M.A.

has more than 20,000 volumes, the second more than 75,000 volumes in its free libraries. The daily average issue at Sunderland is more than 500, at Nottingham nearly 1400.

STATISTICS RELATING TO FREE PUBLIC

A. Name of place. B. Population in thousands (1891). C. Date of adoption of Public Libraries Acts. D. Date of opening of first reading-room or library. E. Rate per pound of assessment, and product in the first year. F. Rate per pound of assessment, and product in 1895-96. G. Important donations and bequests.

A.	B.	C.	D.	E.		F.		G.
				£		£		
Bedfordshire— Luton	30	1894	1894	..	..	1d.	420	Subscriptions towards buildings
Berkshire— Reading . . .	61	1877	1882	1d.	600	1d.	1110	Buildings (=£60,000) erected by public subscriptions; 2000 vols.; £500 for books
Cambridgeshire— Cambridge (one branch)	37	1/3/53	28/6/55	½d.	200	1d.	950	£350 subscribed; 2500 vols.; 4300 vols.; three other small libraries
Cheshire— Chester . . .	37	1874	1877	1d.	532	1d.	777	£100; a new reading-room given
Macclesfield . .	36	6/2/74	1876	..	300	..	360	The Chadwick Library premises, and 5000 books
Runcorn . . .	20	19/11/81	1882	1d.	..	1d.	193	Stock of old public library; a few subscriptions
Northwich . .	15	13/11/83	1885	..	..	1d.	231	The Brunner Free Library; £1000 for books; many other gifts
Altrincham . .	12	6/9/89	1892	..	..	1d.	245	Buildings transferred; £1000 in donations
Sale	10	18/2/90	1891	1d.	205	1d.	233	£100; buildings erected by subscription; 1500 books
Ashton-upon-Mersey	..	1896	..	..	..	½d.	..	....
Hyde	31	1893	18/9/93	1d.	440	1d.	450	Old Mechanics' Library of 3452 vols.; small sums
Dukinfield . .	17	6/8/94	..	..	..	..	215	Building and books given; £280 in donations
Cornwall— Truro	11	7/5/85	1885	..	..	1d.	117	Ferris bequest, £2000; Passmore Edwards building
Penzance . . .	14	-/2/93	1893	1d.	176	1d.	190	Ferris bequest, £2000; 2000 volumes
Camborne . .	15	1893	23/5/95	..	..	..	?	Ferris bequest, £2000; Passmore Edwards building; 1000 volumes
Redruth . . .	10	1894	1895	..	..	1d.	100	Ferris bequest, £2000; Edwards building; 500 volumes.
Cumberland— Whitehaven . .	18	19/2/87	15/5/88	1d.	232	1d.	275	£228 by subscriptions
Carlisle . . .	39	9/6/90	1891	1d.	650	1d.	740	£5000 in subscriptions; books = £500; also a library of 10,000 vols.

LIBRARIES IN THIRD-CLASS TOWNS.

H. The result of special efforts to raise funds. J. Number of hours per week the central institution is open—figures in brackets hours for issue of books (R. L. means in the reference library, L. L. in the lending library). K. Percentage annual cost (a) of central establishment, (b) of branches, (c) of loans and rent. L. Daily average issue of books (a) in lending libraries, (b) in reference libraries. M. Daily average number of visits to reading-rooms. N. Present number of books in libraries. O. Librarian's or other informant's name.

H.	J.	K.			L.		M.	N.	O.
		a.	b.	c.	a.	b.			
A little from lectures	78	..	Nil	19	60	1	300	1,750	David Wootton.
Nil	81	..	Nil	Nil	427	20	2000	25,690	W. H. Greenbough, F.R.S.L.
Nil	69	83½	16½	Nil	280	28	?	43,000	John Pink.
Nil	75	..	Nil	24	200	20	800	?	?
Nil	72	..	Nil	Nil	171	20	400	16,828	Atherton Brunt.
Nil	L. L. 14	..	Nil	20	90	2	..	7,859	J. D. Jones.
Nil	70	..	Nil	Nil	?	?	?	?	T. J. Yarwood.
£200 to £300 per annum from a charity	69	..	Nil	20	250	?	350	6,355	Benjamin Clegg (Secretary).
A little from lettings	75	..	Nil	Nil	185	9	286	6,142	George Bethell.
Nil	56	..	Nil	11	160	?	290	5,460	John Chorton.
Nil	39	..	Nil	Nil	42	?	60	6,165	E. B. Broadrick.
Nil	84 (26½)	..	Nil	Nil	50	?	..	4,000	W. J. Martin.
Nil	78 (48)	..	Nil	Nil	240	12	..	7,000	Charles H. Benn.
Nil	L. L. 38½	..	Nil	Nil	190	..	..	3,500	Jacob Laity.
Nil	78 (27½)	..	Nil	Nil	120	?	..	1,700	William Gifford Hale.
50 vols. from Book Club	42	..	Nil	10	90	10	300	6,037	John Simpson.
Nil	75 (46)	..	Nil	Nil	310	?	1000	22,000	Robert Bateman.

STATISTICS RELATING TO FREE PUBLIC

A.	B.	C.	D.	E.	£ F.		£ G.
Derbyshire— Chesterfield . .	22	8/6/75	1879	1d.	165	1d.	332	£145 by subscriptions
Devonshire— Devonport (one branch)	55	3/11/80	6/2/82	1d.	500	1d.	670	Small
Durham— South Shields (two branches)	78	24/4/71	1873	½d.	608	1d.	1052	Several donations exceeding £100 each
Darlington . .	38	1883	23/10/85	..	639	..	685	Pease bequest = £10,000
West Hartlepool	43	1891	1893	..	650	..	685	Site given
Essex— Colchester . .	35	—/10/91	17/3/92	..	480	..	580	£2700 by bequests and donations
Leyton . . .	63	1891	1892	1d.	700	1d.	880	Books only
Walthamstow (one branch)	46	—/2/92	—/9/94	½d.	258	1d.	650	1000 volumes, and smaller gifts
Grays	12	1893	1894	..	93	..	138	500 vols., and smaller gifts
Ilford	11	1895	Not yet	..	..	..	..	....
Gloucestershire— Cheltenham (one branch)	44	18/7/83	13/10/84	1d.	1037	1d.	1126	Subscriptions, £1989; Buchanan bequest; £500; Miss Stokes, 1000 vols.; Day Library
Herefordshire— Hereford . . .	20	21/7/71	4/12/71	..	276	..	440	Subscriptions, £1840 to pay off debt in 1892
Hertfordshire— Walford . . .	17	1871	1874	1d.	80	1d.	400	Mr. James Rankin gave £6000; building erected by subscription; bequests, £1250; £1150 from local funds
Kent— Maidstone . .	32	20/1/55	..	..	..	..	*80	....
Bromley . . .	22	—/5/92	1894	..	..	..	..	Under £100
Gravesend . .	24	22/10/92	—/10/93	1d.	432	1d.	406	£100; a loan without interest
Rochester . .	26	—/6/94	Jubil. Free Library —/5/88 Under Act 10/10/94	½d.	150	½d.	170	Eastgate House Library; £600 by subscriptions
Lancashire— Warrington . .	53	1848	1848	½d.	77	1½d.	1000	Many books; £2100 subscribed; £450 bequest
St. Helens . .	71	Local Act 1869	1871	½d.	?	1d.	?	Gamble Institute library premises; some subscriptions and donations
Darwen . . .	34	1871		1d.	220	1d.	470	Mechanics' Institute Library
Heywood . .	23	15/4/74	..	..	..	..	380	Some books
Southport (two branches)	41	8/2/75	1875	..	590	..	1145	Atkinson Building = £10,000; and for books from Mr. Atkinson, £5500

* Proportion of rate expended on library.

LIBRARIES IN THIRD-CLASS TOWNS (*Continued*).

H.	J.	K.			L.		M.	N.	O.
		a.	b.	c.	a.	b.			
Small	?	..	Nil	Nil	200	5	..	12,356	D. Gorman.
Nil	69	..	Slight	?	220	50	200	16,000	Fred W. Hunt.
By an exhibition, £50	58	90	10	15	371	58	2000	22,104	Thomas Pyke.
Outside subscribers, £10 per annum	81 (52)	..	Nil	Nil	400	18	1000	21,739	B. R. Hill.
Nil	75 (66)	..	Nil	?	500	70	500	9,600	Albert Watkins.
Nil	78 (48)	86	14	?	230	3	700	6,600	George Rickword.
Nil	?	?	?	?	500	?	?	12,500	Z. Moon.
Nil	85 (L. L. 30, R. L. 69)	..	Slight	48	300	10	700	7,800	?
Nil	12	..	Nil	?	20	0	90	980	Annie George.
..	..	..	..	..	..	..	..	..	..
Nil	69 (53)	..	Slight	33	500	35	1000	24,000	William Jones.
Nil	60 (30)	..	Nil	Nil	154	..	..	..	James Cockcroft.
Small	78 (R.L. 59, L. L. 30½)	..	Nil	Nil	150	10	250	13,039	John Woolman.
..	..	..	..	..	..	..	..	5,000	Frederick James (Curator).
Nil	72 (53)	..	Nil	54	215	5	300	6,379	John Harrison.
Nil	72 (33½)	..	Nil	12½	120	10	380	5,000	Alfred Watkinson.
Nil	15	..	Nil	Nil	100	..	..	3,156	W. R. Bartley.
Nil	69 (60½)	..	Nil	5	237	..	..	25,000	Charles Madeley.
Nil	85 (R.L. 72, L. L. 66)	65½	34½	?	534	18	1398	26,716	Alfred Lancaster.
Nil	78	..	Nil	?	150	25	300	12,000	Albert Cawthorne.
Nil	75	..	Nil	?	70	20	..	11,000	George Chiswell.
Nil	..	82	18	9	500	30	1000	26,096	Thomas Newman.

STATISTICS RELATING TO FREE PUBLIC

A.	B.	C.	D.	E.	F.		G.
Lancas. (contd.)— Wigan (one branch)	55	27/10/76	-/6/78	1d.	£505	2d.	£1489	Taylor gift = £12,000; Winnard bequest, £12,000; branch and £50 per annum from Sir F. S. Powell; subscriptions, £1000; many books
Clitheroe . . .	11	25/10/78	5/4/79	¾d.	75	..	130	£180 for new books
Blackpool (two branches)	24	4/11/79	1880	..	..	..	..	....
Ashton-under-Lyne	40	1880	1881	1d.	480	1¼d.	1028	£620 and 1000 volumes
Barrow-in-Furness (1 branch)	52	20/10/81	1882	1d.	803	1d.	814	£250 in three donations
Bootle . . .	49	19/3/84	22/6/87	1d.	1485	1d.	1709	£360 by bequest; donation of £250
Widnes (one branch)	30	29/12/85	1887	..	410	..	580	£100 for books
Hindley . . .	19	2/5/87	21/6/87	..	..	1d.	220	Building and £50 per ann. from Mr. Eckersley
Middleton . .	22	4/4/87	·1887	1d.	240	1d.	260	Building and furniture (£2000) subscribed for
Denton and Haughton	14	31/5/87	1889	..	..	..	..	Subscriptions
Nelson . . .	23	23/3/89	-/11/89	1d.	253	1d.	379	£450 from a few donors
Leigh	29	1892	-/9/93	..	360	..	450	For buildings and books
Lancaster . .	31	-/11/92	..	1d.	500	1d.	510	Storey Institute and books of old Mechanics' Library given
Colne	..	1894	1895	1d.	240	1d.	250	200 books
Lincolnshire— Lincoln . . .	41	21/1/92	28/3/95	1d.	489	1d.	545	£1200 from Col. Seeley, M.P.; £100 from Mr. W. Crosfield; 1000 volumes
Middlesex— Ealing . . .	24	33/1/83	1/8/83	1d.	415	1d.	716	£92 in donations
Brentford .	14	19/6/89	?	½d.	120	1d.	277	£200 subscribed
Chiswick . . .	22	-/3/90	8/11/90	1d.	383	1d.	454	Small
Edmonton . .	25	1891	16/1/93	1d.	270	1d.	315	Promise of a building by J. P. Edwards
Enfield (two branches)	32	1892	1893	..	..	1d.	420	Nil
Monmouthshire— Newport (two branch reading-rooms)	55	22/2/70	..	..	200	..	1100	2000 volumes
Norfolk— Great Yarmouth (one branch)	49	5/8/85	3/5/86 17/10/87	¾d.	500	1d.	740	£153 in subscriptions; 2000 volumes
Northamptonshire— Peterborough .	25	-/3/91	-/9/92	1d.	400	1d.	440	2500 volumes
Kettering . .	19	-/3/95	1/3/96	..	..	1d.	190	About £120

LIBRARIES IN THIRD-CLASS TOWNS (*Continued*).

H.	J	K. a	K. b	K. c	L. a	L. b	M.	N.	O.
Large from voluntary rate for many years	74 (R. L. 53½, L. L. 63½)	92	8	3½	310*	110		48,000	Henry T. Folkard, F.S.A.
Nil	16	..	Nil	Nil	240†	..		?	James Robinson.
Nil	60	?	?	?	222	..		11,000	Kate Lewtas.
Nil	55	..	Nil	?	206	20		14,000	D. H. Wade.
Nil	78 (72)	..	Slight	..	405	80	2000	20,094	Thomas Aldred.
Nil	75 (66)	..	Nil	22½	251	43	570	15,000	John J. Ogle.
Nil	66	..	Slight	10½	239	12	175	?	Anne J. Proctor.
Nil	58 (53)	..	Nil	Nil	..	..	..	4,447	John Smith.
Nil	78 (66)	..	Nil	3	50	6	250	5,600	F. Entwistle (Town Clerk).
Profits of a bazaar	18	..	Nil	..	70	..	120	2,500	David Smith.
Nil	75 (42)	..	Nil	45	120	2	550	6,914	David Rushton.
Nil	78 (61½)	..	Nil	Nil	143	2	..	5,900	James Ward, B.A.
Nil	49	..	Nil	28	260	50	..	9,000	J. M. Dowbiggin.
Nil	?	?	?	?	109	..	..	3,000	Ernest Crowther.
Nil	77 (66)	..	Nil	Nominal	280	21	680	7,100	Henry Bond.
Small	65 (52½)	..	Nil	12½	544	4	950	10,222	Thos. Bonner.
Nil	65 (55)	..	Nil	Nil	78	?	?	5,395	Fred Turner.
Nil	74 (35)	..	Nil	15	273	4	..	5,253	H. G. Hewitt.
Nil	27 (21)	..	Nil	Slight	250	0	80	2,000	P. W. Farmborough, F.Z.S.
Nil	36	?	?	?	240	..	?	5,600	C. Frederic Harrison.
Nil	48	70	30	?	253	87	..	21,000	Jas. Matthews.
£40 collected from borrowers	72 (60)	88	12	19	484	16	776	14,692	Wm. Carter.
Nil	75 (L. L. 44, R. L. 72)	..	Nil	?	150	2		4,100	L. Stanley Jast.
Nil	78 (33)	..	..	25	100	..	..	1,700	R. B. Wallis (Chairman, Committee).

* Does not include issues to boys' room. † Open two days a week only.

STATISTICS RELATING TO FREE PUBLIC

A.	B.	C.	D.	E.	F.		G.
					£	£	
Northumberland— Tynemouth (one branch)	47	13/7/69	..	..	500	..	750	Building, and books
Nottinghamshire— Newark-on-Trent	14	26/8/81	1883	..	..	1d.	210	Land, building, furniture, 4000 books, and endowment of librarian's salary from Sir Wm. Gilstrap, Bart.
Hucknall Torkard	13	30/4/84	1/1/87	1d.	98	1d.	110	£2000 from Mr. J. E. Ellis, M.P., and Mr. H. B. Paget; 500 vols. from Mechanics' Institute; about £150 in small donations
Somersetshire— Weston-super-Mare	16	28/12/86	-/6/90	..	..	1d.	400	About £300
Southampton— Winchester . . .	19	23/12/50	-/11/51	..	..	1d.	380	....
Gosport and Alverstoke	25	22/9/86	-/2/91	1d.	250	1d.	299	£50; some books
Southampton (one branch)	65	13/6/87	15/1/89	1d.	953	1d.	1144	About 2500 volumes
Bournemouth (one branch)	38	11/3/93	1/1/95	1d.	1000	1d.	1250	....
Staffordshire— Walsall	72	24/6/57	..	1d.	264	1½d.	990	....
Burslem	32	2/9/63	..	..	..	1d.	456	Large subscriptions and donations of books
West Bromwich (three branches)	59	1870	1874	1d.	300	1d.	810	Subscribed for books, £1470; Mr. A. Brogden, M.P., £500
Brierley Hill . .	12	9/11/75	1876	1d.	145	1d.	120	....
Darlaston . . .	14	6/7/75	..	..	..	..	..	2000 volumes
Wednesbury . .	25	1876	1878	1d.	270	1d.	320	£1288 by subscriptions
Stafford	20	-/3/79	1882	..	..	1d.	220	....
*Tipton	29	24/3/83	..	..	..	..	..	
Hanley	55	24/6/84	1886	1d.	630	1d.	685 (?)	Messrs. J. & G. Meakin, £1000; other subscriptions amounting to more than £1000
Tunstall	16	15/8/85	1885	..	..	1d.	150 (?)	The library is in part of a "Jubilee" building raised by subscription
Leek	14	4/10/87	1884	1d.	150	1d.	170	Nicholson Institute a gift (=£20,000); a legacy from Mr. W. Challinor, M.A., £300
Longton	34	-/5/91	-/1/92	1d.	386	1d.	401	Donations, £22; library of old Athenæum; Duke of Sutherland has given a site for new building
Burton-on-Trent (two branches)	46	3/10/94	..	..	..	½d.	135	Books and premises of Burton Institute

* Reading-rooms only.

LIBRARIES IN THIRD-CLASS TOWNS (*Continued*).

H.	J.	K.			L.		M.	N.	O.
		a.	b.	c.	a.	b.			
	?	95	5	..	558	..	?	?	J. S. Edington (Hon. Sec.).
Nil	66	..	Nil	Nil	150	30	200	7,000	George G. Killingley.
Profits of a successful bazaar	78 (10)	..	Nil	Nil	130	10	260	3,970	Henry Dennis.
..	69 (18)	..	Nil	Nil	190	..	?	?	F. W. Coleman.
.. Nil	59 72 (L. L. 63, R. L. 69)	.. ..	.. Nil	.. Nil	100 144	.. 2	.. 280	4,300 5,853	J. T. Burchett. A. Gray.
Nil	72 (54)	?	?	Nil	412	46	1300	19,440	Oswald Tatton Hopwood.
Circular appeal, £10	..	86½	13½	?	490	10	?	6,400	Charles Riddle.
Nil ..	50 48	.. ..	Nil Nil	? ?	285 106	101 ..	1600 411	17,020 7,546	Alfred Morgan. James Rigby.
Nil	55	?	?	?	248	4	600	14,650	David Dickinson.
.. Nil	4 25 78 (66) 18 ..	.. ..	Nil Nil Nil	33 .. 18	? 50 237 180 ..	? 0 33	? .. 700	2,146 4,353 10,264 8,000	Jas. H. Dudley. Annie Simkin. Thomas Stanley. Thomas Jackson.
..	78 (R. L. 55, L. L. 49)	..	Nil	?	208	14	1450	12,093	A. J. Milward.
	75 (30)	..	Nil	..	?	?	?	3,680	M. Flint.
	81 (L. L. 44, R. L. 66)	..	Nil	Nil	109	17	?	9,825	Kineton Parkes.
Nil	78 (69)	..	Nil	5	109	4	800	5,832	Herbert Walker.
..	..	..	..	..	..	..	..	..	J. N. Whitehead (Town Clerk).

STATISTICS RELATING TO FREE PUBLIC

A.	B.	C.	D.	E.		F.	G.
					£		£
Suffolk— Ipswich * (one branch)	57	1853	10/4/88	..	..	..	..
Surrey— Richmond (two branches)	23	18/3/79	18/6/81	1d.	484	1d.	937	Books and subscriptions = £400; Richmond Parochial Library = 2000 volumes
Kingston . . .	27	1/3/81	1882	1d.	325	1d.	500	Mr. Rowlls Rowlls, £1000 consols; Lady Wolverton, £50
Sussex— Hove	26	1/4/91	14/12/91	1d.	1008	1d	1034	Many books
Eastbourne . .	35	3/2/96	7/7/96	..	..	½d.	540	Ald. J. A. Skinner, £75
Warwickshire— Leamington Spa	27	2/12/56	1857	1d.	300	1d.	656	....
Warwick . . .	12	-/2/65	1866	..	..	1d.	220	About £73 collected
Aston Manor (one branch)	69	15/5/77	4/2/78	1d.	458	1d.	680	....
Rugby. . . .	11	30/6/90	8/2/91	½d.	97	1d.	228	Rugby Institute, 1890 vols.; £100; Mr. G. C. Berm, £500
Westmorland— Kendal . . .	14	14/4/91	26/9/92	..	..	1d.	200	£2300 subscribed for altering building handed over by the Corporation and for books; since opening, £405 in eighteen donations
Wiltshire— Salisbury . . .	15	2/6/90	-/12/90	1d.	230	1d.	235	More than £300 in subscriptions; Mr. E. H. Hulse, M.P., 1000 vols.
Worcestershire— Kidderminster .	25	26/2/55	R. L. 1854 L. L. 1881	..	..	..	55	£4000 collected for new building opened in 1894
Worcester . .	43	23/4/79	1881	..	600	..	675	Very considerable gifts towards building the Victoria Institute, which cost £45,000
Yorkshire, N. R.— Middlesborough	76	23/11/70	3/4/71	..	..	..	Expenditure 1000	....
Thornaby-on-Tees	16	18/11/90	9/11/92	..	..	1d.	180	Ald. T. Wrightson presented building; some donations
Yorkshire, W. R.— Rotherham . .	42	16/2/76	1879	½d.	?	1d.	?	....
Harrogate . .	14	17/2/86	1888	1d.	230	1d.	445	
Dewsbury . .	30	3/5/87	21/12/89	1d.	415	1d.	450	Jubilee fund for building and books, £800
York . . .	67	15/10/91	1/8/92	1d.	995	1d.	1017	York Institute handed over on payment of debt; library given by members; £500 raised by subscriptions
Sowerby Bridge	12	19/4/93	1893	1d.	150	1d.	160	About £100

* Acts adopted to maintain a museum.

LIBRARIES IN THIRD-CLASS TOWNS (*Continued*).

H	J.	K.			L.		M.	N.	O.
		a.	b.	c.	a.	b.			
Nil	48	..	..	..	300	..	?	?	W. Fenton.
Voluntary rate 1885-94, about £150 per annum; a monthly shilling book fund since 1888, about £14 per annum	81 (66)	94½	5½	Nil	350	37	1200	22,050	Albert A. Barkas.
..	81 (L. L. 60, R. L. 72)	..	Nil	Nil	180	4	920	8,000	Benjamin Carter.
Nil	69 (59)	..	Nil	Nil	291	17	421	8,669	John W. Lister.
..	72	..	Nil	Nil	?	?	?	1,778	J. H. Hardcastle.
Nil	78 (L. L. 28, R. L. 66)	..	Nil	?	235	20	500	18,438	David B. Grant.
Nil	29	..	Nil	?	100	..	?	10,434	Thomas Haynes.
Nil	78 (L. L. 66, R. L. 72)	90	10	15	283	45	500	15,733	Robert K. Dent.
Annual circular, small result	49	..	Nil	11½	74	2	450	3,500	Jas. W. Kenning.
Subscription fund for new books	84 (48)	..	Nil	Nil	290	20	500	9,329	Robert C. Garner.
	54	..	Nil	25	99	12	300	3,190	Oliver Langmead.
Lectures, football match, concerts, small result	78 (L. L. 60, R. L. 72)	..	Nil	Nil	120	25	800	6,000	Archibald Sparke.
Nil	72 (60)	..	Nil	Nil	200	60	600	30,000	Thos. Duckworth.
Nil	65	..	Nil	21	314	32	?	18,168	Baker Hudson.
Nil	9	..	Nil	?	150	8	600	3,283	N. J. Watson (Town Clerk).
Nil	66	..	?	?	150	..	?	13,000	John Ridal.
Nil	60	..	Nil	..	379	4	?	8,791	George W. Byers.
Nil	60	..	Nil	Nil	222	..	500	10,748	W. H. Smith.
Nil	78 (L. L. 60, R. L. 69)	..	Nil	..	608	7	1219	16,529	A. H. Furnish.
..	30	..	..	..	101	..	?	3,289	J. Edward Ball.

STATISTICS RELATING TO FREE PUBLIC

A.	B.	C.	D.	E.	F.	G.
Wales— Wrexham . . .	13	11/3/78	10/12/79	1d.	£180	1d.	£228 From the National Eisteddfod Committee, £390; £25 annually from the Working Men's Hall Trust Fund
Pontypridd (three branches)	20	14/3/87	1887	1d.	110	1d.	430 Towards building, £903
Isle of Man— Douglas . . .	20	30/5/86	1886	1d.	166	1d.	480 £800 from the managers of the Isle of Man Savings Bank
Scotland— Paisley	66	28/3/67	11/4/71	1d.	500	1d.	1000 Public subscription; Paisley Library, 9000 vols.; Sir P. Coats, two large buildings
Inverness . . .	19	4/7/77	16/6/83	1d.	232	1d.	373 Town Council gave site; public subscriptions, £3925; includes £1750 from Mr. Carnegie; many books given
Hawick . . .	19	16/3/78	1/11/78	1d.	176	1d.	260 £900 in four subscriptions
Dunfermline . .	22	11/2/80	1883	..	?	1d.	300 4000 vols.; £8000 spent on building by Mr. Carnegie, and he gives £50 per year
Dumbarton . .	17	13/10/81	1883	..	?	1d.	229 £150 from Denny Trustees
Ayr	25	6/8/90	1891	1d.	450	1d.	480 A public subscription library, 8000 vols.; building presented by Mr. Carnegie
Peterhead . . .	12	27/2/90	-/10/93	1d.	133	1d.	140 Mr. Carnegie, £1300; and other subscriptions
Kilmarnock . .	28	12/6/93	1895	½d.	205	1d.	434 Kilmarnock Library given; Crawford bequest yields £96 per annum
Perth	30	1/6/96	..	..	..	..	Sandeman bequest, £30,000
Ireland— Cork	75	18/9/55	-/12/92	½d.	269	¾d.	440 Donation of £25
Dundalk . . .	12	17/12/56	-/1/58	1d.	59	1d.	93 1600 volumes from a defunct institute
Sligo . . .	10	1880	1880	..	..	..	.. Large donations of books
Limerick . . .	37	9/5/89	11/12/93	..	..	1d.	264 ....
Waterford . . .	21	26/3/94	1/1/96	1d.	168	1d.	190 £100 subscribed; 850 vols.

The following places have not furnished particulars for this return. The dates of the adoption of the Acts and the population in thousands are given after the names:—
Bedfordshire— Bedford, 30/7/89 (28). *Cheshire*— Stockport, 1860 (70); Staleybridge, 13/3/88 (27). *Cumberland*—Workington, -/4/90 (23). *Derbyshire*—Glossop, 16/5/88 (22). *Devonshire*— Exeter, 6/5/70 (37). *Dorset*— Poole, 30/9/85 (15). *Durham*—Stockton, 14/7/74 (48); East Hartlepool, 1891 (21). *Essex*— Barking, 27/11/88 (14); East Ham, 1895? (33). *Gloucestershire*—Gloucester, 1894 (39); Stroud, 1896 (11); St. George's, 1896 (37). *Hertfordshire*—St. Albans, 1878 (13). *Kent*—Canterbury, 1858 (23); Folkestone, 15/5/78 (24); Tonbridge, 1882? (10); Ramsgate, 1894 (25); Tunbridge Wells, 1895 (28); Bexley, 1896 (11). *Lancashire*—Moss Side, 1887 (24); Stretford, 1893 (22). *Leicestershire*— Loughborough, 21/2/85 (18). *Lincolnshire*—Grimsby, 1894 (52). *Middlesex*—Twickenham, -/2/82 (16); Wood Green, 1891 (26); Tottenham, 1891 (71); Willesden, 1891 (61); Teddington, 1895 (10). *Northamptonshire*—Northampton, 8/10/60 (61). *Nottinghamshire*— Mansfield, 11/4/90 (16); Worksop, 1895 (13). *Oxfordshire*—Oxford, 6/10/52 (46). *Shrop*-

LIBRARIES IN THIRD-CLASS TOWNS (Continued).

H.	J.	K. a.	K. b.	K. c.	L. a.	L. b.	M.	N.	O.
Lectures and entertainments, small result	L. L. 33, R. L. 63	..	Nil	15	120	10	340	3,994	Richard Gough.
Lectures, &c., fair result	?	81	19	19	40	..	600	4,000	George Hughes.
Nil	72 (66)	..	Nil	12	146	43	279	11,250	John Taylor.
Profits of lectures	64	..	Nil	Nil	500	..	?	12,000 (in 1882)	Morris Young (Curator).
Nil	78	..	Nil	..	58	12	?	7,800	S. F. Donaldson.
Nil	78 (26)	..	Nil	Nil	115	..	?	13,000	Geo. S. M'Nairn.
Nil	42	..	Nil	Nil	240	..	250	15,000	....
..	54 (30)	..	..	?	63	..	?	5,400	Archd. Macdonald.
Nil	78 (36)	..	Nil	Nil	377	7	824	15,000 (in 1893)	G. B. Phillips.
Picture exhibition, entertainments, fair success	78 (24)	..	Nil	..	120	..	?	6,500	R. Robertson (Hon. Sec.).
Nil		..	Nil	15	213	..	595	14,950	H. Y. Simpson.-
Nil		..	..	..	..	..	..	..	William MacLeish (Town Clerk).
Nil	78 (L. L. 66, R. L. 72)	..	..	..	245	10	569	6,000	James Wilkinson.
Entertainments, small result	24 (18)	..	Nil	Nil	50	20	Nil	7,000	Mathew Comerford (Town Clerk).
..	77	..	Nil	Nil	10	18	150	1,600	D. Saultry.
Nil	75	..	..	..	..	40	?	3,030	John Hogan.
Nil	72	..	Nil	24	?	?	?	?	Henry D. Keane (Member of Committee).

shire—Shrewsbury, 1/5/83 (27); Bridgwater, 18/5/60 (12). *Staffordshire*—Bilston, -/3/70 (23); Willenhall, 1874 (17); Stoke, 1875 (24); Handsworth, 23/12/76 (33); Smethwick, 18/9/76 (36); Newcastle-under-Lyme, 18/9/84 (18). *Suffolk*—Bury St. Edmunds, 1894 (17); Lowestoft, 1891 (23). *Surrey*—Wimbledon, 1883 (26). *Sussex*—Worthing, 1892 (17). *Warwickshire*—Coventry, 17/9/67 (53); Nuneaton, 1895 (12). *Worcestershire*—Dudley, 25/9/78 (46); Oldbury, 30/7/88 (20). *Yorkshire*—Doncaster, 14/6/68 (26); Barnsley, 17/1/90 (35); Bingley, 8/2/90 (10); Morley, 1892 (21); Rawmarsh, 1892 (12); Todmorden, 1896 (25).
    Wales—Carnarvon, 1887 (10); Barry and Cadoxton, 1891 (13); Blaenau Festiniog, 1894 (11); Penarth, 1894 (12).
    Scotland—Airdrie, 6/10/53 (19); Forfar, 14/3/70 (12); Galashiels, 14/3/72 (17); Alloa, 22/6/85 (11); Arbroath, 1896 (23); Falkirk, 1896 (17).
    Ireland—Kingston, 1884 (17); Rathmines and Rathgar, 1887 (28); Lurgan, 1891 (11); Newry, 1895 (14).

STATISTICS RELATING TO FREE PUBLIC

A. Name of place. B. Population in thousands (1891). C. Date of adoption of Public Libraries Acts. D. Date of opening of first reading-room or library. E. Rate per pound of assessment, and product in the first year. F. Rate per pound of assessment, and product in 1895-96. G. Important donations and bequests.

A.	B.	C.	D.	E.		F.		G.
					£		£	
England—								
Bideford . . .	8	-/4/77	1876	1d.	60	1d.	70	Donations, £150; from Bridge Trustees, £125; legacies and gifts, £550
Buxton . . .	8	11/2/86	-/11/89	1d.	200	1d.	225	....
Millom . . .	9	-/2/87	1887	..	..	..	..	£75 from Trustees of the "Jubilee" fund
Nantwich . .	7	-/8/87	-/12/88	1d.	68	1d.	72	Sir John Brunner, £50
Hinckley . . .	10	-/8/88	..	..	..	1d.	..	Subscriptions, £390; bequest, £30 per annum
Middlewich . .	4	7/2/89	-/3/89	1d.	36	1d.	62	Sir John Brunner, £100 and frequent gifts of books
Woolton . . .	5	17/2/90	1890	1d.	..	¾d.	..	Building presented
Arlecdon and Frizington	6	7/8/91	31/5/92	1d.	91	1d.	94	£12, and 150 volumes
Falmouth . .	5	-/1/93	1894	1d.	130	1d.	143	Mr. J. Passmore Edwards, £2000 for building, 1000 volumes; Ferris bequest, £2000
Middle Claydon (one branch)	Small	-/9/93	-/10/93	..	..	1d.	9	Many books
New Mills . .	7	9/9/95	Not yet	..	..	..	..	£500 promised
Scotland—								
Thurso . . .	4	1872	1873	..	..	1d.	38	Mr. A. Carnegie, £325; £300 North British railway stock
Tarves . . .	2	-/12/83	Old Library, 1878, continued	¾d.	22	½d.	29	Mr. Melvin's bequest of books; Mr. A. Carnegie, £100
Wick	9	10/5/87	16/11/88	1d.	160	1d.	150	A handsome building now being erected; the townsfolk, £1250; Mr. A. Carnegie, £3000; a free site from Mr. Usher of Norton
Selkirk . . .	6	9/10/88	25/5/89	1d.	91	1d.	95	Buildings presented by Mr. T. Craig-Brown; subscriptions and donations, £600
Brechin . . .	9	1/3/90	6/7/93	1d.	100	1d.	120	Anonymous gift of £5000
Elgin	8	1891	1892	..	..	1d.	126	Mr. A. Carnegie, £500; Town Council, £10 per annum
Drumoak . . .	(860)	18/3/93	1894	½d.	15	½d.	15	Donations for building and books; Mr. A. Carnegie, £25
Ireland—								
Coleraine . .	7	20/10/81	Not yet	..	..	..	..	....

From the following places information has not been received, but the dates of adoption, and populations in thousands, except in rural villages, follow the names :—*Bedfordshire*—Leighton, 1891 (7). *Buckinghamshire*—Grandborough, 1896. *Cambridgeshire*—Burwell, 18/2/95. *Cheshire*—Winsford, 4/4/87 (10); Lower Bebington, 9/1/94. *Cornwall*—Bodmin, 1895 (5); Liskeard, 1895 (4); St. Austell, 1895 (3); St. Ives, 1895 (6). *Cumberland*—Penrith, 1882 (9); Cleator Moor, 1892 (9). *Derbyshire*—Pleasley, 1895. *Durham*—Trimdon 1895 (5); Leadgate, 1896 (5). *Herefordshire*—Leominster, 1889 (6). *Kent*—Queenborough, 1887 (1); Sittingbourne, 1887 (8). *Lancashire*—Fleetwood, 1887 (9). *Leicestershire*—Ibstock, 1895; Sheepshed, 1896. *Norfolk*—Shouldham, 1896. *Northamptonshire*—Rothwell, 1894 (3). *Notts*—Carlton, 21/4/87 (7). *Shrop-*

LIBRARIES IN SMALL TOWNS AND VILLAGES.

H. The result of special efforts to raise funds. J. Number of hours per week the central institution is open —figures in brackets hours for issue of books (R. L. means in the reference library, L. L. in the lending library). K. Percentage annual cost (a) of central establishment, (b) of branches, (c) of loans and rent. L. Daily average issue of books (a) in lending libraries, (b) in reference libraries. M. Daily average number of visits to reading-rooms. N. Present number of books in libraries. O. Librarian's or other informant's name.

H.	J.	K.			L.		M.	N.	O
		a.	b.	c.	a.	b.			
£250 from bazaar	Every week day	..	Nil	25	40	20	50	2200	John W. Narraway (Hon. Sec.).
..	38	..	Nil	..	85	3	350	3780	Thomas A. Sarjant.
Nil	60	..	Nil	..	..	..	530	6000	A. J. Hutchinson.
Various, £400	69	..	Nil	..	40	15	120	3642	Annie Jackson.
American Fair, £130	..	..	Nil	..	70	..	300	3000	Peter Payne.
Nil	78 (6)	..	Nil	..	82	..	?	3000	Thos. Lawrence Drinkwater.
Nil	6	..	Nil	Nil	40	..	?	1760	Alfred James Aldred.
Nil	12	..	Nil	..	50	..	?	?	M. Jones.
..	24	..	Nil	..	?	..	?	3000	N. Fox.
..	21	?	?	?	..	..	?	1100	Ellin Verney.
	..	..	..	..	..	..	..	..	Joseph Pollitt (Clerk to U.D.C.).
Bazaar, &c., £608	6	..	Nil	Nil	104	40	64	5620	Henry Manson.
	3	..	..	..	..	..	?	3250	George Argo (Clerk to Committee); John Young (Librarian).
	48	..	Nil	15	53	..	?	?	George Bain.
	78(7½)	..	Nil	Nil	66	Small	?	?	James George Chalmers (Hon. Clerk).
Lectures (failure)	48	..	Nil	Nil	120	..	350	..	James Craigie.
Concerts, &c. (poor)	54	..	Nil	16	147	20	..	4500	Isabella Mitchell.
Nil	2	..	..	..	41	..	..	601	James Burnett.
..	..	..	..	..	..	..	..	..	W. Eccles (Town Clerk).

shire—Oswestry, 19/5/90 (8). *Southampton*—Andover, 1896 (6). *Staffordshire*—Lichfield, 1856 (8); Tamworth, 20/12/81 (6). *Warwickshire*—Atherstone, 1895 (5). *Yorkshire*—Halton, 1895.
Wales—Bangor, 1871 (10); Aberystwith, 1872 (7); Llanuwchllyn; Broughton, 1895 ; Holyhead, 1896 (9); Corwen, 1896 (3); Towyn, 1896 (5); Halkin, 1896.
Scotland—Grangemouth, 1887 (6); Kirkwall, 1890 (4); Jedburgh, 1892 (3); Newburgh, 1894 (2); Kirkmichael, 1896; Campbeltown, 1896 (8).
Ireland—Ennis, 1860 (5); Banbridge, 1890 (5); Nenagh, 1894 (5); Dalkey, 1895 (3); Newtonards, 1895 (9).

INDEX

INDEX

ABBOTT (T. C.), 165
Aberdeen, 7, 41, 42, 53, 69, 114, 239-241, 310
Aberystwith, 41, 272, 325
Abortive adoptions of Acts, 34, 35, 64, 212
Accounts, 81
Accrington, 42
Acts of Parliament (Acts now in force marked *)—
  7 Anne, c. 14, 7
  *6 and 7 Victoria, c. 36, 84
  *Local Taxation (Customs and Excise) Act, 1890, 76
  *Local Government Act, 1894, 77
  Museums Act, 1845, 10
  *Museums and Gymnasiums Act, 1891, 76, 204, 232
  Public Libraries Act (England and Wales), 1850, 12-24
  Public Libraries Act (Ireland and Scotland), 1853, 23, 24
  Public Libraries Act (Scotland), 1854, 24
  *Public Libraries Act (Ireland), 1855, 24
  Public Libraries Act (England and Wales), 1855, 25
  Public Libraries Act, 1866, 35-37
  Public Libraries Act (Scotland), 1867, 37
  Public Libraries Act (Scotland), 1871, 39
  Public Libraries Act (England and Wales), 1871, 40
  Public Libraries Act (Ireland), 1877, 42
  Public Libraries Amendment Act, 1877, 43, 50
  Public Libraries Act, 1884, 54
  Public Libraries Act for Isle of Man, 1885, 56, 270
  Public Libraries Act (England and Wales), 1887, 57, 58
  *Public Libraries Act (Scotland), 1887, 59
  Public Libraries Act, 1889, 71
  Public Libraries Act (England and Wales), 1890, 71
  *Public Libraries Act (England and Wales), 1892, 73-76
  *Public Libraries Act (Scotland), 1894, 63, 81
  *Public Libraries Act (Ireland), 1894, 81
  *Technical Instruction Acts, 76, 232
Administrative questions, 101
Admission to free libraries, 79, 82
Adoption of Acts: a condition of certain gifts, 112
Adoption of Acts: procedure, 72, 77, 81
Adoptions of Acts, 27, 33-35, 37-38, 41, 49, 53, 57, 61, 64-65, 66, 76, 134, 301-325
Aggas's map of the City of London, 130
Agreements, 79, 80
Aikins (the), 256
Ainsworth (Harrison), 286
Ainsworth bequest, 308
Airdrie, 27, 40, 114, 323
Albert Institute (Dundee), 237
Alleghany (U.S.A.), 113
Alloa, 53, 67, 323
Alnwick, 57
Altrincham, 64, 312
Alverstoke. *See* Gosport
American influence on British libraries, 102
American Library Association, 97
American State libraries, 16
Amiens, 16
Anderson (Colonel), 113
Anderson (Mr.), 42

329

Andover, 65, 325
Anglers' books, 215
Annotated lists, 141, 241
Apprentices and the free library, 93
Appropriation of lands, 73, 82
Arbroath, 41, 42, 47, 65, 70, 114, 323
Archer (W.), 191-192
Architecture: books relating thereto, 164, 172, 215
Arguments for the free library (*see also* Speeches), 60
Arlecdon and Frizington, 65, 324
Armistead (Mr.), 40
Arnold (Sir Arthur), 87
Arnold (Matthew), 280
Art books, 252
Art exhibitions, 224, 258
Art galleries, 79, 164, 168, 172, 179, 193, 207, 224, 225, 227, 228, 235, 237, 255, 257, 266
Art schools, 79, 164, 216, 237, 261, 268
Ascham (Roger), 119
Ashton-on-Mersey, 65, 272, 312
Ashton-under-Lyne, 37, 68, 83, 316
Assessments, 243, 301-325
Associates of Dr. Bray, 6
Aston Manor, 41, 248-251, 320
Athenæums, 7
Atherstone, 65, 325
Atkinson Library, Southport, 41, 46, 314
Austen (Miss), 298
Australia, 300
Avery (Alderman), 51
Aylesford collection, 180
Ayr, 21, 47, 64, 113-114, 322

BAGGALLAY (Mr.), 58
Bailey (S.), 306
Bailey (Sir W. H.), 100
Baillie's Institution, Glasgow, 292
Baines (Mr.), 38
Balfour (A. J.), 196, 244
Ball (Sir R.), 196
Ballinger (J.), 101, 234
Bamburgh Castle Library, 8
Banbridge, 64, 273, 325
Bangor, 41, 325
Banksian Library, 121
Bannatyne Club, 290
Barker (Rev. Canon), 299
Barking, 64, 322
Barnard (Sir F. A.), 121
Barnet. *See* Hadley

Barnsley, 64, 68, 323
Barrett (F. T.), 289, 292
Barrow-in-Furness, 49, 316
Barry and Cadoxton, 65, 323
Barter (Dr. J. Boyd), 238
Bass (Sir M. T.), 46, 223, 308
Bataillard collection, 164
Bath, 38, 41, 47, 48, 66
Baumann (Mr.), 71
Bazaars, 238, 279
Beaconsfield (Lord) quoted, 36
Beaney (Mr.), 70
Bebington. *See* Lower Bebington
Bedford, 64, 322
Beer and Spirit duties (*see also* Local Taxation funds), 77
Belfast, 49, 157, 190, 192-194, 306
Benefactions. *See* Subscriptions
Bentley (Richard), 119
Beresford (Lord Charles), 297
Berm (G. C.), 320
Bernal-Osborne (Mr.), 18, 22
Berwick, 35, 40
Beveridge (Mr.), 68
Bexley Heath, 65, 322
Bibliographical books, 179, 253
Bibliographical exhibits, 127
Bibliographical rarities, 121
Bideford, 41, 272, 324
Bills in Parliament (*see also* Acts), 49, 55, 58, 59, 71, 80, 86
Bilston, 37, 323
Bingley, 64, 68, 323
Birkbeck (George), 9
Birkenhead, 33, 83, 217-220
Birmingham, 16, 27, 34, 49, 50-53, 83, 173-182, 306
"Birmingham Free Libraries (1871)," 174
Blackburn, 27, 308
Blackpool, 49, 316
Blaenau Festiniog, 65, 323
Bletchingley, 108
Blind. *See* Books for the blind
Bloxam's "Gothic Architecture," 250
Board of Guardians and parochial land, 79
Board of Trade, 86
Board School and free library (*see also* School libraries), 99
Bodmin, 65, 112, 275, 324
"Boldrewood (Rolph)," 280
Bollandist "Acta Sanctorum," 252
Bolton, 27, 308

INDEX 331

Bond (G. A.), 106
Bonner indicator, 100
"Books for a Reference Library," 182
Books for the blind, 99
Books for the young, 99
Books in free libraries: their wide range of subject, 92
Booksellers and the free library, 92
Booth's "Darkest England," 298
Bootle, 53, 256-260, 316
Borrowing powers of library authorities, 57, 81, 82
Bossuet, 198
Boston: church library, 5
Botanic Gardens, Liverpool, 167
Bournemouth, 65, 318
Bowden, 62
Braddock (U.S.A.), 113
Braddon (Miss), 149, 190, 196, 243
Bradford, 41, 69, 76, 206-209, 308
Bradley's "Dictionary of Miniaturists," 250
Bragge (Mr.), 177
Branch delivery stations, 102, 156, 160, 211, 259
Branch libraries, 98; their cost, 149, 159, 202, 206, 237, 243, 246, 301-325
Brassey (Lady), 149
Brassey (Lord), 67
Brassey Institute, 67
Brassington (W. S.), 181
Bray parochial libraries, 6, 283
Brechin, 64, 68, 273, 276-278, 324
Brentford, 53, 64, 316
Bridgwater, 34, 323
Brierley Hill, 41, 318
Bright (John), 20, 22, 51, 180
Brighton, 28, 83, 310
Briscoe (J. P.), 99, 100, 211
Bristol, 3, 41, 76, 84, 98, 196-202, 215, 310
British Association, 110, 175
British Museum, 7, 10, 110, 116-128, 131, 243
Brogden (A.), 318
Bromley (Kent), 65, 68, 314
Brontë sisters, 298
Brooke (Stopford), 244
Brooks (Maurice), 42
Brotherton (Joseph), 10, 16, 17, 21
Brotherton Memorial Fund, 205
Broughton, 65, 325
Brown (J. D.), 102, 282
Brown (Rev. J. C.), 8

Brown (Rev. William), 8
Brown (Richard), 59, 81
Brown (Samuel), 8
Brown (Sir William), 32, 168
Brown (T. Craig-), 67, 324
Brown Library, Liverpool, 46, 168, 306
Browne (G. W.), 188
Browning, 147
Brunner (Sir J. T.), 67, 71, 312, 324
Bucer's MSS., 119
Buchanan (Miss G. I.), 69, 260, 314
Buck (Mr.), 17
Buckinghamshire charities, 276
Bull (Mr.), 69
Bullen (G.), 44, 125
Bullivant (Mr.), 68
Burke (Edmund), 190
Burney (Dr. C.), 121
Burney collection, 122
Burnley, 66, 195
Burns (R.), 288
Burns' literature, 290
Burslem, 35, 318
Burton (Lady), 302
Burton (Sir Richard), 302
Burton-on-Trent, 65, 318
Burwell, 65, 324
Bury (Lancashire), 66
Bury (William), 128
Bury St. Edmunds, 65, 323
Bute (Lord), 70, 233
Butler (Mr.), 69
Buxton, 53, 76, 273-274, 324
Buxton (Sydney), 71
Bye-laws, 40, 82, 83
Byron literature, 182

CADOGAN (Lord), 67, 87, 137, 302
Cadoxton. See Barry
Caine (Hall), 87, 92, 243
Caldwell (Mr.), 198
Calvin, 198
Camborne, 65, 112, 312
Cambridge, 27, 312
Cambridge University, 146
Cambridgeshire libraries, 283
Cambuslang, 53
Cameron (Dr.), 59
Campbell (E. L.), 69
Campbell (G. L.), 49
Campbell (L. E.), 290
Campbeltown, 64, 65, 70, 325
Canterbury, 10, 11, 34, 70, 322
Card ledger, 99

Cardiff, 34, 40, 54, 70, 76, 88, 101, 230-234, 310
Carlisle, 64, 68, 312
Carlisle (Bishop of), 68
Carlisle (Lord), 68
Carlton (Notts), 57, 325
Carlyle, 120, 135, 190, 196, 244, 299
Carnarvon, 57, 323
Carnegie (A.), 61, 66, 69, 70, 87, 112-114, 187, 240, 278, 279, 280, 306, 322, 324
Carnegie (Mrs.), 69
Carpenter (John), 129
"Cassell's New Popular Educator," 194
Cataloguing rules, 103
Catchpool (R.), 68
Causton (R. K.), 88
Caxton exhibition, 127
Cervantes literature, 177
Chadwick Library, Macclesfield, 41, 46, 312
Challinor (W.), 318
Chalmers (R.), 290
Chamberlain (J.), 42, 52
Charity Commissioners, 73, 79, 214, 287
Charity lands, 73
Chatham, 42
Cheetham (J. F.), 36, 70
Chelsea Commissioners, 71
Cheltenham, 34, 47, 53, 69, 260-261, 314
Chester, 41, 67, 312
Chester (Mayor of), 67
Chesterfield, 41, 314
Chetham (Sir Humphrey), 5, 286
Chetham Society, 165
Children's libraries, 140, 143, 170, 188, 211, 215, 219, 223, 240, 253, 258, 261
Children's reading, 163
Children's reading-rooms, 145, 147, 160
Chinese books, 121
Chiswick, 64, 316
Chivers' indicator, 99
Christie (Chancellor), 74
Church libraries, 5
Circuit libraries, 282
Circulars of information, 219
City Corporation libraries, 3, 4, 5
Clarendon Press, 243
Class lists on special topics, 164
Classical MSS., 126
Classics, 120, 121

Classification systems, 102
Cleator Moor, 65, 324
Clerkenwell, 101
Clifton (C.), 308
Clitheroe, 49, 316
Coats (Sir Peter), 35, 61, 266, 322
Cobden (Richard), 10
Cockburn (Lord Chief-Justice), 25
Cockermouth, 63
"Codex Leicestrensis," 5
Cohen (Arthur), 58
Colchester, 53, 65, 68, 69, 314
Coleraine, 41, 273, 324
Coleridge, 200
Collins (Jesse), 178
Collins (Mr.), 58
Colne, 62, 65
Colonies, 300
Colt Hoare collection, 121
Commission on Free Libraries. See Select Committee
Commissioners of Public Libraries and Museums in Ireland (see also Library authorities), 81
Committees. See also Library authorities
Committees in Scotland and their powers, 82
"Common Good," 277
Commonwealth tracts, 119
Complutensian Polyglot, 198
Conferences of librarians—
London International, 43, 97
New York, 44, 97
Philadelphia, 43, 96
(See also Library Association)
Constitution of Committees, 193
Contemporary Review quoted, 59
Continental libraries, 13, 16
Co-operation of authorities, 73, 79, 272, 282
Corbett (Cameron), 59
"Corelli (Marie)," 135, 196, 243
Cork, 27, 40, 244, 267-269, 322
Cornish towns, 69
Corry (James), 42
Corsar (David), 70
Corwen, 65, 325
Cost of branches. See Branches
Cotgreave (Alfred), 99
Cottonian MSS., 118, 119, 120
County libraries, 282
Coventry, 37, 323
Cowell (Peter), 100, 167
Cox (J. H.), 69
Cox (T. H.), 239

Cracherode bequest, 120
Craig-Brown (Mr.), 67, 324
Crawford bequest, 322
Credland (W. R.), 160, 283
Crewe (Nathaniel, *Lord*), 8
Crockett (S. R.), 196, 243, 280
Croker collection, 121
Crompton, 64
Crompton-Roberts (Mr.), 144
Crosfield (W.), 316
Crossley (James), 159
Croydon, 54, 56, 64, 87, 310
Cultivated lands: deductions for, 80, 81
Cunningham (Peter), 32
Cutter's "Rules for making a Dictionary Catalogue," 102

DA COSTA (Solomon), 120
Dalgleish (Sir W. Ogilvie), 238
Dalkey, 65, 273, 325
Danson (T. P.), 257
Darlaston, 41, 318
Darlington, 53, 314
Darwen, 41, 314
Darwin (Charles), 135, 149, 190, 244, 299
Davy (Sir Humphry), 200
Dawson (George), 12, 175
Day (Francis), his ichthyological collection, 260, 314
De Thou, 121
De Worde (Wynkyn), 130
Debate on Ewart's Act of 1850, 17-23
Debenham (Frank), 299
"Decimal Classification," 102
Deffett-Francis collection, 235
Denmark, 300
Denny trustees, 322
Denton and Haughton, 57, 68, 316
Derby, 37, 223-224, 308
Derby (Lord), 168, 257
Deschanel's "Natural Philosophy," 194
"Devon and Cornwall" books, 221
Devonport, 49, 314
Devonshire (Duke of), 68, 153, 223, 308
Dewey (Melvil), 102
Dewsbury, 57, 320
Dickens (Charles), 149, 196, 243, 244, 298

Dickens' (Charles) speech at opening of the Manchester Free Library, 30
Dilke (Sir C. W.), 67, 137, 302
Disraeli (B.). *See* Beaconsfield
Distribution of parliamentary papers, 85
Dodgson bequest, 308
Dollar (R.), 67
Donaldson (Robert), 240
Doncaster, 37, 323
Douglas (Isle of Man), 53, 56, 270-271, 322
Dover, 11
Downes (Mr.), 55
Downpatrick, 63
Doyle (Conan), 149, 190, 196
Dramatic literature, 121, 131
Droylesden, 56
Drummond, 196, 244
Drumoak, 65, 273, 280, 324
Dublin, 157, 189-192, 306
Dudley, 49, 323
Dugdale's "Monasticon," 252
Dugdale's "Warwickshire," 250
Dukinfield, 65, 312
Dulwich College, 73
Dumbarton, 49, 322
Dumfries, 108
Dundalk, 243, 269-270, 322
Dundee, 35, 40, 61, 69, 85, 237-239, 310
Dunfermline, 49, 61, 112, 113-114, 322
Dunlop (Mr.), 35
"Durham Book," 120
Dutch literature, 128
Dyall (Charles), 99

EALING, 53, 316
Earliest existing city library, 215
Early printed books, 290
East Ham, 322
East Hartlepool, 65, 322
Eastbourne, 65, 92, 320
Eastern topography, 131
Ecclesiastical Commissioners, 79
Eckersley (Mr.), 316
Economy of the library rate, 89-91
Edinburgh, 7, 38, 47, 48, 53, 66, 113, 114, 157, 186-189, 306
Edmonton, 65, 316
Education Department, 50
Edwards (Edward), 11, 95, 96, 104-107, 159, 166, 312

Edwards (J. Passmore), 70, 87, 110–112, 152, 153, 203, 247, 264, 275, 302, 316, 324
Eighteenth-century libraries, 6
Eissler's "Metallurgy of Gold and Silver," 250
Eisteddfod, 265, 322
Electric light in free libraries, 100
Electricity, 299
Elementary Education Act of 1870: its influence on free libraries, 39, 88
Elgin, 54, 65, 324
"Eliot (George)," 244, 298
Elliott (Rev. H. V.), 226
Elliott (J.), 99
Ellis (J. E.), 67, 318
"Encyclopædia Britannica," 97, 106, 299
Endowed Free Libraries, 285–296
Enfield, 65, 316
Ennis, 34, 40, 272, 273, 325
Entertainments, 265, 301–325
Esquilant (Miss J. A.), 144
Estimates, 82
Evans (Sir W.), 223
Evening reading-rooms, 214
Ewart (William), 10, 17–26, 35, 36, 37, 95, 105, 107–109, 166
Ewart Act of 1850: its provisions, 23
Ewart's Bill of 1854 defeated, 24
Ewing (W.), 290
Examinations for library assistants, 101, 202
Exchequer Contribution Account, 207
Exeter, 27, 34, 37, 68, 322
Extended areas of library districts, 170, 218

FALCONER (Judge), 233
Falkirk, 57, 65, 67, 323
Falmouth, 65, 273, 274–275, 324
Fanshawe (Mr.), 75
Faraday (M.), 147
Farley (Alderman), 69
Farrar (Dean), 135, 196, 298
Fathers of the Church, 198
Fénelon, 198
Ferris (A. O.), 69, 264, 275, 312
Field (Justice), 139
Fife (Duke of), 297
Finch (G.), 252
Fine art books, 172

Fires in libraries, 14, 178, 214
First adoption of Ewart's Act, 216
First free library under Ewart's Act, 158
First Public Libraries Act, 12–24
First rate-aided free library, 254
Fisher (Mr.), 86
Fishmongers' Company, 146
Fitzgerald (Seymour), 25
Flechier, 198
Fleetwood, 57, 324
Folkard (H. T.), 253
Folkestone, 49, 322
Forfar, 38, 40, 323
Formby (T.), 70
Forster (W. E.), 39
Fortescue (G. K.), 125
Fovargue (H. W.), 77
Fox (W. J.), 22
France, 300
Francis (J. Deffett-), 235
Fraser (Dr. W.), 290
Free Church of Scotland, 9
Free lectures, 100, 165, 168, 206, 251, 258
"Free Library Movement in Manchester," 160
Free town libraries, 106
French Government, 45
French revolutionary literature, 121
French works, 198, 235
Frizington. See Arlecdon
Froude (J. A.), 196, 244, 280, 299

GAINSBOROUGH, 63
Galashiels, 41, 68, 323
Gamble (Colonel), 69, 314
Gardiner (R. W. A.), 277
Gardiner (S. R.), 120, 149
Gardner (H.), 71
Gardyne (A.), 290
Garnett (Dr. R.), 44, 101
Garrick, 121
Gas profits, 193
Gaskell (Mrs.), 298
Gateshead, 49, 310
Genealogical books, 131
George III., 7
German Government, 45
German works, 235
Germany, 300
Gibbon, 149
Gifts. See Subscriptions
Gilchrist Trust lectures, 217, 225
Gill (Robinson), 69, 287

INDEX

Gilstrap (Sir Wm.), 61, 68, 261, 318
Ginguené collection, 121
Gipsies : works thereon, 164
Gladstone (W. E.), 87, 93, 106, 154, 236
Glasgow, 16, 54, 59, 62, 67, 69, 157, 158, 285, 288-293
Glasgow books, 290
Glasgow University, 290
Glossop, 64, 322
Gloucester, 38, 65, 322
Gloucestershire books, 261
"Golden Legend," by Wynkyn de Worde, 130
Gordon (General), 248
Gore's "Lux Mundi," 244
Goschen (G. J.), 87, 150
"Gospel of Wealth" quoted, 113
Gosport and Alverstoke, 53, 318
Goulburn (Mr.), 18
Government assistance to libraries, 14
Government control, 195
Government grants, 278
Graham (Mr.), 59
Graham (Sir J.), 21
Grammar School libraries, 6
Grandborough, 65, 324
Grangemouth, 57, 325
Grant (J.), 194
Grantham, 63
Gravesend, 65, 314
Gray (W.), 192
Grays, 65, 314
Greek and Latin Fathers, 5
Greek Government, 45
Greek topography, 131
Green (J. R.), 190, 194, 196, 244
Greenock, 67
Greenwood (Thomas), 56
Gregory (George), 40
Grenville (Thomas), 121
Greville (E. E.), 155
Grey (Sir George), 21
Griffits (J. V.), 287
Grimsby, 65, 322
Grolier, 121
Guild (J. Wyllie), 290
Guildhall Library, London, 128-133
Guion (Madame), 198

Hack (D. P.), 227
Hackney Nonconformist literature, 130
Hadley and Barnet, 285

Haggard (Rider), 149, 196, 243
Haggerston (W. J.), 213
Hakluyt's Voyages, 252
Half-hour talks with readers, 100, 211
Halifax, 49, 310
Halifax (Lord), 118
Halkin, 65, 325
Hall (J. M.), 70
Halliwell-Phillips (J. O.), 226
Hall's (Thomas) Library, 181
Halton, 65, 325
Hamilton (G. A.), 17, 19
Handbooks, 164, 289
Handsworth, 41, 249, 323
Hanley, 53, 318
Hanson's (James) Library, 207, 308
Harben (H.), 69, 141
Harcourt (Sir William) quoted, 72
Hargrave collection, 121
Harleian MSS., 118, 119, 120
Harris bequest (Preston), 69, 228, 310
Harrogate, 53, 320
Hart (Sir Israel), 308
Hartley Institution, Southampton, 248
Harvey (C.), 68
Haslingden, 34
Hastings, 47, 48, 62, 66
Haughton. *See* Denton
Hawick, 49, 266-267, 322
Hawkes (Rev. R.), 310
Hawkins (Sir J.), 121
Heald (Mr.), 23
Hebrew books, 120, 130
Heginbottom (G.), 68
Henderson (Lord Provost), 240
Henry VII., 7
Henty, 196, 243, 298
Hereford, 27, 41, 314
Herschell (Lord), 85
Hertford, 272
Hewetson (H.), 69
Heywood, 41, 314
Heywood (J.), 302
Heywood (Mr.), 21
High Wycombe, 287
Highlands and Islands (Scotland), 9
Hinckley, 64, 67, 324
Hindley, 53, 316
Hinton (R.), 218
Historical MSS., 120, 122
Hoare (J. Rolls), 144
Holborn (R. M.), 68
Holyhead, 65, 325
Homestead (U.S.A.), 113

"Hope (Anthony)," 135
Hopwood (Mr.), 55
Hornsey, 65
Horsfall (T. B.), 166
Horwich, 287
Houghton (Lord), 24, 31, 71
Houldsworth (Sir William), 71
Hours of assistants, 202
Hours that libraries are open, 301–325
Hove, 65, 320
Howard (Baron), 21
Howard-Arundel collection, 122
Howard de Walden (Lady), 297
Hucknall Torkard, 53, 67, 318
Huddersfield, 47, 48, 56, 66, 195
Hull, 34, 47, 62, 65, 68, 157, 184–187, 306
Hulse (E. H.), 320
Hume (Mr.), 18, 22
Hume (Rev. A.), 166
Hungarian literature, 128
Huntingdonshire, 66
Huxley (T. H.), 149
Hyde, 65
Hyde (Mrs. Julia), 285, 312
Hythe, 69

IBSTOCK, 65, 324
Ilford, 65, 314
Ilkeston, 63
Illuminated MSS., 120, 126
"Imitation of Christ," 121
Income-tax, 84–85
Incunabula, 177, 198
India, 214
Indicators, 99, 226, 241
Industrial Exhibition at Thurso, 279
Informality of adoption of Acts at Newcastle-on-Tyne, 42
Inglis (G. M.), 68
Inglis (Sir R. H.), 20
Innes (Professor), 290
Inspection of libraries, 50
Intellectual apathy, 91, 92
International Conferences of librarians, 43, 44
International exchange of books, 15
International Exhibition, Edinburgh: application of profits, 188
Inverness, 41, 114, 322
Ipswich, 33, 320
Ireland (Alexander), 87, 88
Ireland: scarcity of libraries, 13
Irving Shakespeare, 250

Isle of Man Local Government Act, 56
Isle of Man Savings Bank, 322
Issues from libraries, 301–325
Italian books, 121, 198, 235
Italy, 300

JACKSON (George), 10, 59
Jebb (Professor), 87, 92
Jedburgh, 65, 325
Jevons (W. S.), 59
Johnston (U.S.A.), 113
Joint-use of library, 79, 80
Jones (R. L.), 129
Juvenile libraries. *See* Children's libraries

KEATS, 250
Kederminster (Sir John), 5
Keiller (J. M.), 61, 238
Kelly (Mr.), 73
Kendal, 65, 69, 320
Kennaway (Sir John), 58
Kettering, 65, 316
Kidderminster, 27, 68, 320
Kilmarnock, 21, 65
Kingdon (Mr. Kent), 68
King's Library, British Museum, 118, 119, 127
King's Norton, 181
Kingsley (Charles), 196, 298
Kingston (Ireland), 53, 323
Kingston (W. H. G.), 196
Kingston-on-Thames, 49, 83, 320
Kingston-upon-Hull. *See* Hull
Kinnaird (Mr.), 40
Kirkcaldy, 68
Kirkmichael (Banff), 65, 325
Kirktown, 279
Kirkwall, 64, 325
Kirkwood (Rev. James), 6
Knight (Charles), 32

LABOUCHERE (Mr.), 19
Lafone (A.), 166
Lamb (A. C.), 238
Lancashire and Cheshire Union of Institutes, 9, 283
Lancashire church libraries, 5
Lancashire works, 164
Lancaster, 65, 69, 316
Land appropriation in Scotland, 82
Land held for free libraries, 79

INDEX 337

Land; held on trust for an open space, 79
Landor (W. S.), 200
Lang (A.), 196
Langford (Dr.), 174, 176
Langley Marish, 4
Langworthy (E. R.), 205, 308
Lansdowne collection, 122
Law (Mr.), 21, 23
Law relating to free libraries: English, 78–80; Irish, 80; Scotch, 81, 82
—— improvements required, 86
Lawson's "Tyneside Celebrities," 245
Leadgate, 324
Leamington, 33, 83, 320
Learned societies' publications, 252
Lectures, 13, 100, 145, 253, 256, 265, 274, 277. *See* also Free lectures
Lee (Edward), 133
Leeds, 16, 37, 157, 183-184, 306
Leek, 57, 68, 318
Legislation. *See* Acts and Law
Leicester, 11, 35, 308
Leigh, 65, 69, 316
Leighton, 65, 324
Leighton (J.), 44
Leith, 67
Lending libraries, 14, 26
Leng (Sir John), 85
Leominster, 64, 72, 324
Letters of royal and illustrious persons, 120
Lever (Charles), 194, 243, 244
Leyton, 65, 314
"Liber Landavensis," 233
Liberty and Property Defence League, 66
Librarians, 242, 263, 303-325
"Libraries and their Founders," 106
"Library (The)," 97
Library Association of the United Kingdom, 45, 49, 74, 75, 85, 86, 87, 97, 112
Library authorities and their powers, 78-80
"Library Chronicle," 97
Library districts, 282
"Library Journal," 97
Library rate, 23, 24, 167. *See also* Rate limit
Lichfield, 33, 325
Lichfield (Master William), 129

Lilford (Lord), 69
Limerick, 64, 322
Lincoln, 65, 69, 92, 316
Lings (Edward), 174
Linlithgow, 288
Liskeard, 65, 112, 275, 324
Littledale (T.), 167
Liverpool, 7, 11, 27, 76, 97, 99, 100, 103, 108, 157, 165-173, 174, 306
"Lives of the Founders of the British Museum," 106
Llandudno, 62
Llanuwchllyn, 65, 325
Loans on free library property, 94, 301-325
Local Acts, 27, 28, 35, 38, 167, 182, 204, 214, 224, 226, 228, 236, 255
Local Boards, 40, 41
Local Government Board, 79, 81
Local history and literature, 93, 98, 129, 138, 140, 143, 145, 151, 155, 156, 164, 171, 177, 189, 198, 199, 208, 215, 217, 221, 227, 233, 236, 240, 245, 247, 250, 252, 256, 261, 267, 271
Local societies, 183, 226, 236, 238, 248, 269, 271, 280
Local Taxation residue fund, 170, 215, 219, 246, 259, 291
Local views, plans, &c., 156, 172, 180, 234, 250, 261
Logan (D.), 290
London, 7, 9, 13, 34, 43-45, 49, 66, 73, 109, 111, 134-156
—— Acton, 57; Battersea, 53, 57, 135-137, 302; Bermondsey, 57, 83, 302; Bethnal Green, 63, 111, 134; Birkbeck Institution, 9; Bloomsbury, *see* St. Giles; Bow, 65, 305; Bromley-by-Bow, 65, 305; Camberwell, 47, 64, 67, 71, 87, 111, 302; Chelsea, 57, 67, 137-139, 302; Christ Church, Southwark, 64, 302; City of London, 27, 34, 78, 152; City: Bishopgate Institute, 132, 287; City: Cripplegate Institute, 132, 287; City: Guildhall Library, 128-133, 287; City: St. Bride's Institute, 112, 132, 287; Clapham, 57, 302; Clerkenwell, 57, 68, 83, 139-141, 154, 302; Deptford, 54, 63; Fulham, 53, 134, 304; Greenwich, 63, 134; Hackney, 47, 48, 63, 134; Haggerston, *see* St. Leonard; Hammersmith, 57, 64, 91,

Y

INDEX

111, 302; Hampstead, 65, 69, 141-143, 304; Holborn, 65, 134, 304; Hoxton, *see* St. Leonard; Islington, 28, 42, 57, 63, 134; Kensal Town, 138; Kensington, 42, 57, 88, 302; Lambeth, 53, 64, 68, 87, 88, 144-145, 302; Lewisham, 64, 304; Mile End, 64, 65, 83, 305; Newington, 62, 64, 146-147, 304; Paddington, 28, 57, 63, 134; Penge, 65, 304; Plumstead, 62, 134; Polytechnics, 138, 287; Poplar, 64, 68, 134, 147-149, 304; Putney, 47, 57, 302; Rotherhithe, 57, 89, 302; Ratcliff, 65, 305; St. George, Hanover Square, 64, 149-152, 304; St. George in the East, 65, 305; St. George the Martyr, 65, 112, 305; St. Giles', Bloomsbury, 64, 65, 134, 304; St. Leonard, Shoreditch, 65, 111, 152-153, 304; St. James, Westminster, 134; St. Luke, Middlesex, 134; St. Margaret and St. John, Westminster, 33, 234, 304; St. Marylebone, 34, 62, 63, 134, 296-299; St. Martin-in-the-Fields, 5, 57, 87, 93, 154-155, 302; St. Olave, 134; St. Pancras, 34, 41, 63, 134; St. Paul, Covent Garden, 65, 302; St. Saviour, Southwark, 65, 88, 304; St. Saviour's district, 134; South Kensington, 126; Stoke Newington, 64, 304; Strand, 134; Streatham, 64, 304; Tenison's (Abp.) Library, 286; Tooting Graveney, 134; Wandsworth, 53, 134, 155-156, 302; Westminster, 134, 286; Whitechapel, 47, 64, 134, 304; Williams' (Dr.) Library, 286
London printers' work, 131
Londonderry, 64
Long (G.), 227
Longstaff (G. B.), 155, 156, 302
Longstaff (Ll. W.), 156
Longton, 65, 318
Lord Chancellor, 85
Lorne (Marchioness of), 88
Lothian (East), 8
Loughborough, 53, 322
Lower Bebington, 65, 294, 324
Lowestoft, 65, 323
Löwy (Rev. A.), 130
Lubbock (Sir John), 42, 49, 57, 59, 71, 74, 75, 87, 89, 109-111, 150

Lugard (Captain), 196
Lurgan, 65, 323
Luton, 62, 65, 312
"Lyall (Edna)," 149, 190, 196, 243
Lyceums, 7
Lynn, 47, 48
Lyons, 16
Lyttleton, (Mr.), 40
Lytton (Lord), speech at opening of the Manchester Free Library, 29

"MABINOGION," 233
MacAlister (J. Y. W.), 74, 97
Macaulay (Lord), 190, 244
MacCarthy (Justin), 58, 71, 75
Macclesfield, 38, 41, 312
Macnaghten (Lord), 85
M'Pherson (D.), 69, 290
"Magna Charta," 120
Maidenhead, 63
Maidment (J.), 290
Maidstone, 27, 33, 314
Maitland Club, 290
Malin (Stephen), 149
Malleson (Colonel), 149
Management of libraries, 96, 102
Manchester, 5, 10, 13, 27, 49, 68, 82, 83, 84, 88, 98, 100, 103, 105, 158-165, 286, 306
Manchester (Bishop of), 32
Manchester Free Library: speeches at opening, 28-32
Manchester School and Charles Dickens, 30
Manners (*Lord* John), 19
Mansfield, 64, 322
Mansfield House Settlement, 202
Manx books, 271
Margate, 238
Margrave (T. J.), 235
Marryat (Captain), 194, 298
Marseilles, 16
Marshall (H. Brooks), 144
Martin (Mr.), 175
Marylebone Free Public Library Association, 296
Masson (Professor), 187
Master of the Rolls, 84
Mathews (E. R. N.), 197
Matthew (Dr. Toby), 4, 197
Maxwell (Sir W. Stirling), 250
Mayer (Joseph), 293
Mayer Library, Bebington, 293-296
Meakin (J. D. G.), 318
Mechanics' institutions, 8, 9, 21

INDEX 339

Mediæval libraries, 3
Medical works, 120
Melvin (Mr.), 279, 324
"Memoirs of Libraries," 96, 105
"Men of Letters," 299
Mercer's School, 129
Merthyr-Tydvil, 47, 48, 67
"Methods of Social Reform" quoted, 60
Metropolis Management Act, 57
Metropolitan districts, 78
Metropolitan Free Libraries Association, 49, 55
Middle Claydon, 65, 273, 275–276, 281, 324
Middlesborough, 38, 320
Middleton, 57, 316
Middlewich, 64, 324
Migné: "Patrologia," 252
Miles (W.), 19
Millom, 57, 272, 324
Mill's "Political Economy," 244
Milnes (R. M.). *See* Houghton (Lord)
Milton literature, 182
Minet (Mr.), 67
Mitchell (Stephen), 288
Mitchell Library, Glasgow, 158, 285, 288–293
Moir (Bailie), 290
Moll collection, 121
Monastic chronicles, 126
Monk Bretton, 62
Monkswell (Lord), 71
Montague (Duke of), 118
Montague (S.), 302
Montague House, 118, 119
"Monthly Notes," 97
Morgan (O. V.), 59
Morison (Rev. Principal), 290
Morley, 65, 323
Morley (Henry), 143
Morley (John), 75
Morley (S.), 211
Morley Memorial Library, 143
Morris (Lord), 85
Morrison (Robert), 121
Moser (J.), 69, 207
Moss-side, 57, 322
Mountain Ash, 57
Mullins (J. D.), 175, 181
Mundella (A. J.), 42, 87
Muntz (Mr.), 21, 22
Murphy (Mr.), 42
Museum rate, where collected, 76
Museums, 33, 34, 79, 151, 172, 193, 200, 204, 207, 224, 227, 228, 237, 246, 254, 257, 266, 274, 279, 293, 294, 295
Museums Act of 1845, 10, 11, 23
Museums and Gymnasiums Act, 76, 172
Music schools, 81, 268
Music scores, 99, 121, 141, 299

NANTWICH, 57, 324
National Library of Ireland, 191
Natural History, 120, 121, 172
Natural History departments of British Museum, 126
Naturalist and Archæological department at Wolverhampton Free Library, 226
Nelson, 64, 316
Nenagh, 65, 273, 325
Nettlefold (F.), 144
New Mills, 65, 324
New South Wales country delivery system, 282
New Testament: Codex Leicestrensis, 5
New York conference of librarians, 44
New York State country delivery system, 282
Newark-on-Trent, 49, 61, 68, 261–262, 318
Newburgh (Fife), 65, 325
Newcastle-on-Tyne, 41, 42, 70, 83, 212–215, 285, 310
Newcastle-under-Lyme, 53, 323
Newport (Monmouth), 37, 316
Newry, 65, 323
Newsham bequest, 228
Newspaper reading-rooms, 25
Newton (H. W.), 212
Newton Heath, 54, 57, 161, 306
Newtonards, 65, 273, 325
Nicholson (E. W. B.), 44, 49
Nicholson family, 68
Nicholson Institute, Leek, 68, 318
Noble (W.), 68, 144
North (Chancellor), 7
Northampton, 34, 322
Northwich, 47, 53, 312
Norton (J. J.), 68
Norton (Mr.), 263
Norwich, 27, 196, 215–217, 308
Nottingham, 37, 83, 99, 100, 209–212, 310
Nuneaton, 65, 323

"ODYSSEY," 120
Official organs of the movement, 97
Ogilvy (Sir John), 37, 40
Oldbury, 64, 323
Oldham, 35, 83, 310
Oliphant, 244, 298
Open access, 101, 102, 139, 141, 154, 182, 233, 240
Open space: land held as such, 79
Openshaw branch library, 161, 306
Opposition tactics, 48, 83
Origin of the Museums Act, 10
O'Shaughnessy (Mr.), 42, 43
Oswald (Mr.), 21
Oswestry, 64, 325
Otley, 69, 287
Oxford, 27, 100, 322
Oxford and Mortimer (Earl of), 120

PAGET (H. B.), 318
Paisley, 35, 40, 61, 265-266, 322
Palmer (Roundell), 20
Panizzi (Sir A.), 106, 120, 123
Paris libraries, 282
Parish Councils, 77
Parliamentary Commission on the British Museum, 96, 124
Parliamentary papers: their free distribution, 85
Parliamentary return of 1856, 33; of 1870, 38; of 1876, 45; of 1885, 61; of 1890, 94
Parr (George), 100
Pascal, 198
Patent specifications, 103, 176
Paton (Thomson), 67
Pecock (Reginald), 129
Peeblesshire travelling libraries, 9
Peel (Sir Robert), 16
Penalties recoverable in Scotland, 82
Penarth, 65, 323
Penny rate introduced, 24
Penny rate: its insufficiency, 157
Penrith, 49, 324
Penzance, 65, 312
Periodical press, 59
Persian MSS., 126
Perth, 65, 70, 322
Peterborough, 54, 65, 316
Peterhead, 64, 114, 322
Philadelphia Conference, 44
Phillips (J. O. Halliwell), 226
Philological books, 290
Photography and the free library, 101

Picton (Sir J. A.), 166, 169, 171
Picton Reading-room, Liverpool, 170
Pierpoint (Gervaise, *Lord*), 5
Piranesi's "Rome," 252
Pittsburg (U.S.A.), 112
Planché's "Cyclopædia of Costume," 250
Playfair (Lord), 58, 87
"Plea for Liberty," 66
Pleasley, 65, 324
"Pleasures of Life," 109
Plowden (Mr.), 22
Plymouth, 41, 220-223, 308
Poll of voters, 78
Polytechnics, 287
Pontypridd, 57, 322
Poole, 53, 68, 322
Popularity of authors, 243
Portsmouth, 38, 41, 310
Potter (Sir John), 158
Powell (Sir F. S.), 68, 75, 76, 316
Preston, 49, 69, 83, 228-230, 285, 310
Priestley (Joseph), 256
Prince Consort, 237
Prince Henry (son of James I.), 119
Prince Leopold, 210
Prince of Wales, 87, 214
Princess Christian, 88
Princess Louise, 88
Privy Council Committee on Education, 54
Prize Draft Library Bill, 74
Professional libraries, 4
Promenade concerts, 224
"Proposals for a Publick Library at Aberdeen," 8
Provisional orders, 83
Pryce (George), 98, 198
"Public Libraries," 56
Public Libraries Acts. See Acts
"Public Library Legislation," 80
Public men and the free library, 87

"Q," 244
Quarterly "Guides," 140, 143, 204
Queenborough, 57, 273, 324
Queen's College, Oxford, 106
Queen's jubilee year, 56, 227

RAMSGATE, 54, 65, 322
Rankin (James), 314
Rankin (Mr.), 72

INDEX 341

Rate limit and rating, 36, 50, 55, 56, 64, 71, 78, 80, 82, 83, 89, 242, 257, 301-325
Rathmines and Rathgar, 57, 323
Rawmarsh, 65, 323
Rawson (H.), 164
Reade (Charles), 190
Reading, 38, 41, 312
Reckitt (Francis), 185
Reckitt (Sir James), 68, 185, 306
Recording indicator, 100
Recreation rooms, 161, 267
Redgrave's "Dictionary of English Artists," 250
Redruth, 65, 112, 312
Redwood (Robert), 4, 197
Reed (E. J.), 111
Rees collection, 233
Reference libraries, 98
Reformation controversial writings, 5
Reg. v. *Morris*, 139
Rejections of the Acts, 27, 34, 38, 41, 42, 62-64, 173
Rents, 246
"Report on Public Libraries in the United States," 96
"Repressor of over much blaming," 129
Requisition to compel authority to act, 81
Rice (H.), 308
Richmond, 49, 320
Riddell bequest, 214, 310
Ripon (Marquis of), 87
Roberts. *See* Crompton-Roberts
Robertson (H. W.), 240
Robertson indicator, 100
Robertson's "Reign of Charles V.," 201
Robinson (Phil), 231
Rochdale, 37, 308
Rochester, 65, 314
Romances of Chivalry, 126
Roscoe (William), 167
Rosebery (Lord), 87, 91, 188
Rosebery's "Life of Pitt," 201
Rossetti's "Ballads," 201
Rossetti's "Memoirs of Shelley," 201
Ross's "Arctic Expedition," 201
Rotheram, 41, 320
Rothwell, 65, 324
Rouen, 16
"Round the World," 113
Rousseau's "La Nouvelle Héloïse," 201

Rowlands (J. H.), 235
Rowlls (Rowlls), 320
Royal Dublin Society, 191-192
Royal Library, 7, 119
Royalty and the free library, 87-88
Rugby, 64, 320
Runcorn, 49, 262-263, 312
Ruskin, 135, 196, 201, 244, 250, 299
Russian literature, 128
Russian travelling libraries, 9
Rutland, 66
Rutland (Duke of), 19

ST. ALBANS, 49, 322
St. Austell, 65, 275, 324
St. George, near Bristol, 65, 322
St. Helens, 38, 69, 83, 314
St. Ives (Cornwall), 112, 275, 324
St. Petersburg, 8
Salaries of assistants, 183
Sale, 64, 312
Salford, 11, 16, 33, 83, 204-206, 308
Salisbury, 64, 111, 320
Salomons (Philip), 130
Salomons (Sir David), 130
Salt Society, 250
Sandeman (Professor), 70, 322
Sandhurst (Lord), 75
Scarborough, 57
School libraries, 183, 216, 222, 259
School of science and art, Bromley, 68
Schools of design, 10, 107
Science and Art Department, 10, 54, 80, 107, 191, 192
Science classes and schools, 79, 213, 255, 261, 268
Scotch works, 267
Scott (Sir Walter), 196, 243, 244, 298
Scottish Church: General Assembly, 6, 9
Scottish libraries, 13
Scottish poetry, 290
Seaforth. *See* Waterloo
Seeley (Colonel), 69, 316
Selborne (Lord), 20, 133
Select Committee on Public Libraries, 7, 8, 11-15, 105, 107
Selection of books, 176
Selkirk, 64, 67, 324
Sendall (Alderman), 227
Servell (R. C.), 220
Sevenoaks, 63
Seventeenth century libraries, 4

INDEX

Shaftesbury (Lord), 32, 36
Shakespeare collections, 177–179, 181, 218
Shakespeare's autograph, 130
Sharp (A.), 68
Sharpe (John, *Archbishop*), 8
Sheepshed, 65, 324
Sheffield, 16, 27, 82, 306
Shelley, 250
Shelving at Birkenhead, 220
Shepheard's Library, Preston, 285
Sheppeard (Mr.), 101
Shipley (Joseph), 169, 306
Shouldham, 65, 324
Shrewsbury, 53, 323
Sibthorp (Colonel), 17, 22, 23
Sittingbourne, 57, 324
Skelmersdale, 57
Skinner (J. A.), 320
Slaney (Mr.), 20
Slatin Pasha, 196
Sligo, 49, 322
Sloane (Sir Hans), 116
Sloane Library, 120
Smethwick, 41, 249, 323
Smiles (Samuel), 12, 190, 196, 244, 280, 298
Smirke, the architect, 118
Smith (Miss Durning), 68, 144
Smith's " English Gilds," 250
Somerset (Lord Protector), 128
South Africa, 300
South Shields, 41, 213, 245–247, 314
Southampton, 57, 243, 244, 247–248, 318
Southend-on-Sea, 63
Southern (J. W.), 164
Southey (R.), 200
Southport, 41, 314
Sowerby Bridge, 65, 320
Spalding Club, 290
Spanish literature, 121, 235
Special lists, 209, 215, 220
Specialisation in free libraries, 103
Speeches quoted, 51, 52, 72, 88–93
Spencer (Herbert), 212, 298
Spenser Society, 165
Spooner (Mr.), 20, 25
Stafford, 49, 318
Staleybridge, 64, 70, 322
Stanford (Mr.), 23
Stanley (H. M.), 149
Stationery Office, 86, 243
Statistics, 301–325
Staunton (J.), 177

Stephen (Sir James), speech quoted, 31
Stephenson (Mr.), 70, 310
Stevens (Henry), 44, 101
Stevenson (J. B.), 246
Stevenson (R. L.), 196, 243
Stevenson (Rev. W.), 290
Stirling's Library, Glasgow, 292
Stockport, 34, 322
Stockton-on-Tees, 41, 322
Stoke-on-Trent, 41, 323
Stokes (Miss), 314
Storey Institute, Lancaster, 69, 316
" Story of the Nations," 299
Stow, 129
Stowe collection of MSS., 122, 126
Stretford, 65, 322
Stroud, 62, 65, 322
Subscription libraries, 7, 238, 254, 255, 270
Subscriptions, gifts, &c., 33, 51, 61, 67–70, 111–114, 158, 162, 166, 168, 169, 227, 228, 230, 243, 246, 247, 250, 266, 301–325
Summer school of library science, 101
Sunday opening, 148, 163, 177, 220, 253
Sunderland, 11, 83, 310
Surrey topography, 145
Sutherland (Duke of), 318
Sutton (C. W.), 165
Swan (Annie), 280
Swansea, 37, 40, 82, 235–237, 310

TALBOT (J. G.), 40
Tamworth, 49, 325
Tarves, 53, 273, 279–280, 324
Tate (H.), 68, 144, 302
Taunton, 53, 62
Taxation of libraries (*see* also Income-tax), 26
Taylor (Joseph), 69
Taylor (T.), 251, 316
Taylor bequest, Wigan, 61
Taylor the Platonist, 147
Technical instruction, 77, 170, 188, 209, 215, 232, 256, 258, 268, 274
Technical literature, 140, 236, 238, 250, 253, 259
Tedder (H. R.), 44, 97
Teddington, 65, 322
Tenison (Archbishop): his library, 5, 286
Tennyson, 196

INDEX 343

Thackeray (W. M.), 196, 298
Thackeray (W. M.), speech at opening of the Manchester Free Library, 30
Thomas (E. C.), 97, 107
Thomason tracts, 104, 120
Thomlinson Library, Newcastle, 214, 285
Thompson (H. M.), 233
Thompson (Sir E. M.), 44
Thornaby-on-Tees, 64, 320
Thurso, 38, 41, 272, 278-279, 324
Tinworth, 147
Tipton, 53, 318
Todmorden, 65, 70, 323
Tonbridge. *See* Tunbridge
Tong, 5
Tottenham, 62, 65, 322
Tovey's "Bristol City Library," 196
Towns that have not adopted the Acts, 66
Towyn, 65, 325
Trades Union Congress, 66
Traill's "Social England," 244
Travelling libraries, 8, 282-284
Trimdon, 324
Truro, 53, 69, 111, 112, 263-264, 312
Trustees of the British Museum, 123
Tudor (R.), 257
Tunbridge, 49, 322
Tunbridge Wells, 62, 65, 322
Tunstall, 53, 318
Twickenham, 49, 322
Tynemouth, 37, 318
Tyssen collection, 130

UNITED STATES, 9, 13, 18, 43, 45, 70, 88, 96, 300
Universities and the free library, 22
University College, Nottingham, 210
University extension, 217, 224, 248
University Press, Cambridge, 243
Urban districts (*see* also Local Boards), 66, 76, 78, 81
"Use of Life," 109
Usher (Mr.), 324

VAUGHAN (Rev. Dr.), 32
Venetian presses, 198
Verard, 119
Verney (Lady), 276
Verney (Miss Ellin), 276, 277
Verney (Sir Edmund), 276

Village libraries, 14, 61, 281-284
Visits to reading-rooms, 301-325
Volumes in free libraries, 301-325
Voluntary free libraries, 230, 296
Voyages and travels, 121

WALES, 40, 264
Wallis (George), 10
Walsall, 33, 83, 318
Walter (Mr.), 22
Walthamstow, 65, 314
Ward's "Robert Elsmere," 298
Warrington, 11, 15, 16, 33, 82, 254, 256, 257, 314
Warwick, 35, 320
Warwickshire collection, 177, 180
Waterford, 65, 322
Waterhouse (A.), 252
Waterloo-with-Seaforth, 65
Waterton collection, 121
Watford, 41, 314
Watts (Thomas), 128
Wednesbury, 41, 318
Welch (Charles), 131
Welsh literature, 233
Welsh MSS., 70
Welshpool, 57, 272
Wensley, 69
West Bromwich, 37, 69, 318
West Cowes, 62
West Ham, 57, 64, 202-204, 310
West Hartlepool, 65, 314
Westminster (Duke of), 150
Weston-super-Mare, 53, 318
Weyman (Stanley), 135, 196, 243
Wheatley, 53
Wheel catalogue, 154
Wheelhouse (Mr.), 85
Whitehaven, 57, 312
Whitworth (Sir Joseph), 161
Whitworth legatees, 68, 306
Whityngton (Richard), 128
Wick, 57, 324
Widnes, 53, 316
Wigan, 41, 61, 68, 83, 108, 243, 251-254, 316
Willenhall, 41, 323
Willesden, 65, 322
Williams (Rev. Rowland), 235
Williamson (Alderman), 246
Williams's Library, 286
Wills (Justice), 139
Wilton (Lord), 32
Wimbledon, 53, 156, 323
Winchester, 27, 33, 318

Winnard bequest, Wigan, 61, 252–316
Winsford, 57, 67, 324
Wisbeach, 5
Wolverhampton, 37, 38, 69, 82, 99, 224–226, 308
Women assistants, 202, 241
Wood (Miss), 190, 196
Wood (Mrs. H.), 135, 149, 243
Wood Green (Middlesex), 65, 322
Wood's "Natural History," 299
Woolton, 64, 324
Woolwich, 57, 62, 65, 305
Worboise (Miss), 196, 243
Worcester, 41, 42, 49, 55, 320
Working-class libraries, 13 14
Workington, 64, 322
Worksop, 65, 322
Worthing, 65, 323
Wotton Wawen, 5
Wrexham, 49, 264–265, 322
Wright (W. H. K.), 98, 99, 221
Wrightson (T.), 320
Wycliffe Exhibition, 127
Wyld (Mr.), 21

YARMOUTH, 53, 316
Yates (J.), 99, 183
Yonge (Miss), 298
York, 47, 57, 65, 320
Yorkshire books, 208
Yorkshire Union of Mechanics' Institutes, 9, 283
Ystradyfodwy, 67, 195

THE END